Advance Praise for The Story of Latinos and Education in American History

"This book is not easy to read because it is so packed with useful but frequently ignored information. At the same time, it is essential reading precisely for the same reason, as it is packed with useful and frequently ignored information. Pro-educational change agents must read Dr. Noboa-Ríos's work. Understanding why schools continue to fail US Hispanic students and to learn how they can excel is a must for today's educator. Practitioners must listen to and learn from the most informed voices of the nation to change tragic and shameful outcomes for Latinos. Advocates, policymakers, school of education professionals, and educators at all levels now have access to an indispensable resource for transformational leadership."

Samuel Betances, author of *Winning the Future through Education: One Step at a Time*

"Throughout US history, Latinos have been marginalized and discriminated against. Not surprisingly, the experiences of Latinos, particularly in education, have been obscured and rendered largely invisible. In this important new book, Dr. Noboa-Ríos begins the process of excavating that history, drawing attention to the many ways in which schools have been used to maintain the subordination of Latinos in American society. As the Latino population grows and as its influence increases, understanding this history will be essential for creating a better future. This book will serve as an important step toward ensuring that the past is not repeated and that the future for Latinos in education is better and more promising than the past."

Pedro A. Noguera, Distinguished Professor of Education, UCLA Graduate School of Education and Information Studies

"Not simply the story of Latinx in U.S. education, Noboa-Ríos tells a rather more comprehensive story of public education with a focus on various Latinx groups, particularly Mexicans and Puerto Ricans. This valuable history will put into perspective the complex, flawed, aspirational but nonetheless segregated, racialized, unequal, and inequitable education of Latinx students in our public schools. It will also put to rest the conventional wisdom that Latinx students in U.S. public schools are a recent or new phenomenon. This book should be required reading for teachers, administrators, teacher educators, and policymakers responsible for the education of Latinx students."

Sonia Nieto, professor emerita, College of Education, University of Massachusetts at Amherst

"The author demonstrates a passionate and practical approach to develop an understanding of Latino educational challenges and assets. Dr. Noboa-Ríos provides a comprehensive and useful tool with unique insights to achieve educational success for the future of Latinos and America. The author articulates an explicit rationale which emphasizes the urgency of his findings with a call to action. He communicates the depth and breadth of his topic in a powerful manner."

Carlos Azcoitia, professor emeritus, Educational Leadership Program, National Louis University

"*The Story of Latinos and Education* is one of the most comprehensive, compelling, and passionate analyses of the education of Latinos in America, inextricably linking the persistent disparity in the education of Latinos to the long history of racial and social segregation, division, and inequality that remains to this day."

Ron Blackburn Moreno, National Executive Director, Aspira Association

"Dr. Noboa-Ríos's panoramic detailing of Latino education history provides a niche for placing our episodic recollections of the events we lived through or read about. That context augments our understanding of current realities and provides reasons to hope we will, at last, be able to change the course of the trajectory."

Rosa Castro Feinberg, retired faculty, Florida International University; former member of the Miami-Dade School Board

"In a much needed and long-awaited book, Dr. Noboa-Ríos has interwoven the most comprehensive tapestry of the Latino American quest to navigate success in American society. A historical gem, certain to become the standard work in its field for many years to come."

Rosita López, Professor Emerita in Educational Leadership, Northern Illinois University

"In this detailed and thought-provoking book, Dr. Noboa-Ríos offers a unique perspective on the historical barriers within our educational system and an insightful chronicling of the struggles faced by Latinos across the country."

Eduardo Padrón, President, Miami-Dade Community College

"Abdin Noboa-Ríos's story is a bold exploration of a topic that resonates ever more loudly in American higher education. It constitutes a comprehensive examination of the subject. His observations are incisive and on the mark."

Arturo Madrid, Murchison Distinguished Professor Emeritus of the Humanities, Trinity University

The Story of Latinos and Education in American History

Yolanda Medina and Margarita Machado-Casas
General Editors

Vol. 21

The Critical Studies of Latinxs in the Americas series
is part of the Peter Lang Trade Academic and Textbook list.
Every volume is peer reviewed and meets
the highest quality standards for content and production.

PETER LANG
New York • Bern • Berlin
Brussels • Vienna • Oxford • Warsaw

Abdín Noboa-Ríos

The Story of Latinos and Education in American History

PETER LANG
New York • Bern • Berlin
Brussels • Vienna • Oxford • Warsaw

Library of Congress Cataloging-in-Publication Data
Names: Noboa-Rios, Abdin Israel, author.
Title: The story of Latinos and education in American history / Abdín Noboa-Ríos.
Description: New York: Peter Lang, 2019.
Series: Critical studies of Latinxs in the Americas; vol. 21
ISSN 2372-6822 (print) | ISSN 2372-6830 (online)
Includes bibliographical references and index.
Identifiers: LCCN 2019014099 | ISBN 978-1-4331-6736-2 (hardback: alk. paper)
ISBN 978-1-4331-6735-5 (paperback: alk. paper) | ISBN 978-1-4331-5926-8 (ebook pdf)
ISBN 978-1-4331-5927-5 (epub) | ISBN 978-1-4331-5928-2 (mobi)
Subjects: LCSH: Hispanic Americans—Education.
Educational equalization—United States. | Multicultural education—United States.
Education—Aims and objectives—United States.
Classification: LCC LC2669.S76 2019 | DDC 371.829/68073—dc23
LC record available at https://lccn.loc.gov/2019014099
DOI 10.3726/b14394

Bibliographic information published by **Die Deutsche Nationalbibliothek**.
Die Deutsche Nationalbibliothek lists this publication in the "Deutsche
Nationalbibliografie"; detailed bibliographic data are available
on the Internet at http://dnb.d-nb.de/.

The paper in this book meets the guidelines for permanence and durability
of the Committee on Production Guidelines for Book Longevity
of the Council of Library Resources.

© 2019 Peter Lang Publishing, Inc., New York
29 Broadway, 18th floor, New York, NY 10006
www.peterlang.com

All rights reserved.
Reprint or reproduction, even partially, in all forms such as microfilm,
xerography, microfiche, microcard, and offset strictly prohibited.

Printed in the United States of America

TABLE OF CONTENTS

Foreword: Infusing U.S. Latino History into the Future of Education		vii
Antonia Darder		
Preface		xiii
Acknowledgments		xvii
Introduction		1

Part I.	**American Education**	
Chapter 1.	The Birth of American Education	15
	Colonial Education	17
	Education as a Right	20
	Educating Populations of Color	27
	Asian Exclusion	28
	Latino Exclusion	30
	Public Schooling	31
	Growth and Expansion	38
Chapter 2.	Dual Systems of Education	51
	Emancipation Becomes Segregation	53
	The Stain of *Plessy*	59
	Dual Systems	62
	Reformers Miss the Point	69

	Testing and Profiling	76
	The Fallacy of Reform	81
	Segregation as Disenfranchisement	83
Chapter 3.	*Brown* and Beyond	91
	Calamitous Times	92
	The Era of *Brown*	95
	The System Flounders	105
	Major Warts	107
	A New Century	109
	The Other Education	111

Part II. Latino Education

Chapter 4.	The Miseducation of Latinos	117
	A Glimpse of the Past	120
	Latino Beginnings	126
	Education Began in Spanish	129
	Latinos in the U.S.	132
	Education in the U.S.	135
	Excluding Latinos from Public Education	138
	Education and Imperialism	147
	Counting the Latino	150
Chapter 5.	A Tripartite System	157
	Polarization During *Plessy*	157
	Educational Contradictions	162
	Unabated Segregation	164
	Second-Class Schooling	168
	Identity and Race	174
	The Color of Reform	179
Chapter 6.	Contemporary Issues	189
	School Funding	189
	Language, Pedagogy and Rights	191
	High School Dropouts	193
	Back to the Future	196
	Higher Education	201
	New Century Struggles	206
	Epilogue: Learning from History	215
	Bibliography	229
	Index	245

FOREWORD

Infusing U.S. Latino History into the Future of Education

Antonia Darder
Loyola Marymount University

> *Indeed, it seems that while the natural inclination of scholars interested in intellectual history is to explore the known, central, established centres, we must not forget to also explore the accumulation, development and distribution of ideas and knowledge in more distant and less well-known hubs...*
> Jonathan Rubin

Exploring *less well-known hubs* is, indeed, an illuminating way to characterize the underlying intent of Abdín Noboa-Ríos' outstanding book, *The Story of Latinos and Education in American History*. To accomplish this, he effectively utilizes a creative and innovative approach for engaging the myriad conditions that have resulted in the gross miseducation of Latino children, since the inception of the "New World"—a Eurocentric misnomer that has supported the historical misperceptions and distortions of Latino populations, who (as Noboa-Ríos reminds us) actually predate the pilgrims in this country. In so doing, the book provides a well-crafted and systematic examination of the social, political, and economic roles Latinos have played in the formation of U.S. life. By including intimate bits and pieces of his personal history as a Puerto Rican migrant and locating these experiences within the larger fabric of U.S. Latino life, Noboa-Ríos offers us a rich counternarrative to the troublesome Black/White binary of race, which has conveniently and tragically rendered Latinos ambiguous and invisibilized within most spheres of daily life, despite our growing numbers and unswerving contribution to every facet of U.S. society.

Hence, the story that unfolds across the pages of this volume serves to unveil the deleterious impact of racism, and economic impoverishment as part of a systematic project of colonization, linked to a determinist history of racialization meant to preserve the power and privilege of the White ruling class. By focusing on the schooling of Latinos, the book also speaks to a significant pedagogical challenge, which is becoming more and more evident as the Latino population in the U.S. continues to gain prominence across new geographical zones within the nation and, therefore, within large educational school districts as well. Moreover, what is made stunningly clear is that not only has the Latino population been here since before the establishment of the nation but is now poised to become the majority population in a society that remains exceedingly ignorant of the complexities of our histories and our contemporary existence.

The Inevitability of the Browning of the U.S.

You can cut all the flowers but you cannot keep spring from coming.
Pablo Neruda

At the core of Noboa-Ríos' story of U.S. Latinos and education, is a plainspoken argument about the inevitability of the browning of America and the evasion of social justice (Sundstrom, 2008). Centering on Latinos as the future of the nation, he unequivocally inserts Latinos back into the historical continuum across the western hemisphere and across time. Just as the Chilean poet, Pablo Neruda, reminds us, we *cannot keep spring from coming*, so too, it is impossible to keep Latinos from soon becoming the majority population. Noboa-Ríos' treatise is then a powerful political wake-up call, particularly with respect to policy considerations and practices linked to the education of Latino children. Through a brilliant twist of narrative, *The Story of Latinos and Education in America History* inserts Latino children—who have often been ignored or driven unrelentingly into an assimilative culture of forgetting—more fully into the educational discourse of *all* children. By so doing, Noboa-Ríos confronts the inevitable changes that are taking place within the ethnic landscape of the United States and within our schools.

Use of popular historical references gives a sense of palpable familiarity to the persuasive narrative. Noboa-Ríos' personal experience, for example, with the politics and consequences of gentrification, brings a compelling description that catapults the reader out of abstraction, into the realm of very real conditions played out upon the lives of living human beings—a reality that is so often obscured by the abstract language of policy briefs and economic priorities that drive gentrification discourses. As he moves back and forth in his narrative of history, Noboa-Ríos sheds light on the persistence of societal inequalities and cultural disrespect, countering celebratory social mobility arguments within education that prefer to remain rooted to the lie of meritocracy, rather than to face the damning truth: an enduring legacy of racialized economic inequality and educational abandonment, which has only intensified as Latinos continue to grow in overwhelming proportions. The consequence, moreover, is that the schooling of Latino children is caught within the crosshairs of rancorous educational policy debates that tend to accomplish little beyond further eroding the emancipatory promises of diversity discourses.

Reclaiming the Essence of Life

Like bones to the human body, the axle to the wheel, the wing to the bird, and the air to the wing, so is liberty the essence of life.

José Martí

Noboa-Ríos rightly argues that schools evolved "under assumptions of inequality" and as spheres of social control for Latino communities—although the project of Americanization (or assimilation) was seldom posed in this manner. Nevertheless, assimilative curricula and pedagogy were consistently implemented as a recurrent practice linked to the colonization of non-European children in the United States. This phenomenon often intensified during periods of economic decline and political strife, although more recently reconsolidated under the ethos of neoliberal multiculturalism, which claims to recognize (and even celebrate) ethnic minorities, although undermining fundamentally the significant gains made during the civil rights era. Hence, it is not surprising that the recognition (and commodification) of Latinos in the U.S. never led to the political and economic empowerment anticipated by educational and community activists of the past. Noboa-Ríos addresses aspects of this phenomenon eloquently, pushing the sociological discourse further, by naming the detrimental impact that racialized inequalities have had across all populations, to make the case that we must move to reclaim the essence of what has been lost.

That said, I would argue, that the distinct story of Latinos and education that unfolds in this volume invites readers to embrace Martí's notion that liberty is the *essence of life*. As such, Noboa-Ríos' rendering of the history of Latinos and education highlights a variety of concrete example of policies and practices that over the years have, wittingly or unwittingly, functioned to impede the essence of liberty for Latino populations within both society and schools. As such, he demonstrates how such impositions work against the very democratic principles that have so often been declared as cornerstones of American life. By guiding us to better comprehend the obstructions that have been perpetuated against this emancipatory essence of Latino life, Noboa-Ríos' resounding message to educators, at all levels, is clear and decisive: we are all (Latinos and non-Latinos) implicated in determining the future schooling and well-being of Latino children.

History as Invaluable Memory

> *Write what should not be forgotten.*
> Isabel Allende

In his dynamic storytelling, Noboa-Ríos (re)captures history as an undeniable fountain of knowledge and as invaluable memory, which can assist us to better understand how Latinos arrived to our current social location and status in U.S. society. To do this, he repeatedly fills in missing pieces significant to the story of Latinos and education in the U.S. and uncovers misperceptions and distortions, which not only impede the education of Latino children but also prevent the establishment of an educational system able to contend with their actual needs. Noboa-Ríos further insists that old approaches to the persistent educational and economic oppression of Latinos requires very different solutions than those of another time—solutions that must be rooted in an authentic quest for a culturally-democratic nation. Also, well-emphasized is a perspective of history as a deeply forceful and changing phenomenon—*an adventure of history in the making*—that can offer us many promising and exciting possibilities for the future, if we heed its warnings and valiantly contend with contemporary conditions with new eyes and a new commitment to our common liberation. This view further speaks to an understanding of freedom or liberation that is born fundamentally from the recognition of our shared humanity and an abiding respect for and commitment to our many ways of being human in the world.

Made painstakingly clear by this provocative account is how the erosion of Latino history and thus, the erosion of freedom in our lives is precisely the legacy of colonization—a legacy which has left U.S. Latinos dangling on the great stage of human evolution, uncertain and often confused about our legitimate place in the social fabric of the nation. Accordingly, the damage has led many Latinos on a quest to "pass for White"—whether acknowledged or not—in a desperate attempt to feel some sense of belonging or feeling of acceptance. This debilitating dynamic can also be connected to what Noboa-Ríos calls *a cloak of invisibility*, which seems to plague us within our most mainstream educational settings. Hence, the book is also about freeing ourselves—personally and collectively—from this brutal assimilative grip and, by so doing, opening ourselves to those pieces of our histories obscured by the whitewashed portrayals of humanity by the West.

And finally, the radical hope at the very core of this book is resolutely linked to an underlying belief that if we can understand the history of Latinos and education in the U.S. as a powerful living force, we can use this force to go to the root of the problem and, thereby, stop repeating history. It is through new perspectives and fresh solutions that emerge from an accurate (re)reading of Latino history that we are encouraged to work to dismantle the current system of education that preserves the colonial structures of capitalism and holds us all hostage to an outdated, repressive, and bureaucratized institution of schooling. There is no question that Abdin Noboa-Ríos' great passion for history and commitment to the education of Latino children is profoundly felt in his scholarly rendition of *The Story of Latinos and Education in American History*. As such, the book's timely message is truly a formidable example *of what should not be forgotten*, if our nation is to genuinely embrace a culturally, politically, and economically just future for all.

References

Allende. I. (2004). On "Why I Write". Stanford Presidential Lectures in the Humanities and Arts. Retrieved January 5, 2018, from https://prelectur.stanford.edu/lecturers/allende/interviews.html

Martí, J. (2016). *José Martí: Quotes & Facts*. B. Kivov (ed.). CreateSpace Independent Publishing Platform (back cover).

Pablo Neruda Quotes. (n.d.). BrainyQuote.com. Retrieved December 28, 2018, from *BrainyQuote.com* Web site: https://www.brainyquote.com/quotes/pablo_neruda_381705

Rubin, J. (2018). How the Latin East contributed to a unique cultural world. *Aeon Magazine* (January).

Sundstrom, R. (2008). *The Browning of America and the Evasion of Social Justice*. New York, NY: SUNY.

PREFACE

EVERY BOOK HAS A PURPOSE AND THIS VOLUME ATTEMPTS TO ADDRESS THE STORY OF THE LATINO* REGARDING AMERICA'S PAST SO AS TO BETTER FOCUS ON ITS FUTURE. Rather than a broad history, education is used as the lens by which to examine the Latino reality in American life, as this has been how Hispanics have experienced this country. For the most part, life in school and its consequences has been the schoolmaster that has taught the Latino child what this country is about and what it represents. Through education, this book will show how this history has impacted and shaped the Latino experience and why this knowledge is important for today.

All too often many of us view events as they readily appear rather than seeing them as a continuum of a long past. While many know Latinos did not appear yesterday, some act is if Hispanics just appeared on the horizon. Somewhere Latinos got lost in the narrative. Yet, the Latino is endemic to the history of this nation and goes as far back as the Pilgrims; in fact, back to

---

* The terms Latino and Hispanic are used interchangeably throughout the book. In Spanish lexicon, the terms are generic unless specific to females in which case they will follow the Spanish female designation.

the original Spanish colony of St. Augustine in 1565 and even farther back to San Juan at the start of the 16th century, both part of the United States today.

Here the story of the Latino is presented with an assumption that may be surprising. Bluntly stated, the future of America is now inevitably linked to the future of the Latino population as major demographic shifts have considerably altered the landscape of the country. Latinos are now the largest racial group in America and together with Blacks, Asian/Pacific Islanders and other people of color represent more than half the elementary and secondary school enrollment nationwide. While most demographers and many educators are aware of this change, it is not clear how many policymakers believe it or fully know what this information may imply for policy. One thing is to be aware of impending trends the other is to be able and willing to act upon its ramifications. As such information hinges strongly on demographic realities, it also conveys a major responsibility for the education of this nation. In very real terms, this is both a pedagogical challenge and a political reality facing American education. As important as nuclear proliferation, it concerns the future wellbeing of the country and its posterity. If the country does not pay close attention, a perfect storm will appear by stealth, catching everyone by surprise. Here timing is important and knowledge is essential.

This book aims for a deeper understanding about the role Latinos play in the context of the social and economic realities that are shaping the nation. Three critical topics interrelate. One concerns *education*. The other is about timing, how the Latino *past* relates to the *future* of this nation, with the third fully focused on the *Latino* presence. All three interweave as they together represent an important, multidimensional portrait. In a very real way, this is a counter narrative to dominant thinking, and also a wakeup call for better planning and clearer policy formulation around these topics.

Ultimately, the book is about all children in America, not just Brown children. It is also about everyone, as it concerns the future of the country. At the same time, it is fully about education. Though seemingly independent, these topics highly interrelate as they intersect in very complementary ways, albeit at times conflictual. Quite importantly, the country's destiny is dependent on how the topics work in tandem. *Bottom line*: our nation is facing a new period, as it confronts a new reality based on population shifts and educational achievement that demand different approaches to resolution because it now finds itself in a different context from the past. Understanding the past makes this evident. The remaining decades of the twenty-first century predict a different future about which we must be more knowledgeable and more ready to confront. This is not about educational or social reform, but an altogether different framework for examining the Latino population and America's role in asserting responsibility.

In assessing these conditions, this is not so much my book as it is yours. It is meant for the general public, everyday Americans as well as professionals, especially those wanting to learn more profoundly about the complexity of the America of today. This is not about racialization, any more than it is about nationalism. These are destructive forces that can polarize. It is also not about a zero-sum game, where some win at the expense of others. It is neither about who has the largest numbers or who has the votes. Not quite. This is about all winning or we all lose! We must work together or each will stand alone. The story is inclusive. It is about all of us.

For educators, my intent is to also reach you, but maybe differently. You represent the vanguard in this movement. You are the hard-working and diligent learners—from paraprofessionals to superintendents, from community workers to parents, from public to private institutions, from preschool to university. As you equip yourself with information gathered from this book, it is important that you reflect from where you work, worship, party, and play. There will be considerable information from which to share at conferences and social gatherings as well as at your children's athletic events, around coffee machines, at the bar, at home, and abroad. Responsible thinking and civic action are important about this topic. When educators get together much is learned and important things happen. Welcome to the adventure of history in the making, but commencing with deep introspection.

ACKNOWLEDGMENTS

As with any book of this type, it is always difficult to acknowledge all the persons that encouraged me to write this book as well as many others that contributed in strengthening the manuscript. Equal thanks go to those that have gotten on my case to finally write a book on the story of education. While nagging seldom achieves intended results, it did prove successful in my case.

Somewhat different from other books, I am highly grateful and deeply indebted to literally hundreds of colleagues that provided personal input to much of the thinking behind my writing, most especially interviewees that shared their wisdom. As it was, this latter group was to be 25 individuals, but eventually grew to 112 persons that lent valuable time and shared great insight. Each patiently acquiesced to in-depth questions regarding myriad issues around the topic of Latinos and education—all "*en vivo*," most face-to-face and several via Skype. Few are quoted in this volume, as most appear in my next book. Throughout, their invaluable insights were very helpful in reviewing the history of Latinos in American education, both current and past.

Seldom is a book written from the collective wisdom and insightful perception from so many elders that were interviewed, not to mention many colleagues and friends. In this instance, their sage advice and wise feedback made this a collective enterprise, as there is much to be said about "our" shared history as Latinos in education (book one) and more about what this history implies for our collective future in the 21st century (book two). Voluminous information required separating data into two distinct books. This first book focuses on a formative understanding of the role and history of Latinos in American education. Such a baseline establishes the necessary foundation from which a second book on 21st century issues in education emerged: *The Challenge of Latinos and Education in 21st Century America: Where Are We?* As it takes a *village* to write a book, I benefited from the wisdom and valuable input from a *community* of sages to compose this book and its companion volume.

Special gratitude goes to the several few that more specifically contributed particular critiques. Support from this final group of eyes merits special attention. Absent their contribution, my work would suffer from oversight and not be as carefully crafted. At the same time, very special thanks first goes to my editor, Yolanda Medina, as Series Editor of Peter Lang's Critical Studies of Latinx in the Americas. Her guidance was invaluable in putting these tomes together. Very special thanks are also due to historian Victoria-Maria MacDonald for her wise and thoughtful counsel to a non-historian like me. She steered me away from errors of fact and flippant comments, though I likely did not catch all of them.

Special thanks are also extended to my esteemed colleagues and friends that provided another pair of eyes in review of my work: Tony Báez, Margarita Benítez, Samuel Betances, Sarita Brown, Consuelo Castillo Kickbusch, Rosa Castro Feinberg, Ricardo Fernández, Barbara Flores, Richard Medina, Ric Murphy, Julio Noboa Polanco, Deborah Santiago, Lew Smith, and Angela Valenzuela.

I would be remiss not to mention my wife whose attention and dedication to my passion in education has always been my bedrock and guiding support. This book could not have been possible without her love and infinite patience throughout the process, at times into daylight hours. This includes many hours where I read passages out loud, anxiously expecting her approval, even grunts. She always guided with the right orientation, even in disagreement, as we now chuckle about some of them. I am also thankful for support from my children, most especially my youngest daughter María who holds definitive opinions about communication and writing style. These all have been invaluable as they also have been quite salutary.

INTRODUCTION

In repositioning Latino history and its impact today, I am reminded of actor-comedian John Leguizamo's personal search for identity from an interview with *Time* magazine (2017) which described his one-man play at a New York theater as self-reflection. He talked about how important the play was for him as a primer on the "history of a people of Latin descent in the Americas."[1] As portrayed, it is a "comedic lament for the pain of knowing" how his people's contributions have been minimized in U.S. history. During the interview, he deeply reflected by saying: "If I would have read in a textbook as a kid that 10,000 [Hispanics] participated in the Civil War and Cuban women in Virginia sold their jewelry to feed the patriots, people wouldn't feel so confident to disrespect me." He then concluded by saying, "I wouldn't feel as victimized because … this is my country, too."[2]

Upon reflection, he confessed: "I'm writing this for me, because this is how I take care of myself, with how invisible we Latino people are in the media." He shared the fact that others may feel similarly, almost like a kind of healing as Latino* vignettes should be shared. The play is more of a plea for Latinos to understand their role in this country's history, as an important part

---

* The terms Latino and Hispanic are used interchangeably throughout the book.

of the story that needs to be known and more fully internalized before it can be fully celebrated.

In a similar way, I hope this book further adds to the legacy of the Latino population, as it is important for Hispanics to know who they are and where they have been. Equally important is for the country to be apprised and aware that 1-in-5 residents are now Latino, with 1-in-4 enrolled in public schools (preK–12) as well as among today's newborns.[3] The population pyramid is quickly becoming Latinized.

For Latinos, I hope the book helps remove the cloak of invisibility, as it also may heighten pride in learning about a collective past and its continuing contribution to American history. For educators, it should help them become more knowledgeable about the Latino experience and its role in education. Such knowledge also helps equip teachers and practitioners with new information they can pay forward to advance their practice to meet today's demographic reality.

In deeper reflection after completing this writing, I find myself agreeing greatly with historian Ira Berlin (2015) in reviewing the history of the long emancipation for African Americans when he affirms that "History is not so much about the past, but more about arguments we have about the past."[4] As he well illustrated in his book, history is all too often slanted by those who survive and later triumph, with others left out of the story. This is not dissimilar to Jeff Long's documentary on the Alamo in *Duel of Eagles* (1991), about the various battles over the Alamo, as few survived the last major battle like Juan Seguín, the Mexican who later narrated his version of what happened. History is most important from which to learn fully from all sides.

Raised in one of Chicago's notorious "barrios," nearly half a century after the Spanish-American War, I was one of many Puerto Rican children enrolled in "mainland" schools. This was during the early 1950s, when many Puerto Ricans first came to the "mainland," as we called it.[5] This was after Mexican Americans had settled in the Southwest, with some migrating to the Midwest generations later, just before the Puerto Rican migration. While struggles for the newcomer Puerto Rican was historically different than for Mexican Americans such as citizenship rights, equally difficult circumstances were encountered in adjusting as well as learning English sufficiently fast enough to excel in school that first generation for most of us. Over time, an affinity was developed among Hispanics, as all battled with language, culture, color, racism, and basic re-adjustment into an American and Mainland way of life, albeit differing by region, skin tone, migration patterns, and citizenship.

My *barrio* sector of Chicago was where the Puerto Rican community first moved, a sliver of a neighborhood, thinly sandwiched between Little Italy and the tracks of Van Buren Street, before Congress Expressway existed, but a stone's throw from Al Capone's headquarters, as depicted in the movie, *The Untouchables* (1987). These portions of neighborhoods were strongly defended between gangland turfs that snaked all the way to Chicago's famous Maxwell Street and across the swath of the Almighty Ambrose Italian gang, not far from iconic Al's Beef on Harrison and Laflin Streets. This was also from where other gangs like the Latin Kings, Latin Counts, Rampants, and Taylor Dukes ranged, and to where the Blackstone Rangers later encroached from the south.

After years of adaptation, our community was urban removed to make room for Chicago Circle Campus, now the University of Illinois at Chicago (UIC). At that time, it seemed like the entire Puerto Rican community had been relocated *en masse* to move nearby Studs Terkel's old neighborhood around Division Street.[6] Over time, the community eventually spilled onto Humboldt Park, the near Northwest Side of Chicago known as Saul Bellow's neighborhood, author of *Humboldt's Gift* (1975) for which he received the Pulitzer Prize in 1976. This was the new hood—another *barrio*—where Puerto Ricans eventually nestled the following decades, also the new home of the Latin Kings ... with the old neighborhood now undergoing gentrification.

For much of my family, it was a scary but adventurous period, as it dealt with accommodation, great frustrations and rough periods of survival. Some of us made it through school, others survived in the streets, still others got roughed up in the concrete jungle, with most heading in two primary directions—prison or a dead-end job—with hardly anyone going to college. We survived, somehow, but with different scars, each with stories to tell and legends to share.

Today, while many relatives and acquaintances confront a different reality in that windy city, many living between Division Street and Logan Square, all too many of their offspring are now now struggling with school, more than we ever expected. Somehow, the struggle for the second and third generation had become nearly as difficult as it was for my family two generations earlier. We expected it would have become easier by now, but it was more like "*déjà vu*," with upward mobility almost frozen.

Here I asked "Why?" What had happened? Why did they not leapfrog into social mobility as we expected? While education had been the salvation for some, it was more a condemnation for most others. Too many were not making it. Again I asked, "Why?" What had gone wrong? Puzzling questions all. These enigmas revealed my search. They eventually exposed my journey, as I wrestled with the paradox.

During this migratory history, Latino newcomers were landing as another stop in a long journey, coming from migratory shifts that were increasing the rates of racial minorities, hopping from one barrio landing to another, trying to find the right job and the right home. But no one knew that at the time. This was when Mexican Americans starting moving to the Midwest, with Blacks moving up North and Puerto Ricans landing after the Second World War, descending from the largest airborne migration in U.S. history. Today, the majority of preK–12 students in these *barrios* are racial minorities, with Latinos multiplying faster than all others. For many of us at the time, it felt like we were the very few, truly a minority among a majority of others. It is astonishing to contemplate how fast we became a majority-minority in many of the schools. As I look back, our schools eventually suffered not because of the students, but because of deteriorating facilities and the quality of teaching. All of a sudden what seemed like prime schools to us went from bad to worse due to White flight. The more Latinos and Blacks, the more the best teachers went to teach elsewhere. Our schools, which we thought were OK at the time, had deteriorated through no fault of the teachers or the students.

Conditions changed with racial population shifts. Schools were now identified as schools for the "children of color." They had been abandoned by the system, no longer a priority. Today, it seems that Latinos at urban schools are now facing an equally tough academic environment as well as a social, political, and highly-polarized setting. Schools had become worse than when we were there. If I did not know better, I would say my teachers of yesteryear were better, as were our schools. Could I be wrong? Is this accurate? How can that be? Not only was this the story for many parts of Chicago, but it also had become the template for other cities across the country. It was like a national movement was afoot with no one realizing it. This occurred as if in slow motion by stealth.

Today, with a majority-minority public school enrollment in most urban and many suburban areas, the country wrestles with persistent achievement gaps between Whites and most other racial groups, with patterns becoming seemingly stagnant and long-standing. While proficiency scores have risen a bit, the gaps between Latinos compared to White and Asian children has not narrowed. While the tide has increased everyone's score, Latinos and Blacks are not much much better, with Latinos in a worse relative position. Internationally, gaps have widened for the U.S., with minorities at rock bottom. Is it the fault of my progeny or is something else going on? Have our kids gotten worse? What has truly changed?

Among schoolteachers, racial disparities in the education workforce also seem to have continued, with large disproportions increasing between minority students and White teachers, and also between minority teachers and nonminority peers, with Latino stagnation in school leadership. Fearsome to some and conflicting for others, these shifts, regardless of ideology, are creating a more entrenched status quo, while Latino numbers keep growing and gaps remain stagnant. Chicago is no exception, as these patterns and trends now impinge on policy and equity across the country, as if a negative contagion effect.

For education, there are countless battles over the improvement of failing schools, certainly among Latino enclaves. The pattern is becoming obvious. Many schools have been downgraded, but for no fault of my family or anyone else. In fact, the more of my relatives, the worse the schools have become. Despite this fact, some relatives are now middle class. This means that cousins attending suburban schools have seen performance scores increase dramatically. Yet, they are the same kids, are they not? Is it the kids or is it the schools? Obviously, we know the answer. Reflecting on former days, it may be equally hard to now thrive in the same streets where I once upon grappled, as I now fear for the education of children from this generation that are still attending these schools. Maybe I should be thankful I lived then rather than now, but this is not progress over time.

As the nation acclimates to or recoils from these realities, it tussles with unresolved problems from former days, not yet shed. Meanwhile, Latinos confront the twin realities of high growth with poor progress. As the paradox of the two meet, confront, and conflict, they may exacerbate, even burst. Latinos together with African Americans are caught in the midst of school changes, culture wars, and class battles of major proportions. These fissions create storms of inequality and imbalance that only ignite current politics in dramatic ways, with students caught in the crosshairs and inaction surviving. This is not same old, same old. It is actually worse, as policies and practices seem to have deteriorated. This reality is no longer hidden. It is now fully front and center, and facing a new America. Are we going forward or is it back to the future?

There is no question that how we understand the past will profoundly affect how we plan for the future, both as minorities of color and collectively as a nation. In education, the system of public schools that developed two centuries ago was deliberate and intentional when it came to the advancement of certain groups. Has it changed? What happens if we play the tape backwards? Are there continuing patterns of old, like an old vinyl record that repeats with minor scratches? As the country becomes more racially diverse, will education policies become more highly polarized? By now, such a recipe would have become ruinous.

There was a considerable difference when racial isolation in schools was ten percent and many were kept out, versus the minority school-age population of today that is still racially segregated, but with half the preK–12 enrollment representing "students of color." While conditions have changed, maybe policies have not. If truth be told, in some ways they have deteriorated and in other ways improved, but overall not much improved, mediocre at best.

With the nation's future now dependent on the wellbeing of every citizen, not just White children, the national context is quite different. Approaching this new phenomenon with the tools and mindsets of yesteryear is calamitous. It is high time old formulas changed. For education practitioners, it is important to well understand what political processes and conditions must change to avoid pitfalls from continual repetition. But learning has been slow, with too many schooling officials stumbling and others anxious to retire but meanwhile as lumps on a log.

Looking back, public schools operated under peculiar assumptions of inequality, backed by racial superiority. In point of fact, they are still highly unequal and largely segregated, with similarly unchanged assumptions. Wow, is this true? Some of my peers will argue with straight faces how much better conditions have become. I may be from the hood, but it seems some of them may be living in planet Pluto, if it is still a planet. They do not see my world. Of course not! They never lived it! As such, it is important to know how these conditions persist so as to stop them for the foreseeable future. In actuality, an educational process that was insensitive to color must now wipe it out to make it more tenable this century, but with public schooling already out of joint and vastly out of step, how can this be accomplished?

Schools are operating as rather complex and convoluted systems, highly bureaucratic and rather dogmatic, unfortunately not unlike the body politic of larger systems or even the nation. While this paints schools as ineffective, it does not mean they cannot improve and beat the devil. While public schools provide opportunities for some, it rationalizes injustice for too many others, even at the ridicule of some. While not necessarily intentional, institutional miseducation is bearing seeds of inequality throughout, with no one to blame, but with everyone responsible. With public schools operating as closed systems, dominant groups will not be able to advance for long at the expense of another, most especially as Whites are numerically diminishing. While undoubtedly education is broader than schooling, these concepts operate in tandem, with major reliance on the public school sector for the education of nearly all children.

In much of the history of school improvement and educational reform, the education reality is that reformers have too often crafted rather simplistic solutions to problems, showing much absence of knowledge or total misguidance for policymaking. For whatever reasons, they have much too often arrived at irrelevant if not shameful solutions.

In preparing this book, I was less concerned about finding culprits than seeking understanding and uncovering solutions. Searching for villains and enemies does not undo the past nor does it cure the deficits of our kids. This is not to blame any group, but to understand the wider system, and in the process help push education in a better direction so that more students succeed. If any culprit is to blame, it is most assuredly the system, not the student.

As with some books of this ilk, I differ at not seeing public education in decline, but as stagnant and stale. It is not so much that schools are performing more poorly than before, though some truly are, but that they must operate more responsibly, more effectively, with the system more greatly supporting failing schools rather than closing them down. After all, it is the responsibility of the system to ensure schools function properly in the first place. How can they fail when well monitored? School closures affect the lives of hundreds of thousands each year, often as untold history. Yes, schools may get overhauled several years after closure, at times, but still at the expense of too many kids whose lives are wrecked in the meantime. Worse than our most laggard students, it is the schools that are on trial.

The history we will undertake takes a closer look at the lessons our public schools are still learning. We have miles to travel in redressing fundamental problems, but I am getting ahead of the story and an untold history. Public schools should ensure that the advantage of American education does not merely represent a better system, but that it stops operating lackadaisically, with bureaucratic structures that are inefficient, inequitable, and dastardly difficult to change.

The description historian David Tyack provided a long time ago in *The One Best System* (1974) captured well the view that urban schools were more like the Great Wall of China than the walls of Jericho that tumbled.[7] Over time, this wall has thickened. For this reason, removing the wall may not yield desired affects. The challenge is to understand how to work with the wall, by penetrating it as well as moving around it or just plainly climbing over it. For every tall wall, there is an equally tall ladder, as we learned from the *barrio*.

The challenge here is not to undo the system, but to instill a rebirth, a special renaissance, a renewal, as the system must improve profoundly from within if it is to keep in step with the country's needs and remain at par with global advances. The system needs to wake up. Its stupor is worrisome for researchers and practitioners alike. For the system to improve it must change substantially; for it to be effective, even greater modifications will be needed. But for it to reach Latinos and other "hard-to-reach" students of color, it must change dramatically, radically, and rapidly.

I agree with many observers that Americans have all too often perpetuated social injustice by blaming the victim, particularly in the case of institutional racism. But I am also struck by Tyack's cogent assessment of years back about the system when he stated:

> Despite frequent good intentions and abundant rhetoric about "equal educational opportunity," schools have rarely taught the children of the poor effectively—and this failure has been systematic, not idiosyncratic.[8]

Yes, this is an old statement; but by that very reason it is a major concern, as it still applies today. By all means necessary, as this appears endemic, failure must be upturned for our schools. If our children are to succeed, a more rigorous and equitable system is necessary.

Chapters for this book's journey appear in progressive order chronologically, one which contains the traditional milestones in the typical story of American education, and the other that introduces the parallel story of Latinos based on this history. Too many historical misperceptions interfere with accurate knowledge about people of color in this country, most especially the Latino. We are full of fear and anxiety primarily because we lack knowledge about each other. Poignantly stated, the Latino reality has been unknown and too often distorted. It seldom enters the American landscape of discussion, lost in the traditional story.

Part I of the book emphasizes the traditional American version of education history, with the first chapter tracing how American education developed from colonial days and then broke away from the traditional English system, Chapters 2 and 3 focus on how American education eventually became a dual system of education, one for Whites and the other for nonwhites and how this broke apart after *Brown*, leaving vestiges that were equally devastating. *Part II* focuses on education history once again, but this time bringing the Latino into that history. Chapter 4 provides a brief overview of how Latinos were treated at different periods, including their gross miseducation, with chapter 5 depicting how this became a tripartite system of education, one for Whites another for Blacks, and eventually another for Hispanics. Chapter 6 shows how this past is related to contemporary issues yet unresolved.

Lastly is a short epilogue that analyzes the implications of this history as a continuing saga that deeply affects the current status of Latino educational attainment. Ten specific Challenges arise from a cogent summary of prior chapters, as they logically emanate from this learned history. Nearly every issue is a vestige from the past, but in new molds, sizes, and shapes. These remain part of the unfinished business confronting the education of Latinos for both preK–12 and higher education. Welcome to the adventure.

Turns out, the epilogue became more a summary rather than an analysis, as its broader scrutiny eventually resulted in another book. In this subsequent volume, each of the ten topics is covered in greater detail. This book is also published by Peter Lang Publishing, *Critical Issues of Latinos and Education in 21st Century America: Where Are We?* (2020).

Notes

1. Berman, p. 50.
2. *Ibid.*
3. Number of births, 2017, Henry J. Kaiser Family Foundation, https://www.kff.org/other/state-indicator/births-by-raceethnicity/?currentTimeframe=0&selectedDistributions=black--hispanic--total&sortModel=%7B%22colId%22:%22Location%22,%22sort%22:%22asc%22%7D
4. Berlin, 2015.
5. The major Puerto Rican migration to the continental USA referenced as the "mainland" started soon after WWII, with major waves during the late 1940s and 1950s. They first went to New York City and Chicago then later the Northeast Coast and east of the Mississippi River. Today, destinations are quite varied, with Florida, New Jersey, Texas, and sectors of the South as leading destinations.

6. Renown Chicagoan, author of *Division Street: America* (1967) and Pulitzer Prize winner in 1985.
7. Tyack, p. 11.
8. *Ibid*.

PART I

AMERICAN EDUCATION

> *An educated citizenry is a vital requisite for our survival as a free people.*
> Thomas Jefferson

THERE IS A LATINO VOID IN AMERICAN HISTORY. This book responds to a critical part of that void, as innumerable omissions exist. In fact, there is less knowledge about Latinos in the context of American history than for any major demographic group nationwide. Given that Latinos represent the largest racial presence in America, this is a troublesome statement for this century. As this condition presents a major challenge, it also represents a tremendous opportunity.

The Latino history in the American context has countless stories from which to learn, as the legacy of the Hispanic is considerable. Such a heritage should be examined carefully, for there is much to be gained from this knowledge. As every book charts a new path, it is my hope this volume will provide an enriching opportunity and an enjoyable experience to learn from this past with the aim of forging a stronger knowledge about this rich history and a greater understanding about the present. The history of Latinos in education is a major case in point.

As America's public schools reflect a rapidly changing complexion, few schools are adequately prepared to meet the challenges of racial students, even less the Latino child. While the number of minority students has increased rapidly the past four decades, growth rates are even more astounding for the new century.

Racial minorities or students of color reflect an American landscape of cultures and races that must be more fully understood among education circles, as preK–12 enrollment has become one where the majority (>53%) of students are now racial minorities. This majority began academic year 2014–2015, with the largest racial increase now being the Latino child, representing more than 1-in-4 (28%) students nationwide.[1] Such trends are not expected to reverse for the rest of the century. Latino student growth continues to increase faster than the overall enrollment of all other groups, including recent Asian/Pacific Islander immigrants.

Another growing trend concerns the educator workforce of both teachers and administrators. This group reflects diametrically opposite demographics, almost the flip-flop for students, with more than 8-in-10 (82%) teachers of Anglo background and over 9-in-10 (93%) White principals.[2] Trends in the composition of students when compared to staff represent near polar opposites, with predominantly minority student populations facing an educator workforce that is principally Anglo.

While numbers are increasing for both groups, minority students are growing at a faster rate than minority teachers, further widening the gaps between them. For Latinos, such increases are even more sharply evident, with rates increasing more rapidly than for other demographic groups. Rather importantly, lest trends be misconstrued, data are fully independent of recent immigrant numbers. Instead, they are predicated on birth rates, the result of a lower median age and larger households. This means changes in immigration trends will not significantly affect current trends.

These statistics create further concern when coupled with persistent achievement gaps—now decades old—that most directly affect students of color, with Latinos and Blacks ranking at the bottom of overall achievement as well as lower graduation rates. Given the lack of minority staff representation among public schools, the educational system is ill-informed about racial-minority students and less prepared for the Latino student, now the most populous entrant. In retrospect, districts are poorly informed about Latino students today as they had poor knowledge about African Americans at the start of the last century, even after civil rights.

As such, the education system finds itself somewhat at a loss. Most definitively, many staff are not ready to reframe policies and practices to more adequately reflect the needs of these students. For Latinos that are English language learners (ELLs) knowledge is worse as is the data, as there is a greater scarcity of ELL teachers than for nearly any other category of teacher except special education. Of equal concern is that public schools have fewer teachers per capita serving the needs of ELLs than it had 15 years ago, as service gaps have increased substantially. The latest available data from the National Center on Education Statistics (NCES) indicates that "the percentage of public school students in the United States who were … ELLs was higher in fall 2015 (9.5 percent, or 4.8 million students) than in fall 2000 (8.1 percent, or 3.8 million students)."[3] This means that nearly 1-in-10 students nationwide are ELLs. In addition, over 3-in-4 are Hispanic (77% of ELLs or 7.6% of all K–12 students).[4] Astonishingly, many non-Latino educators are unaware about these statistics. More disconcertingly, some do not think the data are important.

Before responding to multiple barriers about Latino educational progress in later chapters, it is imperative we first gain a fuller understanding of the educational past, especially as it affected the overall progress of Latino and Black youngsters. As such, the first chapter will review the general context of American education relative to the Latino population. Part of the review will focus on particular antecedents and themes that will later resurface contemporaneously, as history oftentimes shapes a troublesome path from which we struggle to escape and overcome.

This context will then direct pathways for subsequent chapters that examine the education of Latinos in greater detail, as the Hispanic portion of the narrative needs to be well understood. Implied is the fact that past conditions sometimes intervene against progress, as particular events and antecedents can slyly dawdle their way into the present, almost as historical grandfathering. This is critically important to comprehend in examining the future progress of education. Gathered information will then be synthesized in a closing epilogue that bridges this learning with the current challenges Latino students are facing in education.

Notes

1. Lesli Maxwell, 2014.
2. U.S. Department of Education, *The State of Racial Diversity in the Educator Workforce*, 2016.
3. https://nces.ed.gov/programs/coe/indicator_cgf.asp
4. *Ibid.*

· 1 ·

THE BIRTH OF AMERICAN EDUCATION

The truth which makes men free is for the most part the truth which men prefer not to hear.
Herbert Sebastian Agar

As history and education intertwine, it is important to understand how past policies and practices have shaped our schools. In the United States, the role of public education is to provide society with a competent and highly-informed citizenry that can help sustain its democracy and ensure it flourishes. One of the articles of faith by the founding fathers is that the American republic will survive only if its citizens are educated.[1] To this end, the common schools movement of the 19th century became a major source that fed the industrial revolution. Economic growth was fueled by immigrant labor and nurtured by public schools, with an achievement in American education midcentury onward that eventually surpassed the education of European nations by the end of that century.[2]

So then, what should we know about public schools? What are the antecedents that have resulted in today's successes as well as challenges? While times have changed, education has not always changed along with it, and seldom as quickly. What does this mean? Simply put, education has changed more slowly the past half century than it did during its heyday during the mid-19th century. In other ways, education has taken a back step. More recently, it has nearly stalemated, often reactive and minimally adjusting to current trends.

There are good reasons why this has been the case, as there are equally valid reasons we should review such a formidable legacy and learn its lessons. Given today's considerable pressures such as increasingly low achievement and global competitiveness, it is important to learn how best to bring about a more effective process by which to generate higher levels of achievement and first-rate learning for our young.

To better comprehend how public schools have reached such major levels of inequality, it is crucial to take several steps back to reconstruct how education has evolved over time. Equally important, it is critical to then sketch patterns by which the antecedents of miseducation for children of color became formalized. To frame such a history it is necessary to start with traditional underpinnings of how a system for the children of the privileged and then for the Anglo student developed. This provides a needed backdrop by which we can then overlay the framework that has guided schooling in America. Such a context is needed before inserting any narrative about racial groups and their struggles over time.

When systems don't know what to do, they do what they know. In such instances, they operate with uncanny human tendencies, at times regressively and at times defensively, but all too often repeating past errors. Here the phrase from a 19th century Spanish philosopher from Harvard, George Santayana, rings true: "Those who cannot remember the past are condemned to repeat it." Point being, history will repeat itself if we do not change it; and we cannot easily change it "if we do not learn from it." This partly explains why educational change at times reverses itself, even backtracks. Today's patterns and trends are no exception. As there are lessons in this quest, it is essential we learn to get them right this time around.

In continually putting out fires, systems limit their capacity to focus on new conditions. For this day and age, with incessant bombardment of new information and instant communication, the educational quagmires we are encountering are unacceptable. Progress gets swallowed when complacency overrules and status quo is reaffirmed, as it is hard to change when rushing to keep up with the mandates of yesterday. Current status prevails when conditions that require essential change are ignored. While no doubt change is difficult as stagnation breeds comfort, unless the status quo is pushed the likelihood of forging new initiatives is in doubt.

In weathering storms, many educational systems operate as if current challenges are merely temporal, hoping problems resolve of their own accord, with limited interference from courts, policy, structure, or practice. Such attitudes expect that what worked yesterday will continue tomorrow, as if conditions do not change over time. Resistance to evolving conditions and non-adjustment to new and pressing realities greatly dogs advancement, yielding limited progress.

When it comes to learning about nontraditional populations and what they imply for the learning context, more specifically for students of color, resistance will encounter negative reactions. What worked well for the modal student likely works poorly today and worse tomorrow, with past models, approaches, practices, and theories remaining fully intact and undisturbed. Meanwhile, yesterday's small minority population is today's majority enrollment, confronting major disparities that still lag as they were never fully resolved. By logical extension, the system must adjust and change to regain balance and remain relevant.

As the past can never be the model for the future, much can be gained in reflection. Churchill once remarked, "The farther back you can look, the farther forward you are likely to see."[3] In securing the future, systems must be ready and willing to advance new knowledge to the next level, with great reflection and learning from past accomplishments as well as misjudgments. For this day and age, public schools must seriously work to adjust and self-correct if they are to meet societal needs and global challenges.

Granted, if the system has barely budged under past difficult circumstances, from where comes the hope to chart a new future in needed time? This query presses related questions such as "What lessons have been learned?" "What has worked well?" "What efforts can be scaled up?" and "How soon should we act?" There is always hope, as this is not about the demise of American education, but about revival and renewal. With significant hurdles to overcome, resolutions to problems can focus on renaissance rather than piecemeal reform.[4] To do so, we must first go way back as Churchill once suggested, to "see" how to better relearn and reframe.

Colonial Education

PRIOR TO THE REVOLUTIONARY WAR, EDUCATION INITIALLY RESTED ON THE FORTUNES OF THE RICH. This worked well for the education of aristocrats, where those that had the means could afford superior education. Despite the inaccessibility of schooling for everyone, estimates indicate that over half (60%) of New Englanders between 1650 and 1670 were able to read, since a good many had been taught at home and in Sunday school. However, literacy rates were lower among the middle-Atlantic colonies and still lower in the South.[5] But even these rates were not maintained. Literacy dropped considerably during the early 1700s, when more of the common class arrived on Eastern shores. Thereon, educational achievement was more limited, reaching its lowest levels around the 1800s.

Despite downturns, education remained continually at the forefront of the American colonies. This was such an important asset that Harvard University, the first institution of higher education among colonists, was founded barely a year after the first secondary public school was established—Boston Latin—and just two decades after the mooring of the Mayflower, indicating the high importance of education for colonists.

By 1642, two decades after the Mayflower, the first compulsory school attendance law was enacted for the Colony of Massachusetts among townships of 50 families or more, where provisions had to be made for the instruction of reading and writing. For townships with 100 families or more, community requisites were even higher, as grammar schools also had to be provided.[6] Without question, the importance of education along with religion as per the Deluder Law were the two institutions most strongly tied to the welfare of the colonies. Education played a major role in the ultimate success of the colonies.

Over time, however, as education developed among colonists, especially those without provisions like Massachusetts, it became principally for the well-to-do. Education held onto its British origin as it would be another century before colonists would shed the British system, when more people were ready to reflect the values of the evolving American culture. This occurred near the start of the 19th century, recognizing education as the strength of the new republic, but this time for average citizens. Even prior to this period, a major exception was made for "paupers," children of widows and other dependents as this had become a responsibility of the state.

Uppermost for the founding fathers was the critical connection between citizenship and education. Nonetheless, the break from only an aristocratic and privately-held education was difficult, as it was tightly held only for the elites, even after the Revolution. But as the dangers of ignorance were strongly felt, especially among leading colonists, the need for universal education slowly became preeminent in both *advancing* the new democracy (Republic) and for *keeping* it together. It was the growth of the population that further prompted the need for greater access to schooling and enfranchisement.

Believing that only when people are "well informed" can they be "entrusted with their own government,"[7] Thomas Jefferson and Dr. Benjamin Rush, both signers of the Declaration of Independence, led the educational charge, with Jefferson strongly advocating for a national education system, affirming that an educated citizenry was a vital requisite for the survival of a free people, and with Dr. Rush pushing for a national system of universal education. Both subscribed to the notion that the nation could not be both "ignorant and free," as this would be a contradiction. Such thoughts were again referenced by Jefferson in a letter to a friend (1816) when he asserted: "If a nation expects to be ignorant and free … it expects what never was and never will be."[8] Education had become so vital to the founders that several went on to establish their own universities. This included Jefferson himself as well as Franklin, Rush, and Adams, among others.

After the Revolutionary War, the country was highly debt-ridden, with a population of barely four million and mostly rural. With barely five percent living in cities, it was difficult for a universalized system of education to take hold.[9] Slowly, education began to be perceived as essential to economic survival, as the nation faced a rather fragmented and more poorly educated population as immigration began to grow among the colonies. An integrated system did not exist where a youngster could progress naturally from elementary school to secondary school and onward to college. Interestingly, it was during this period that slavery also reached its peak, having climbed rapidly from barely 20,000 in 1700 (representing less than 8% of the population) to that of 575,420 by 1780,[10] reaching 21% of all colonists within half a century, its highest percent.*

It was the election of George Washington in 1789, after several faltering Continental Congresses that the country began to regain its composure. In fact, this was a time when the nation began growing rather rapidly. It doubled in size after the Louisiana Purchase of 1803, with more massive immigration at its heels soon after. Growth occurred so quickly that by mid-19th century (between 1830 and 1860), over 4.5 million Europeans arrived, almost tripling the U.S. population in barely 30 years.[11] By the Civil War over 93 cities had the distinction of having more than 10,000 or more residents

---

* The slave population increased nearly eightfold during the next 80 years. Ninety percent of all African Americans were in slave bondage by 1860, when the slave population neared a total of 4 million.

when just four decades earlier (1820) only 13 cities could boast populations of that size.¹²

Given such gigantic growth, the need for public education rose, and the topic of universal education fast became an issue of public debate. Still operating in the mode of revolution during the first third of the 19th century, general thinking about education was shaping differently from the standard; one which was against religious, private, and elitist schools as propagated in Europe. The newly-developing ideal was that schools for a "democratic" republic should be guided by three principles: "public, free and non-sectarian."¹³ As such, it was to be government-sponsored and publicly-supported through some form of taxation and public representation. This new system was to become an American success story by mid-19th century.

This new ideal, shaping a "Democratic Republic" for the "common man," became real when the Democratic-Republican Party of the Jeffersonians became factionalized in the 1820s. This occurred when the election of Andrew Jackson broke the cycle in 1828 of six consecutive and elite presidents. He was the first to triumph over aristocracy as the "champion of the common man." But education was not all driven from the top, as there was already a push by industry from skilled workers by the second third of the century. Several working men's organization in the cities of Philadelphia and New York composed of skilled workers, for example, advocated for strong public education as a form of social mobility for their children. The bifurcated system of private schools for the elite and state funded, but not yet tax supported for the masses was being carefully scrutinized.

By midcentury it had become reasonable for educational reformers to hope that "common" schools for "common" folks [White] would work, as it was endorsed as a movement that would make education available for "everyone." Yet racial minorities were never part of the plan, especially with the entrance of the *Mejicano* after the Mexican-American War. Minority entrance into education became tougher with increased immigration by the Chinese at about the same time midcentury. This condition worsened after the Civil War mid-1860s, as it had after the Trail of Tears for Native Americans early-1830s.

Education as a Right

LOOKING BACK, THE FORMALIZATION OF K–12 EDUCATION HAD EVOLVED SLOWLY ACROSS SEVERAL CENTURIES, BEGINNING WITH THE FIRST PUBLIC SCHOOL IN

1635, AS IT TOOK ANOTHER TWO CENTURIES BEFORE MASS ELEMENTARY EDUCATION CAME ONTO ITS OWN DURING THE FIRST THIRD OF THE 19TH CENTURY. The common schools movement came into formation when it strongly boosted the push for public elementary education with industrialization, eventually becoming the *first transformation* in American education. Growth was so rapid that by mid-19th century over half of all White youth were enrolled in elementary schools compared to negligible representations at the start of the century.[14] Early ungraded classrooms of multiple students crowded into one-room schoolhouses gave way to that of larger facilities with more students in a more structured and manageable manner soon after.

In looking back, it was 1805 when the New York Free School Society was founded to provide education for poor children. This was when the provision of free schools for all children was first tackled in New York City. At the time, there were 141 teachers for a city population of just over 75,000, with most teachers maintaining private schools, while others taught in charity schools run by churches.[15] In fact, it was not until 1821 that the first tuition-free public high school opened its doors in Boston, not New York City. Soon after, it was the State of Massachusetts, renowned for progressive stances in education, that passed the first state law in 1827 that made all grades of public school open to students free of charge.[16] But even by 1830 standards, education was still at its infancy in development, greatly limited in outreach to the general public, but soon to take a great leap forward and one that became rather rapid.

In retrospect, from colonial days to the present, distinct periods denote the development of the public schools. At the inception, it was the British educational system that shaped the entry of elites into positions of leadership, but only among those that could afford schooling, as this was the passport to positions of high influence and status. Already by 1820 the English High School in Boston had become the template for a complete education, as it also began spreading into other parts of the Northeast. Up until then, it had been for the select few that were college-bound.

While the system had lasted several centuries with fairly high levels of literacy, it came to a head by the early 19th century with lower literacy rates increasing in areas outside the Northeast as well as with growing immigration and the rapid development of urban centers, as earlier mentioned. As a result, fears of social disorder sparked from rapid changes and the expansion of industrialization heightened concerns about increasing crime rates and truant youth. In response, schools became the logical solution for merchants and skilled workers, as it also aided the onrush of the Westward Movement and the need for greater specialization. For the growing nation, schools also represented another form of social control for population growth and potential urban decay. Schooling the illiterate also became a solution for the increasing number of lower classes with limited skills.

As a result, a new period of academic growth began to sprout for common people, when schools became freely available to anyone (Whites) that wished to attend. This was when "public schools," as known today, "were born mid-19th century."[17] Rather quickly, education became the expense of the state.[18] This new radicalized education was to be a "right" for anyone that could "access" schooling. It was also midcentury (1848) when differentiation by graded classes came into practice, later denoted as the "egg-crate school." The process of grouping students according to age appropriateness seemed more effective, advancing one full grade for every year in school and with high school (grades 9–12) culminating the next level of advancement.[19]

Pushed by industrialization, progress also increased by way of another logical addition, this time preschool education, with kindergarten also introduced midcentury. Initially, kindergartens were offered as a form of social welfare for children whose parents were working or in poor circumstances, but middle-class parents saw its benefits and also demanded their provision. But preschool education did not advance rapidly, as kindergarten classes among public schools only came to enroll 6% of the nationwide kindergarten-aged population by 1900. It was twenty years later during the next century that it was able to expand, when every major city boasted having kindergarten in their district and in tandem with compulsory attendance laws.[20] This could not have occurred half a century earlier, as conditions were still in the process of expanding elementary schools.

Another example of how far enhancements flourished was when enrollment in the early 1900s grew more rapidly at the upper grade levels primarily to meet the demands of the workforce, causing the median level of educational attainment to increase substantially. This was independent of any educational reform, as it was principally pushed by industry. Such increases also led to related growth higher up the education ladder, propelling departments at universities, colleges, professional schools, and junior colleges to raise enrollment. Between 1900 and 1930 university enrollment rose sevenfold, with more students enrolled in collegiate departments in 1930 than all students that had attended secondary school by 1900![21]

With educational growth all around, state laws began to mandate schooling as a legal obligation so that by 1900 education had become indispensable to the general progress and wellbeing of the nation. Elementary schools were seemingly available everywhere. Compulsory attendance began advancing when it started becoming the national norm in the 1880s for children typically between the ages of 6 and 14, with Southern states the last to pass compulsory education in 1918.

In tandem, though somewhat independently, the high school began to move away from the narrow, private-school model that had functioned as college preparatory.[22] With impetus from schools like Boston English, the "classical" curriculum that had led for nearly two centuries began to surface out of the private academy into a wider and more public audience through the public high school, with the industrial sector beginning to then reinforce the entrance of more students into collegiate institutions. This also helped reframe elementary curricula to become more rigorous because many would not be going to college. Greater rigor was also beneficial to better prepare the few that continued onto university study, almost as backwards mapping.

During this period, debates brewed about the standardization of public education, as it had become uneven. With the growth of the high school, however, competing academic philosophies between "academic" versus "traditional" education for the elementary level, for example, and the concept of "terminal" versus "continuing" education at the high school level exacerbated. Among high schools, for instance, the curriculum had changed in both content and rigor, as secondary instruction—via the private academy—had been the primary vehicle by which the rich had attained their education. Arguably, the public schools were now taking on this role.

Given continuing and unprecedented population growth, with major immigration waves starting once again in 1880, the need for resolution of the curriculum had become important. Just before, a nascent organization called the National Teachers Association (later the NEA) was founded in 1857, precisely when reading was a luxury for White students and a crime for enslaved and free Black children in Southern states. It was within this climate that one of the major contributions of the new organization was the formalization of two expert committees, one at the elementary level and the other among secondary schools, to deal with related curricular issues.

As it turned out, this rightfully brought resolution to debates among critical educational topics that had endured from many decades earlier. The group sponsored to realign and correlate *elementary* school studies was called the "Committee of Fifteen on Elementary Education." It reframed requisites for the training of teachers and helped provide guidelines for the organization of city school systems (1895). By contrast, the "Committee of Ten" that had been formalized to resolve competing academic philosophies, offered alternatives to the *high school* curriculum, as per their report of 1892, exclusively focusing on the high school curricula. These two committees, although at times conflictual, created major complements to the K–12 continuum. The century that had first witnessed disparate schools lacking in uniformity and consistency was now moving toward a more uniform system, where a large percent of students were enrolled in elementary school with a more responsive, aligned, and nationally-directed educational system guiding the high school.[23]

In a short time, the high school curricula became highly differentiated, adding options for studying multiple occupations. Growth was such that by the 1880s the total number of public high schools surpassed in number all private and costly academies for the first time. As demand for still more subjects increased, high schools became the bridge between primary and college education, as it continually expanded its offerings.[24] Over time, especially for those not advancing to college, it became "the people's college" by default, eventually becoming the most major contributor to K–12 educational advancement the first third of the 20th century, nearly equivalent in impact to what common schools had become mid-1800s. However, this was short-lived as the Committee of Ten's conception of the high school as the people's college was ultimately rejected. This spawned a proliferation of various high schools, English, Latin and Vocational that sorted students into sectors of society, with the working classes, Mexicans, and Blacks more frequently slotted into vocational high schools. As a result, they were not able to reach the traditional high school until decades after Whites. This occurred most strongly in the South and the Southwest, where the bulk of both African American and Mexican populations resided. For Whites, a major growth spurt occurred in education the first half of the 20th century, as high school graduation rates zoomed from 7% at the turn of the century to nearly three-fourths (73%) by 1940,[25] quickly becoming the *second major transformation* in American education.

It is important to not lose sight of the fact that K–8 education was seen as a "must" for the economic growth and wellbeing of the country. While high school education was still not as common until the turn of the century, it could not have expanded so widely had it not been free. In retrospect, had it stayed privatized, the nation would not have made the great leaps witnessed by the turn of the century nor could it have advanced as rapidly against European countries in extending literacy and basic education to non-elites. Similar arguments are being made today when it comes to free college education, certainly for community colleges nationwide.

For teachers, their enhancement came through the normal school (from the French "l'ecole normale" begun in the 1790s France) and as early as 1823 in New England accompanying the start of the common schools movement and expanding dramatically after the Civil War. The need for more teachers resulting from the common schools movement encouraged the system to fill needed slots with the surplus of young, middle-class women with high educational levels, but with few vocations matching their qualifications. Although men were first hired for the newly-emerging schools, the shift to women was quick and permanent. School districts, eager to save money, found they could pay women half the price of men. In addition, they employed better pedagogic practices and warmth, especially for young children. Together, these factors resulted in major shifts for a gendered workforce.

While the majority of teachers were male at the start of the 19th century, this was no longer the case mid-19th century, with many more female teachers in all states except for the South. Ratios increased even more for females soon after the Civil War, from 59% in 1870 to 70% by 1900.[26] The shift did not occur at the district administrative levels, however, raising the question decades later of "Why do women teach and men manage?" Latest statistics for female teachers today hover eerily slightly higher than that ratio, with about three-in-four (77%) being female today.[27] While women have made inroads into administration since then, a gendered pyramid remains with higher levels of men employed at each stage of education, from elementary schools, middle schools, high schools, all the way to superintendent.

As traced, the first educational transformation was ushered by the common schools movement midcentury, soon followed by the high school movement. By the start of the new century, a *third major transformation* in American education was taking place, namely that of higher education. This latter emphasis occurred in part to compete with the German higher education in terms of science, mathematics, and what we would call today the STEM areas. More importantly, however, it was the passage of the federal Morrill Land-Grant Act of 1862 that provided funds for every state to establish at least one public university, the origins of what became the Midwestern "Big Ten" schools. For the more rural Midwest, higher education through the original Morrill Act was to help farmers improve crop yield and assist with animal husbandry as well as to reinforce the mechanical arts and general education, as distinct from the more narrowly private Ivy League schools. It was also a place where the sons and daughters of farmers and mechanics could attend. Normal schools, once separate institutions, were absorbed and transformed into state schools of education and then state universities as credentials for teaching increased to a minimum of a bachelor's degree.

The second Morrill Act of 1890 further assured that race was not a criterion for enrollment, as it more specifically related to the former confederate states now back in the Union. Expansion of higher education was so rapid that by end of the century some 977 institutions of higher education (IHEs) had been formalized when barely four decades earlier, at the start of the Civil War in 1860, barely 381 IHEs were operational.[28]

With advances from multiple fronts, public schools greatly improved as a result of these changes, promoting K–16 education considerably. This was so much the case that by the 1940s, as less attention was needed for the addition of school facilities, most especially the construction of high schools, greater focus could now be directed back to the classroom. This propelled the enhancement for quality teacher education, the organization of instructional content, and the expansion of opportunity for more youth to attend junior colleges.[29]

Altogether, as great strides had been achieved in education, the nation celebrated its preeminence in educational prowess and achievement like never before. Looking back, within less than one hundred years, between mid-19th to mid-20th century, education had been advanced by three major transformations, with a student population that had moved from an elite institution of education to one where nearly 4-in-5 students were attaining high school diplomas freely and where a university system had been radically altered.

Notwithstanding, this rapid level of growth hid a growing disturbance that had been surfacing during this highly segregated era, as it had ignored barriers that had developed for racial minorities. The expansion of education had been so fast and furious that there was seemingly no political will and less urgency to ensure a level playing field. In plain fact, it was to prioritize White students for access to quality schools. Students of color from all racial/ethnic groups were marginalized. When included, it was only to meet minimum standards for student funding. With the elimination of child labor and more years for compulsory attendance (for many states up to 16 years of age) enrollments boomed and large school districts were compelled to run double sessions during the day. As a result, it was seemingly easy to ignore a stigmatized segment of the population. While partly true, the real story was more pernicious and fully racialized. The exclusion of different racial groups followed an altogether different pattern. The next subsections briefly review this history for distinct racial groups.

Educating Populations of Color

DESPITE ACADEMIC ADVANCES, THE PARTICIPATION OF RACIAL GROUPS WAS LEFT BEHIND, GREATLY EXCLUDED FROM ALL THREE TRANSFORMATIONS, BUT PARTICULARLY THE HIGH SCHOOL AND HIGHER EDUCATION, AS THE RIGHTS OF CHILDREN WERE IGNORED FOR THIS CLASS OF CITIZEN. Unable to overcome a 19th-century racist mentality, the start of the next century was made even worse with the rise of White nationalism and resistance to equality. This grew to major heights by the 1920s, coincident with the growth of scientific racism as well as an immense rate of European immigration and an emboldened KKK. This resulted in multiple sectors celebrating a heyday of educational growth and development with the needs of racial groups fully ignored. As this "other" issue grew away from any watch, it was dismissed by White governing bodies as less important, even bothersome.

This was also a time when reformers got so caught up in methods and how schools could reform society that they lost sight regarding education "for all." The period epitomized the fact that racial groups had been greatly missing from the educational process, giving impetus to a series of challenges against the status quo.[30] Upon reviewing the state of affairs during this period, W.E.B. Du Bois reminisced at a Georgia teachers' convention in 1935 that there had been one way to "cure society's ills," this was by making people "intelligent" through schooling, but that the process had left behind a critical sector of the population, creating a gaping hole in American education and a devastating gulf in social justice. Here he clearly emphasized that to do this "the school had again but one way … first and last, to teach them [students] to read, write and count."[31] Yet at the same time, the widespread exclusion of nonwhite racial groups from nearly all schools fully disallowed this option for all peoples. A trend had been set, and a gap had been created that was to form a void that continued beyond mid-20th century. This was not only leveled against Blacks and Latinos, but also for Asian and Pacific Islander populations as well as for Native Americans. It is important to note, however, that to combat these trends, Mexican

Americans attended Catholic schools when afforded and Blacks created some private schools or attended missionary schools to provide their own remedies of exclusion and low quality. For the most part this was exceptional to the trend, as it occurred for only a very small population of nonwhite students.

Asian Exclusion

FOR ASIAN AMERICANS, THE CHINESE HAD BEGUN ENTERING THE COUNTRY IN LARGE NUMBERS AROUND THE 1850S, DURING THE CALIFORNIA GOLD RUSH OF 1848–1855. This continued when large construction projects demanded hard labor such as the building of the First Continental Railroad between 1863 and 1869. Not long after that came the Chinese Exclusion Act enacted in 1885. This was the first significant law restricting immigration into the United States. The act provided an absolute 10-year moratorium on Chinese labor immigration.†

In school desegregation cases involving Chinese students, two are of particular note, one before *Plessy* and the other after *Plessy*. In *Tape v. Hurley* (1885), the California Supreme Court decided against the San Francisco Public Schools, as it had completely excluded Chinese, Indian, and Blacks for over ten years. While the Court ordered the district to admit students despite ancestry, it did not require the district to admit these students with Whites, thus creating the rationale for Chinese segregated schools.

In *Gong Lum v. Rice* (1927), the U.S. Supreme Court ruled unanimously that a Mississippi school board had not violated the Fourteenth Amendment's equal protection clause when it classified a student of Chinese descent as "colored," as she was from the "Mongolian or yellow race" and could not be considered White. In adhering to *Plessy*, the decision barred Gong Lum from attending a White high school.

Following the Chinese Exclusion Act, young Japanese laborers started reaching the thousands around the 1880s. Together with smaller numbers of Koreans and Asian Indians, these groups began arriving on the West Coast, replacing the Chinese as cheap labor. But anti-Japanese legislation and violence soon followed. By 1907, Japanese immigration was also restricted between the United States and Japan by a "Gentleman's Agreement." It was around that time

---

† Incredibly, it took more than half a century (58 years) for the law to be repealed by the Magnuson Act on December 17, 1943.

that larger numbers of Korean immigrants started coming to Hawaii and the U.S. mainland, at times serving as strike-breakers, at other times as railroad builders and agricultural workers.[32] Not unexpectedly, these groups also were eventually excluded. For the Korean immigrant, they not only faced racial exclusion in the U.S., but also the double whammy of Japanese colonization at home.

Asian Indian immigrants followed a similar path when they entered the United States as laborers. Settling down soon after Chinese exclusion, they also became victims of denigration with phrases like "Hindu invasion" by exclusionists and White laborers. This "tide of the Turbans," as it was called, was outlawed from entry in 1917, when Congress declared that India was part of the Pacific-Barred Zone of excluded Asian countries. But by then, all Asian immigrants had been barred, including Chinese, Japanese, Koreans, and Indians. All were fully excluded by law, denied citizenship and naturalization, even prevented from marrying Caucasians or owning land. During the Second World War, it was the Japanese internment camps that further exemplified U.S. attitudes toward Asian American citizens, as different from White German Americans.

Ironically, with all other Asians excluded, thousands of young, single Filipinos began migrating in large numbers to the West Coast during the 1920s to work in farms and canneries, filling the continuing need for cheap labor that the Mexican population could not fill alone, as Filipinos could not yet be legally excluded by immigration laws, since the Philippines had been annexed as a result of the 1898 Spanish-American War. But as racism and economic competition intensified with the Depression of 1929, it led to severe anti-Filipino violence and passage of the Tydings-McDuffie Act in 1935, just when the government of the Commonwealth of the Philippines was enacted. It was this Act that reclassified all Filipinos, including those who were living in the United States. They became "aliens" for the purposes of immigration to America. Astonishingly, a quota of 50 immigrants per year was established thereon. Before the Act, Filipinos had been classified as U.S. nationals, but not as citizens. While allowed to freely migrate, they were denied naturalization rights within the U.S., unless they were citizens by birth in the U.S. mainland.

According to Takaki (1993), pioneering Chinese, Japanese, Koreans, Indians, and Filipinos each faced conditions of exclusion that forged a common, shared Asian experience in America. The term "perpetual foreigner" was coined to reflect both the historical exclusionary immigration acts against Asians as well as the continuing legacy of American society's perceptions of Asian Americans.[33]

It was along blatant racial lines that the National Origins Act of 1924 was passed by Congress creating a system of national quotas that deliberately discriminated against immigrants from southern Europe and virtually excluded Asians. To a lesser extent, also excluded were immigrant Eastern Europeans, Arabs, and Jews. One important country was exempt from this law, Mexico. Resultingly, we will see how the U.S. has continued to have the door open to Mexicans when their labor was needed for agribusiness in the Southwest and industrial plants in the Midwest, but shut during periods of low employment. The Johnson-Reed law of 1924 continued in effect until Congress enacted the Immigration and Naturalization Act of 1965 that abolished the quota system during President Johnson's term.

Latino Exclusion

FOR THE LATINO, RACIAL STIGMA HAD BEEN AN ONGOING SAGA SINCE BEFORE THE CIVIL WAR, AND THIS WILL BE MORE THOROUGHLY REVIEWED IN A SUBSEQUENT CHAPTER. But it is important to know that during this period and throughout the three critical decades leading to civil rights (1930–1960), George I. Sánchez, also known as the "Father of Chicano Psychology," had come to similar conclusions regarding the exclusion of Latino populations from traditional education, as he strongly fought against many injustices being forced upon the Hispanic American. Having served as a teacher, principal, district administrator, and later as university professor, author, and civil rights leader, he strongly advocated that the Fourteenth Amendment protected Mexican American rights not solely because of the race-creed-color category, but also for being classified as a "class apart." This came to fruition in the High Court's unanimous ruling in *Hernández v. Texas* (1954), weeks before *Brown v. Board of Education* (1954). Later, in upholding similar arguments before a Texas commissioner during the late 1950s, Sánchez expressed that Texas could not be considered a "great" state as long as one-third of its population was separated by a wide gulf from the others in the areas of education, health, and economic wellbeing. Professor Sánchez was not only a major educational leader, but also served as the first national president of the advocacy organization, the League of United Latin American Citizens (LULAC), and later as special consultant to the U.S. Bureau of Indian Affairs (BIA) as well as in multiple other capacities until his death in 1972.[34]

In the trajectory of traditional American education, it was not until mid-20th century that a *fourth transformation* became reality, one that was to assure in writing legal equality for every child through the courts, removing more than half a century of constitutionally-approved segregation since *Plessy v. Ferguson* (1896). The term "separate but equal" required that segregated facilities nonetheless remain equal in quality, a hallow reality for Black and Mexican-segregated schools.

In the case of Latinos midcentury, a state-level California decision, *Méndez v. Westminster* (1947), successfully challenged the racial segregation of Latino children. Building on *Méndez* and the federal level case of *Brown*, it was not until the mid-1960s that ground-breaking legislation established fresh ground, almost as a "new" Reconstruction, as the first ten years after *Brown* witnessed bitter legal battles over desegregation and an almost barren decade of progress for integration in the public schools. As was the case, it was only after these initiatives that some progress became noticeable, as evidenced by minor incremental gains in minority achievement.

Progress, however, was subsequently deterred by new educational wars. From today's vantage point, the educational gap has barely narrowed since the 1970s, now separated by half a century. Indeed, petty struggles over trite reforms swallowed up the field. Though education should be as basic as fire and police protection as a human right, it has taken turns that have derailed the more important focus of equity. As but one example, educational progress greatly slowed in its pace toward equity when debates began to rage around privatization and then with charter schools 1990s onward. In retrospect, issues like these became a ruse, leaving behind the more basic concerns about equity and equality in American education.

Public Schooling

PUBLIC SCHOOLING STARTED AN EDUCATIONAL MOVEMENT IN AMERICAN HISTORY THAT WAS DIAMETRICALLY OPPOSITE TO THE MORE FORMALIZED AND ELITE SYSTEMS ORIGINALLY PLANTED BY EUROPEANS, THROUGH BOTH THE SPANIARD AND ENGLISH SYSTEMS, EXCEPT FOR RACIAL GROUPS. Catapulting on White success, the effectiveness of the public schools caught on, eventually serving as a major influencer back to Europe, as an unexpected contributor back at the mother continent. As we consider education's current role on society, we realize how impactful it was for America's unique history. American educational Influence increased after the country's expansionist period, when economic growth catapulted to national dominance in the international arena.

Certain processes cannot be easily glossed over, as particular factors are important to understand and interpret in their wider context. In point of fact, they continue in development, albeit within newly formalized settings this current century.

Such interplay with history places the evolution of education front and center as one of America's greatest contributions as well as its most valuable asset in its development as a major power. In an almost parallel manner, this century now represents another turning point—a *fifth transformation* in the making—as it once did when the country went from near bankruptcy in its early days after the Revolution, again during the depression of the 1890s,[35] and once more with the Great Depression of the 1930s to world leadership due to enlightened educational opportunity and consequent economic development by the end of World War II.

Since the start of the 19th century, the country had gone through a Second Great Awakening and had been torn by racial intolerance on one side and imperial expansion on the other. This century also led to several wars, one with Mexico, another war with Spain, and a Civil War in between—all racially-centered. It was also a time when the nation was expanding westward, after the Louisiana Purchase, the acquisition of Mexican territories, and the Alaska Purchase, among others.

By midcentury the country had been fueled by an ideological belief in "Manifest Destiny" that the United States was chosen by God to spread from the Atlantic to Pacific coasts. Manifest Destiny led to additional lands to cultivate and prosper for both slaveowners and non-slaveowners that contributed to major sectional tensions. During this tumultuous period it was the public schools that became the engine that fed innovation, expansion and industrialization. Altogether, these were the major drivers that operated in tandem, molding the country like a production factory. In the midst, education had become indispensable. In considerable ways, it paved the way for many changes to play a formidable part in American progress. It was this impetus that hurled the country into an important world power by the end of the 19th century.

With the 19th century as a transitional century, let's step back a bit and take a closer look at what transpired inside the engine that drove the industrial revolution and led different waves in the process of nation-building. Let's examine what can be learned from this history that provides valuable insights into today's educational challenges.

While America's public schools grew out of the political context of schooling arguments and debates during the middle third of the 19th century, the establishment of public schools for common people became an important turning point in American life. It referred to the majority of the population, the White working-class and aspirational lower-middle classes. This occurred when particular reformers were taking it upon themselves to advocate for "common schools" that would be available to the public free of charge.[36] In turn, the movement to other changes was to reshape the educational landscape, while holding back students of color.

This period was also a time when educational leaders strongly advocated before state legislatures and pushed for a "public" system of schools against many skeptical listeners. In particular, Horace Mann in the Massachusetts legislature and later as educational reformer himself, firmly held that education, if widely dispersed, could speedily affect social reform. Starting as a state legislator, he strongly upheld the voices of previous advocates from the turn of the century like Noah Webster and Benjamin Rush, correctly asserting that democratic values could not be fully upheld by an undereducated public. As he saw it, schooling was the most critical factor that could bring about social equality. It was his ardent belief that "Education ... beyond all other devises of human origin is the great equalizer of the conditions of man—the balance-wheel of the social machinery."[37] This motivated him to lead the change for what became the common schools movement.

Guided by indefatigable leadership toward this end, and after becoming the first Secretary of Education in the nation for Massachusetts, Horace Mann was eventually christened the "father of American public education." He represented a major break from the elite establishment during a period of great inequality, even turmoil in the 1830s, near the height of the Second Great Awakening.[38] It is interesting to note that it was his rhetoric that redefined terms like *public*, *free*, *pauper* and *common*, all roughly synonymous to the common schools movement. Without question, he asserted education was "for all." Within two decades of ardent leadership, a rather large system of publicly-supported elementary and middle schools were founded in many Northern and Midwestern states, soon after expanding to the frontier.

By midcentury, push from reformers of his ilk created a formidable imprint nationwide. After leading the common schools movement, he later advocated for compulsory school attendance legislation nationwide, with Massachusetts passing the first such law in 1852.[39] While it took a while for counterpart laws to take effect in other states—nearly half a century—all states would later boast having passed comparable laws.

Such foresight and leadership was radical. Mann's first three ideas about schooling in America continue to remain at the forefront of education today. The *first* major concept in his thinking was that education was the great leveler, the *equalizer* for everyone to succeed and achieve to their greatest potential.

This has become an avowed principle of the American republic supportive of educational "equity." The *second* concept was that everyone should be enrolled in school—*schooling for all, public and free*—as it tried to move away from exclusionary practices, contrary to the informal establishment of both a segregated and exclusive system, one formal and the other informal. The *third* belief was that *every individual can be educated*, giving credence to the fact that everyone can learn. While debates still abound about nuances around these fundamental concepts and precepts, latter arguments relate more to their actual substance and basic meanings and the details of implementation than to its general principles.

The common schools movement swept the nation so quickly that by 1860 it had become the ladder to university education, providing impetus for higher education to serve more than the elite. While all 33 States of the Union had established at least one university by the start of the Civil War with a total of 381 colleges and universities, the passage of the Morrill Land-Grant Act of 1862 greatly bolstered the state-of-the-art in higher education by century's end. In actuality, higher education had already initiated enormous changes among Normal Schools the previous decade as the gateway for schoolteachers of common schools. As earlier referenced, higher education spread rapidly after the Civil War with nearly one thousand IHEs established by end of the century. It was the Second Morrill Act of 1890, also mentioned, that required former Confederate states to either admit Black students to colleges funding the Morrill Act or establish separate institutions for Blacks. Thus, state universities for Blacks such as Texas A&M Prairie View, became part of the 67 Historically Black Colleges and Universities (HBCUs) by the end of the 19th century that received federal funding.[40]

As common thinking was that the best way to turn the "nation's unruly children into disciplined, judicious" citizens was through education,[41] its teaching force had grown into such a national movement that it had given impetus to the formation of today's NEA by mid-19th century in support of schoolteachers. Also, the magnitude of education had grown to such heights that a national Bureau of Education was established in 1867, just after the Civil War, administered by Henry Barnard, former schoolteacher and one of Mann's assistants from prior years.[42] By end of the century, the country had established a robust K–12 public education system and was on its way to creating a first-class higher education system that would become the envy of the world.[43]

In retrospect, what is important to remember about leaders like Horace Mann is the ability to transform powerful ideas into plain language that people could easily understand, embrace, and readily put into practice. There is no question that he convinced the middle classes through fear-mongering that if they did not support education for all—including the poor and working classes—these young people would spread their damage to society in multiple ways. Mann's hope was that schooling would transform youth from violent behavior to model citizens. It was believed that with education they would, by contrast, greatly contribute back to society. With many families moving away from the country to the cities, thinking was that functional literacy would add to specialized labor and more favorably give back to society. Here education had become the answer to much of the nation's needs. Preponderant belief was that education was not just for moral development, but also for community wellbeing and economic advancement, each complementing the other, with all three working immeasurably for the common good.

However, the gap remained for the African American. In 1838, having been influenced by Horace Mann and in his defense of common schools for the State of New Jersey, Bishop George W. Doane of the New Jersey Episcopal Diocese is noted to have made the following declaration by taking Mann's precepts to their logical conclusion: "We utterly repudiate as unworthy, the narrow notion that there is to be an education for the poor as such. Had God provided for the poor a coarser earth, a thinner air, a paler sky? Does not the glorious sun pour down its golden flood as cheerily upon the poor man's hovel, as upon the rich man's palace?"[44] In his ardent defense for the establishment of common public schools in New Jersey he further stated: "The common school is common;" but "not as inferior" nor as a "school for poor man's children, but as the light and air are common."[45] Here the Bishop vehemently asserted that the time was ripe for fuller educational access for all classes of children.

It is notable that common schools went beyond the three Rs, as they also included such subjects as geography and history. Reaching beyond basic academics, the curriculum also prepared a responsible electorate, promoting the moral values of a non-sectarian, Judeo-Christian philosophy in moral and character development as well as citizenship and academics. As the educational establishment developed, it shed much of its British curricula from prior years, though homespun American curricula were still scarce. Such a vacuum had been slowly filled by educators like Noah Webster, whose *American Spelling Book* was first introduced in 1789, later known as the "Blue-backed Speller," as Webster had been in strong opposition to a British curriculum.

Years later, Webster's spelling book was coupled with McGuffey Readers that appeared in 1836, with both becoming big sellers and both described as fully "American." According to one author, "The McGuffey Readers played an important role in American education, as they also helped shape that elusive quality we call the American character."[46] In fact, the *Readers* sold to so many generations of Americans that by 1890 its sales were estimated to have exceeded 107 million,[47] becoming by default the American handbook of virtues and morality. This was later coupled with Horatio Alger novels, with their peppered stories about success against adversity. Horatio's stories were about impoverished boys that rose from humble backgrounds to become successful through hard work, honesty, and fair play. These were key factors that also helped them leapfrog from rags to riches. But these strong factors were also aligned with White, working-class values, not depicted by Black or any other racial, nontraditional member.

The division of classes and grades for the common schools that was so strongly dependent on age and achievement was taken from German practices overseas and introduced during this formative period.[48] Starting in 1848, graded classrooms helped group pupils into more homogeneous clusters as well as assist teachers in attending to smaller groups, with more focused approaches. Interesting also is that kindergarten, another German import, began to take shape around this period, introduced into the United States in the German language in 1855 by Margaretha Meyer Schurz, wife of Carl Schurz.[49] By 1860, the first English-speaking kindergarten opened in Boston,[50] with major practices flourishing in other cities and educational settings by the end of the century, but as earlier stated not catching the attention of the middle classes until much later.

Another German import was bilingual education (or dual language instruction) which was significant in particular states early on, dating back to colonial days. As a result, bilingual or non-English language instruction was being provided in some form or another in many public and private schools by the second half of the 19th century, where by 1900 nearly 600,000 children—about 4% of the elementary school population—were receiving all or part of their instruction in German, as well as other languages.[51] In New Mexico, for example, it was not untypical for either Spanish or English or both to be used as the language for curricula.[52] A number of other languages were also utilized for instruction.[53] According to Ovando (2003), it was a policy of "linguistic assimilation not coercion" that prevailed during this time. According to educators from that time, this seemed as a reasonable and sound pedagogical approach; basically, to adequately reach children that were not English speakers. Notwithstanding, given the xenophobia against Germans at the height of World War I, including language usage, the bilingual school and legal records were to revert to English only. This was the case for Texas and Colorado around 1918, with similar local laws following for many parts of New Mexico and Arizona soon after they entered the Union in 1912.

The concern regarding education drove many debates regarding cost and public alternatives, as "public" schools were competing with the better and more private academies and institutes. Over time, public elementary schools got stronger and more competitive, even to the point of having its high schools be later recognized by ornate architectural facades and splendorous auditoriums to convey a similar specter of prestige as equal competitors to private schools. Apparently, this seemed to have worked in many sectors.

The rapid growth of common schools had forced the issue about who would *finance* these schools and what *content* would drive the curriculum. It was the 1787 Northwest Ordinance that had clearly captured the sentiments of the new nation declaring, "Religion, morality, and knowledge being necessary to good government and the happiness of mankind, schools and the means of education shall forever be encouraged." The ordinances required that every prospective township reserve a plot of land for education, funding came through land sales in the new Northwestern territories. Local and state communities provided minimum funding for public schools, but the notion of citizens being taxed on their property or income was novel.

The concern regarding school financing came to a head in the Midwest, as common schools mushroomed throughout the newly-developing territories of the West and Southwest. In 1874, the Michigan Supreme Court ruled in favor of Kalamazoo's School District #1 to allow the school board to collect taxes in support of its public schools. This judicial decision on the rights of a state to tax individuals for a public good like education spread throughout the country, including "frontier" settlements, as it became the rule of law. Buttressed by this decision, K–8 education became rather universalized by end of the century, with many of the larger systems later adding kindergarten. As it turned out, public schools had become a permanent fixture, with citizens no longer dependent on fee-based, private academies for the future of their children or previously stigmatized "pauper" schools.

With the spread of free schooling becoming universal, there came the concern about high-quality teachers. Though the acceptance of female teachers came about because it was thought they were more sensitive to children's needs, it was likely more because female teachers kept costs down since female employment was rare, *not* for social equity.[54] This was aided by the development of the Normal School for the preparation of teachers, though still insufficient to meet the demand.⁵⁵ As the teacher profession became more standardized, it still was not until the start of the 20th century that more than a high school diploma was needed for entry into the teaching profession, as teachers had been formerly scarce.

Growth and Expansion

IN BROAD PERSPECTIVE, THE COUNTRY HAD GROWN EXTREMELY FAST BY THE FIRST QUARTER OF THE 19TH CENTURY. There were just 26 cities in 1830 with a population of 8,000 or more. School districts were small, with poverty, disease, and child labor widely prevalent.⁵⁶ That year, only three states had committed legislatively to support schools that were tuition free. Schooling for every child was a startling new concept, as it was breaking precedent with the way elite schools had been established in Europe. At the time, a New England educator proclaimed that "tuition free schools were the nurseries of the public mind."⁵⁷ Yet in a very real way, education was beginning to be perceived as the best safeguard against autocracy by the first third of the 19th century, as it was expected to combat the ills of ignorance and oppression.

Yet by the end of the century, schooling was so strongly embedded in the America psyche that it began to lead many aspects of American thought. It was just that Whites did not care to provide education to nonwhites. Even after the Civil War, it was barely 10% of Blacks and an even lower percent among Mexican Americans that received any education beyond the eighth grade. Among those few, all were receiving more than their share of Americanization classes at the expense of the 3R's.⁵⁸

It was both ironic and disheartening that while the U.S. was becoming the vanguard in leading the charge of free education on the global stage together with a broader curriculum, it was also upending freedom for racial groups. As the "White" portion of the nation moved toward education reform and advancement, racial groups were kept away from schooling altogether, exacerbating an abject gap and creating an underclass that would be long-lasting and fully contrary to the nation's founding precepts and the aims of education for "all."

Highly influenced by Horace Mann, schoolteacher Henry Barnard mentioned earlier, had become a major force in the common schools movement. Also, Catherine Beecher and Prudence Crandall contributed mightily to the common schools movement, as they furthered the expansion of education for nontraditional students, including racial groups and women, to the consternation of peers. They also championed the training and development of teachers through Normal Schools and related institutions. In fact, it was through their efforts and those of fellow crusaders that a law was passed in 1855 abolishing segregation in the schools of Massachusetts just three years after compulsory legislation, with both laws representing firsts across the nation.

Catherine Beecher, later overshadowed by her sister, Harriett Beecher Stowe, author of *Uncle Tom's Cabin*, represented an indefatigable worker and crusader as well as a woman of letters. Older by eleven years, Catherine literally raised her sister, taking over domestic duties of the household upon her mother's death, when Harriet was but five years of age. As someone who had written curricula and had extensive teaching experience, Catherine was likely the single greatest influence in her sister's life. Over time, it was Catherine who went on to organize societies and events for the development of teachers and worked with institutions to develop and expand the teacher supply for the ever-increasing frontier schools of the West. She also founded the American Women's Educational Association in 1847, a decade before NEA's formation.

In her review of teacher movements, Dana Goldstein (2014) confirms that in 1800 some ninety percent of American schoolteachers were men, but that by the end of century the vast majority was women. Much of this turnaround was due to the efforts of Catherine Beecher alongside those of sister crusaders like Prudence Crandall. Ironically, it was the "feminization" of the profession that Goldstein attributes to how education became one of the few white-collar unionized professions in the U.S. The "ugly reality of pay discrimination,"[59] however, has come back to haunt a century later; as low pay for schoolteachers continues to suffer precisely because it was relegated as a "woman's profession." Initially, politicians tried to force this as a wedge for cost reductions in schooling, with the assumption that women deserved lower wages, with the hiring of women balancing school budgets. Over time, however, the pattern got stuck in a time warp, difficult to undo and haunting to this day. Teachers now constitute nearly 4% of the total U.S. workforce, nearly 4 million teachers, nationwide.[60]

From this vantage point, the advancement of women during this period was more propelled through education than by any other avenue. It was precisely because of the teaching profession that other opportunities for women also became available. This resulted in some of the most prominent women leaders rising from the teaching profession later in the century such as Susan B. Anthony and the likes of Belva Lockwood, the first schoolteacher to argue before the Supreme Court and the first woman to run for U.S. President in 1884.

In the push for the inclusion of women into the teacher workforce as well as for the inclusion of African Americans, Beecher and Crandall became strong leaders as well as intellectual giants for the efforts of Horace Mann and Henry Barnard. Catherine Beecher was an enigmatic figure, though at times representing ironic contradictions. While an advocate for women being more than domestic workers at home, she never backed women's suffrage. Also, while she pushed for more women to enter the teacher workforce, she did not advocate for their participation in the disciplines of science, medicine, law or engineering.[61]

The likes of someone like Prudence Crandall was also rare. While advocating for education reform, she also pushed for racial equality, as both abolition and the inclusion of women in higher education had been declined up until then. In 1831, she helped found the Canterbury Female Boarding School in Connecticut that admitted a Black student the following year to the consternation of the community. When parents protested and took their daughters out, the school was shut down. Undeterred, she later reopened the school as an academy for African American girls, with the town again retaliating and the school again closing in 1834. It is interesting that while there were no previous racial laws in the state, townspeople responded with the first of the racial laws, all aimed against Crandall's actions. As it was, racial discrimination was very evident in both the North and in the South, merely expressed differently.

Alexis De Tocqueville observed and described these racial conditions. As a French diplomat and political scientist, he came to the United States in 1831 to document the conditions of prisons and penitentiaries. He traveled extensively across the country for nearly nine months and provided keen perspectives as an outsider about the American way of life and its democratic ideals. As a prolific writer and methodical observer, he made extensive observations and later published them as a book, *Democracy in America* (1835). Almost apologetically in chapter 18, he expressed concern that he did not have time to document the relationship between the three races he encountered—the "Europeans," the "Negroes" and the "Indians"—except to conclude that there was much animosity and little interracial contact, as each operated distinctly apart and independently everywhere he went in the North, with blatant subjugation in the South. Later as an abolitionist back home in France, he was concerned about this separation, but didn't hazard to state any opinion about what this meant when in the U.S., except in conveying grave concern about the condition, long-term.

On the other hand, he saw liberty and religion marching together everywhere, with religion at the top of the political institutions in this country. He believed that the America of the 19th century saw in religion a "utility for democratic government," but to a great extent it also "exploited" others.[62] The obligation to a religious stance all too frequently influenced a community's schools, yet seldom advocated for minority rights.

Rather ironically at the same time, many of the public schools receiving church assistance were differentiated from missionary work by groups like the American Board of Christian Foreign Missions (ABCFM) and the Quakers that established schools by the dozens in the North for Blacks, as they also sent teachers by the hundreds to teach Native Americans in the Southeast. Also, assistance from the Catholic Church with the education of the Mexican American in the Southwest was considerable, though not all church related. Altogether, efforts of these types operating away from the mainstream affirmed that dominant public school education was for the Anglo American, as some church and charitable groups tried to make a difference.

Post-elementary education before the common schools and in preparation for college had been provided primarily by academies and seminaries during the earlier part of the 19th century, especially among the more elite, as there were still very few public high schools. Many of the academies were privately conducted and strongly under church control. Over time, this cycle was difficult to break even by the end of the century, when common schools were dominant and when a more secular education was being provided. As such, let's briefly step back to review the academies, their sister institutions, and what they represented.

After religion, it was education that gave life to the 19th century. Nevertheless, its foundational basis was religious, despite its "secularized" curricula.[63] For example, when great religious fervor swept the nation between the 1790s and the 1830s during the "Second Great Awakening," more than 6,000 academies were founded, with more than a quarter million students enrolling during that period.[64] Also, with the growth of seminaries, it was during the second quarter of the century that colleges began to flourish, as the high school movement was still half a century away.

Higher education found a major proponent in Horace Mann who helped establish the second Normal School for the training of teachers in 1839 in Massachusetts, after the first normal school opened in Concord, Vermont in 1823. In his push for colleges, Mann was highly respected in his zeal for a university system and was quoted to have said: "The relation which [sic] colleges bear to the community is but little less than that which the brain bears to the rest of the body."[65] Given that the first Normal Schools started taking off more strongly during the 1840s, it was the guidance and push from reformers like him that advanced the teaching profession into a semi-professional status, certainly for women.[66] Normal Schools became so acceptable that by 1860 some 13 publicly-supported Normal Schools had been established.[67]

Undoubtedly, the teacher movement was fed by the Normal Schools, as many new teachers were needed for the Westward expansion. "Like itinerant preachers, teachers often served at these frontier schools for two years at each place."[68] Ripples of the Second Great Awakening also headed Westward in slow-moving stagecoaches, traveling together with teachers and in the same direction. Education philosophy led by teachers of the frontier schools represented this perspective to a great extent, as these educators were undoubtedly rather traditional in their views with a good many seeing education as a "mission," at times bordering on evangelical fervor.[69]

With Normal Schools already in operation by the Civil War, other colleges began to be created soon after the war. In contrast to the original concept of a liberal arts college curriculum from many private universities, there was a need to establish practical studies in agriculture, science, military science, and engineering in response to the U.S. industrial revolution, with federal assistance for these university systems having been provided by the Morrill Acts.[70] After the Civil War, a rapid expansion of colleges sprung throughout the Midwest and west of the Mississippi, as urban areas sprouted when land holdings became available.

Founded in 1837 by a Quaker philanthropist, Cheney College (now university) in Pennsylvania was the first Historically Black College. Unusual for its time, the growth of colleges did not create a major dent toward racial inclusion until later, when alternative colleges were principally established after the Civil War as Black colleges, later denoted as HBCUs. These came to prominence because Blacks were not being admitted into traditional institutions of higher learning, but for several exceptional institutions like Oberlin College.

Quite different from HBCUs, there was never a Latino college equivalent. Not until the last third of the following century were there any Latino colleges, barely half a dozen, some which were both Latino and Native American from the mid-1960s to the early 1980s, as part of the self-determination movement.[71] They were short-lived, as most folded or were coopted by other institutions.[72] Also, Tribal Colleges and Universities (TCUs) were established during the latter half of the 20th century as a result of the Higher Education Act of 1965 and its subsequent amendments.[73]

As a consequence, Latino and Native Americans lagged in their progress toward higher education, as admittance into college was by exception and under special circumstances. As few colleges or universities would admit them, they trailed African American collegiate achievement for decades. With Latinos not able to fall back on institutions of their own, even different from the TCUs that started in 1978 with federal funds, Latino college numbers were much fewer than expected for their overall numbers, with handfuls of graduates highly selected for nearly a century. For Blacks, despite HBCUs, it was not until another century before any African American was admitted into a White public university until James Meredith and the integration of the University of Mississippi in 1962.[74]

In contradistinction to the trend, coeducation in higher education and the admission of Blacks was achieved at Oberlin College in Ohio in 1837, with Oberlin becoming the first collegiate institution to open its doors to all comers, as it inaugurated both the co-education of higher education and the admission of Blacks.[75]

Not long afterwards, Antioch College was founded (1852), with Horace Mann as its first president, serving until his death in 1859. His final commencement speech became the college motto: "Be ashamed to die until you have won some victory for humanity."[76] His niece, one of ten original faculty members at the college, was the first female professor nationwide to have obtained the same rank *and* pay as her male colleagues. Antioch College was also the first college to allow women to *publicly* accept their graduate diplomas. Turns out, the vast majority of IHEs did not catch up in many respects until after the Civil War and in other respects not until the civil rights era.

Other reform efforts were underway during the 19th century. Early in the century, reformers like Noah Webster, also a former schoolmaster and author of *An American Dictionary of the English Language* (1828), emphasized the role of education as important for the "fragile nation," but in the context of an American culture. He later became involved in higher education and founded Amherst College in 1821 to educate "indigent young men of piety and talents." From its start, the college enrolled students who might not commonly have had access to higher education. Webster saw the role of education as "central for the working of a free government," declaring it as "the most important business of civil society."[77] Quite a dynamic figure in education, he had earlier railed against overcrowded, one-room schoolhouses (versus those for the elite), with underpaid staff, no desks, and unsatisfactory textbooks that came from England.

The work of Henry Barnard is another example of someone who was involved in multiple levels of education midcentury onward. He established a board of "commissioners of common schools" and served as Secretary of the Board where he worked to reorganize the common school system for the state of Connecticut. From there he worked in Rhode Island where he became the first Commissioner of Public Schools and instituted some of the same reforms as in Connecticut. After various posts in education, including Chancellor of the University of Wisconsin at Madison, he became the first U.S. Commissioner of Education when the Bureau of Education was established in 1867.

During most of the 19th century, the idea of schooling was still rather novel and unproven. Few governments then existed where *all* children were expected to attend school. On the down side, it was thought that overtaxing the mind was not good for mental health. It was felt by some that the mind was something to be cultivated, but not exhausted.[78] Schooling was therefore not to be held for long periods of time, and certainly not the full year. It was commonly accepted that educational learning must be balanced with other chores like work as a farmhand picking crops during season and duties and responsibilities for the household. As a result, the school year was truncated. Some of these former patterns linger, as the U.S. continues to maintain one of the shortest school years among industrialized countries. It clings to an antiquated agricultural cycle, where children were needed to pick crops. A class split has occurred in today's urban, post-industrial society where children that come from means attend high-quality camps with trips to the ocean and around the country as well as abroad versus children of lower incomes that languish without enriched experiences, thus facing incredible summer learning losses at the rate of nearly two months loss for every month out of school.[79]

Other forms of the schooling process were also introduced. While many have since been modified, some of the legacies still continue. For example, uniformity was emphasized, with everyone taught in a similar manner, using the same text, reading aloud and in unison. Students were to follow distinct rules of behavior and conduct; otherwise, they would be punished for not paying attention. Students worked silently and separately from individual desks arranged in distinct rows, equidistant from each other. Corporal punishment was common, and many teachers literally ruled the classroom with a yardstick. Students had to wear a "dunce" cap if highly disruptive or inattentive. Parents were not to participate in the learning process, as teaching was between teacher and student. And teachers were not to be questioned by parents, as parents were not to be involved in the learning process. For today's baby boomers, several of these practices may conjure up painful memories, with others not so dormant.

By mid-19th century, the educational system, still a product of its times, had become deeply entrenched in remaining White, Christian, and Protestant. While certainly nowhere as harsh and intolerant as the pilgrim and puritan schools of centuries earlier, there remained limited tolerance for differences among White communities, most of which were rather fundamental in their religious views. Even schools and secular institutions that were not highly religious played along and pretended,[80] as contemporary journals of the time attest such as writings by Elizabeth Dusenbury, friend of Luisa May Alcott and Emily Dickinson, as she indicates in her personal diaries during the 1850s.[81] She struggled greatly with intolerance and fanaticism that delimited most of her activities.

Even Horace Mann and many of his fellow crusaders were fervent Christians that, while they had encounters with fellow believers, strongly abided by general church principals and were careful on how far to push the envelope of social justice and morality when it came to particular racial topics, but made glib pronouncements when it came to temperance, morality, and other social issues that were more universally accepted and not as controversial. These were delicate boundaries. Notwithstanding, Mann was to fill the Congressional seat vacated by the death of John Quincy Adams in 1848, with his first speech to Congress advocating for the duty to exclude slavery from the territories, as he was against its expansion in the new territories. He was re-elected as an independent and anti-slavery candidate where he served until his death. Incredibly, these qualities distinguished him from nearly all other educational crusaders for most of the next century.

American society was so set in its culture and ways of conducting classes that even outsiders like then immigrating Irish Catholics were seen as disruptors to the status quo. They became highly suspect when they began arriving in great numbers in the 1840s. Ironically, the Irish had arrived to America in earlier waves and had participated in the Revolutionary War, with several signing the Declaration of Independence. Yet, these earlier emigrants had been predominantly Protestant, a distinct difference as Scot-Irish. Between 1840 and 1860, over 1.6 million Irish entered the country, mostly escaping hunger and political oppression as well as the potato famine.[82] The adjustment to American society was difficult in many quarters for them, primarily due to hostility against Catholics by the WASP religion, as public schools were seen as Protestant institutions. Once the new immigrants lost their accent and adjusted to society, as Noel Ignatiev documents in *How the Irish Became White* (1995), these immigrants were generally accepted. Oscar Handlin also documents in *The Uprooted* (1951) that within a generation or two the Irish, among other European Whites were accepted by the dominant members of society and were able to assimilate into the American milieu.[83]

As it was, Catholicism created conflicts and tensions between Protestant-founded schools or the basic Protestant character of public schools and the Catholic Church which later required parishioners to enroll their children in Catholic schools.[84] Under these circumstances, the status of these "minorities," had a different meaning, as their conditions were truly short-lived. Upon later recall early in the 20th century, persons of darker hue reflected that losing an accent when keeping your color was easy for "Whites," but not for them. This is echoed by many Hispanics today in reflecting a darker shade of brown, among other traits found to be different from the dominant mainstream culture.

As the nation grew, divisions grew alongside, creating friction and difficulty when it came to equity, fairness, and justice. The plea for schools to inculcate these values even for trailblazers like Mann and Barnard was not easily shared among the educational elite. It was not an educational issue, as it was more religious and social, but affecting schooling nonetheless, as schools were becoming the very heart of middle-class morality, social acceptability, and the Protestant ethic.[85]

Notes

1. Tyack, 1974.
2. Ibid.
3. Churchill quote, https://www.goodreads.com/quotes/535242-the-farther-back-you-can-look-the-farther-forward-you
4. Over the years, reforms have been about single issues like curriculum, child-centered approaches, school configuration, constructivism, testing and measurement, accountability, and the like, rather than holistic change.
5. Lockridge, 1974.
6. Ibid.
7. Letter from Thomas Jefferson to Richard Price, January 8, 1789.

THE BIRTH OF AMERICAN EDUCATION

8. Letter from Thomas Jefferson to Charles Yancey, January 6, 1816.
9. Sol Cohen, Book One, 1974.
10. U.S. Census Bureau, Historical Statistics of the United States, 1975. It is important to note that the Black population diminished to 13% by the Civil War, and has remained at roughly that percentage to this day.
11. Decennial census for the years 1830 to 1860.
12. U.S. Bureau of the Census, *Population of the 61 Urban Places: 1820*; and *Population of the 100 largest urban places, 1860*.
13. Non-sectarian did not mean non-religious; rather, non-denominational and non-partisan, while subscribing to moral, Judeo-Christian values.
14. Data from NCES (provided January 1993) indicates 57% enrollment just five years after the Civil War in 1870.
15. See article, "New York Free School Society, 1805" *Encyclopedia.com*, at http://www.encyclopedia.com/history/news-wires-white-papers-and-books/new-york-free-school-society-1805
16. Documented in 2006 by "Historical Timeline of Public Education in the U.S.," *Encyclopedia.com*, available at: http://www.encyclopedia.com/history/news-wires-white-papers-and-books/new-york-free-school-society-1805
17. Mondale & Patton, 2001.
18. Tyack, 1974.
19. Ibid.
20. See for example kindergarten history, available at: http://www.faqs.org/childhood/Ke-Me/Kindergarten.html
21. Edwards, 1939, p. 24.
22. It was in 1821 that the first public high school was established in Boston. By 1890, the public high school had surpassed the private academies. It was later in 1873 that the first kindergarten was established to take care of children one year prior to entering first grade.
23. Sol Cohen, Book 2, p. ii.
24. Cubberley, *History of Education*, p. 756.
25. Goldin & Katz, p. 195.
26. Tyack, p. 61.
27. NCES, fast facts, 2017 (for school year 2012–13).
28. Snyder, 1993, *120 Years of American Education*. It must be noted, however, that many so-called colleges were barely colleges, but mostly high schools, especially in rural areas and for Blacks. As accreditation was not in place at this time it is hard to ascertain how many were at the standard of what we would call colleges today.
29. According to Tyack (1974), high school enrollment nearly doubled every decade since 1890.
30. Ravitch, 2000, p. 223.
31. Du Bois' address to the Georgia State Teachers Convention, "Curriculum Revision," April 12, 1935.
32. This included several large groups of agricultural workers that were sent from Puerto Rico to work the fields in Hawaii during the first decade of the 20th century.

33. The term denotes a persistent view that Asian Americans were not quite "real" Americans. It posits that members of certain minority groups (Africans, Asian Americans, Hispanics), as per Devos & Banaji (2005), will always be seen as the "other" in the White Anglo-Saxon dominant society of the United States.
34. See Carlos Blanton's (2014) excellent biography on George Sánchez.
35. This occurred during the panic of the American depression (1893–1897), when J.P. Morgan & Co. led a bond offering that helped rescue the United States from a severe two-year depression in 1895.
36. Mondale & Patton, 2001.
37. Taken from the Twelfth Annual Report to the Secretary of the Massachusetts State Board of Education, 1848.
38. This was a protestant religious revival movement that took place between 1790 and 1830. The First Great Awakening was during the 1730s and 1740s. These were part of much larger religious movements sweeping Europe, principally England, Scotland and Germany.
39. The Massachusetts Bay Colony was the first British colony to enact a compulsory attendance law in 1642, with the State of Massachusetts the first state to pass legislation on compulsory attendance in 1852, two centuries later.
40. Snyder, 1993, *120 Years of American Education*.
41. Who is Horace Mann? https://www.silentwordministries.org/2011/07/21/the-written-word-who-is-horace-mann/
42. The Department of Education was not established as a Cabinet-level department until 1979, becoming operational the following year.
43. Katz, 2001.
44. Murray, 1899. Doane made the statement at a state assembly in defense of adoption of the common school, January 27, 1838.
45. Ibid.
46. Sol Cohen, Book 2, 1974, p. xiv.
47. Ibid.
48. Ibid.
49. He served as an Army General in the Civil War, also becoming Secretary of the Interior soon after the war. He was the first German-born American elected to the United States Senate.
50. Peabody, 1882.
51. Kloss, 1998.
52. Leibowitz, 1971.
53. German was utilized for instruction in the states of PA, MD, OH, IN, IL, MO, NE, CO, and OR; Swedish, Norwegian and Danish in WI, IL, MN, IA, ND, SD, NE, and WA; Dutch in MI; Polish and Italian in WI; Czech in TX; French in LA; and Spanish in the Southwest, as per Carlos Ovando, 2003, p. 4.
54. Paid one-third to one-half as much as much ... with women teachers outnumbering men post-Civil War, 1870.
55. This was highly influenced by the Prussian teacher-training seminaries visited by Horace Mann and others in the 1820s. By 1865, there were at least 15 state normal schools (p. xix). Actually, the normal school was initially little more than a higher elementary

school. It was not until 1894 that a high school diploma was required for admission to normal schools.
56. Morgan, 1938.
57. Ibid.
58. Tyack, 1974.
59. Goldstein, 2014.
60. NCES, 2017.
61. Biography of Catherine Beecher, https://www.britannica.com/biography/Catharine-Beecher
62. De Tocqueville, 1831.
63. Ibid., p. 237.
64. McGaha, p. 144.
65. Horace Mann quotes, taken from Brainy Quotes.
66. It was almost a century later (around the 1940s) that Normal universities began to expand to other fields and develop past their initial mission of training teachers.
67. Tyack, 1967.
68. McGaha, p. 243.
69. Morgan, 1938.
70. This meant granting federally-controlled lands to the states for them to sell, to raise funds, to establish and endow "land-grant" institutions.
71. The exceptions are the universities in Puerto Rico, namely the University of Puerto Rico (UPR) that was established in 1903. It was considered an insular university, not part of the U.S. mainland schools.
72. Universidad Boricua (now Boricua College) and Hostos Community College continue to this day. National Hispanic University was founded in 1981 in Oakland, CA, but had to cease operations in 2015.
73. These educational institutions are distinct by being controlled and operated by American Indian tribes. The first was founded by the Navajo Nation in 1968 in Arizona, with several others established in the 1970s. As of 1994, they have been authorized by Congress as land-grant colleges. There are currently (2018) 32 fully-accredited Tribal Colleges and Universities in the U.S.
74. Private, Ivy League universities like Harvard, Princeton, the University of Chicago, among several others, admitted select minority students under exceptional circumstances.
75. Up until this time, only four African Americans had graduated from a university, as per the *Journal of Blacks in Higher Education*. In sequence, these included Middleburg College (1823); Amherst College (1826); Bowdoin College (1826); and Dartmouth (1828), respectively.
76. Taken from Mann's address at Antioch College, 1859.
77. Horace Mann quotes, http://www.famousquotes123.com/horace-mann-quotes.html
78. Sol Cohen, 1974.
79. In her research on summer loss, Barbara Heyns (1978) was one of the first to document that for low-income children as much as one moth was lost for every two months out of school.
80. Morgan, 1938.

81. *Ibid.*
82. U.S. Census data, 1840 and 1850.
83. Handlin, 1951.
84. As but one example, Catholics and Jews were barred from certain higher education institutions such as Harvard, as President Charles Eliot later broke the mold; but one that was re-established by his successor.
85. Morgan, p. 54.

· 2 ·

DUAL SYSTEMS OF EDUCATION

Since when do you have to agree with people to defend them from injustice?
Lillian Hellman

IN TRACKING THE GROWTH OF THE COUNTRY AFTER EMANCIPATION, WHERE SOME FOUR MILLION BLACKS SHED CHAINS OF SLAVERY, IT APPEARED LIKE THE ENTIRE NATION HAD BEEN LIBERATED. But such was not fully the case. Reconstruction was too brief. Much was left uncompleted. It was insufficient to enter mainstream society. Education was highly unresolved for Blacks. Also, the promise of forty acres and a mule for the protection from abuse to former captives had become mythical as it was rescinded by President Andrew Johnson, Lincoln's successor, in the fall of 1865.

Meantime, illiteracy was rampant and education hard to find. For Blacks, there literally was no education, as it was a new construct for most Blacks. Adequate systems were not in place. As systems started developing, the idea of same schools for children of different races was anathema, intolerable. Dual systems had to be constructed as Blacks could not enter White schools.

As it turned out, many new freedmen and women were figuratively re-enslaved as sharecroppers. Many were trapped by an unfair peonage system that Congress had to outlaw in 1876, and then again several times outlawed by the courts. In order to maintain an inexpensive and controlled labor source,

Southern states after Reconstruction enacted a variety of laws restricting the mobility of Black labor in the late 19th and early 20th centuries. At the time, social conditions greatly determined the educational options for former slaves, with all but handfuls attending school.

As state laws continued to force workers into involuntary servitude in order to pay off debts to their employers, the U.S. Supreme Court intervened in the 1905 case of *Clyatt v. United States* to uphold the federal Peonage Act of 1867. This was a rare but noticeable instance of judicial protection of African American rights during a highly racist era of the early 20th century, virtually impossible to enforce after the federal government withdrew involvement in the South in the Compromise of 1877 ending the Reconstruction Era. To redress rampant abuses, the High Court invalidated an Alabama peonage law in *Bailey v. Alabama* (1911) on the grounds it violated the 13th Amendment that banned involuntary servitude. Then once more in 1914 the High Court struck down another pillar of the peonage system in the case of *United States v. Reynolds*. This was when states were giving convicted criminals a choice between paying a fine, serving time, or working for a planter in exchange for funds to pay off the fine.

Additional to flagrant violations against Blacks, Mexican Americans were also increasingly subjugated, with outright violations of their civil rights. At the same time, Native Americans were also being pushed almost to extinction. In effect, every minority was undergoing suppression. Meanwhile, the South remained devastated after the war, not fully recovering until middle of the next century, after World War II.

Concurrently and already underway even before the Civil War was another revolution that continued to spread its influence quite strongly. This was the industrial revolution. As it came to be, a Northern wave of industrialization literally colonized the South after the Civil War in its building of railroads, imposition of tariffs, and the buying and transplanting of textile mills. These growing industries were able to profit even more greatly by keeping wages low, as they ruthlessly abused child labor and fiercely fought against labor unions. By the end of the century, American industrialization had surpassed even that of England, catapulting this country beyond other nations across the globe on the backs of former slaves and lowly paid immigrants.

The four major sectors of industry and agriculture that fueled this growth were that of steel manufacturing, railroad construction, coal production, and grain harvesting.[1] By the start of WWI, the U.S. had outpaced the world by producing more steel than any other industrial nation, surpassing rival England and Germany; laying more railroad tracks than even Russia, its closest competitor; producing more coal than England, the largest producer; and harvesting more bushels of grain than either Russia or France.² By the end of the century, the U.S. led in nearly every major economic indicator available for the first time ever.

Linked by railroads, fueled by oil, fed by innovation, and built by steel, corporate industry had become a giant. The titans of industry had become a symbol of everything that was both right and wrong with America. The Golden Age of capitalism became so powerful that a mogul like J. P. Morgan could single-handedly rescue the U.S. government in 1895 from a severe two-year economic depression, as a national crisis had triggered a series of bank failures and a run on gold. During this time, the growth of corporate industry (and greed) had become so profitable that its original christening in 1873 by Mark Twain, the "Gilded Age," has been emblazoned ever since.³

Emancipation Becomes Segregation

ACCORDING TO BILLINGSLEY (1992), "THE VICTORY OVER SLAVERY WAS SWEET, BUT THE FORCES OF OPPRESSION WERE SWIFT."⁴ After 1877, barely a decade after the Civil War, it had become clear that the era of reform for African Americans as well as for other racial groups was to be short-lived. Despite the Freedman's Bureau, a federal effort to transition Blacks from slavery to freedom, and the passage of the Thirteenth, Fourteenth, and Fifteenth Amendments to the Constitution,* it was barely a decade in most places of Reconstruction before the struggle for real freedom from economic dependence and educational opportunity would be lost for another century.⁵

After the Civil War, conditions were difficult for African Americans, not fully rescued from past exclusion from formal systems of education. For one, Jim Crow took over Reconstruction. For another, groups like the KKK starting in late 1865 were established to promote terrorism throughout the South, with tremendous increases in lynching peaking in 1892.⁶ Further, 1868 was the peak of voting for Black men that did not reach an equal level until after the start of the civil rights era in the 1960s. A series of voter restriction laws such as the poll tax, grandfather clauses, and extralegal terrorism denied polit-

---

* These were known as the Reconstruction Amendments, designed to ensure equity for recently emancipated slaves. In sequential order they abolished slavery, provided equal protection under the law, and prohibited voting discrimination.

ical power and democratic processes thereon. Equally important, Reconstruction programs like the Freedmen's Bureau, among others, were eliminated before their time, with the road to recovery quickly eroding for Blacks. By the 1890s, progress had come to a near halt.

Rather specifically, the Freedman's Bureau at its peak of operations in 1869 had 150,000 students enrolled in Bureau schools,[7] mostly in urban areas. As it turned out, the educational impact was far less than expected. Few adults benefitted from Bureau schools. Somehow, the process of transition was not long enough, deep enough, or sufficiently responsive enough in its provisions for change, with many Blacks later viewing the process as highly inadequate and symbolic at best of White paternalism. The end of the war did not bring full emancipation nor did it usher in an era of equity and social justice. It was more of the same, but without the indicia of slavery. As a result, the improvement of African Americans after the Civil War was short-lived, literally truncated.

Unchanged conditions eventually led to northern migration, though the majority of Blacks stayed put through the turn of the century, with about 11 of every 12 Blacks continuing to reside in the South.[8] It was not until World War I that an outward migration primarily to the urban areas of the North spurred the beginnings of a larger northern migration that continued until the 1970s, known as the Great Migration. For the vast numbers staying behind, it was efforts from the Black community itself, not the federal government or the Freedman's Bureau, that helped make the difference, including that for schooling..

During the latter part of the 19th century, much remained in disarray for Blacks and other racial minorities. The economic situation was catastrophic and the education for racial minorities a negligent failure. Despite earlier efforts from reformers like Horace Mann and Henry Barnard, "Universal forces," as one author explains, "were aligned against universal education for Black children in the Reconstruction era that were still in existence at the dawn of the 20th century."[9] For the Black worker in the South, as it was for Latinos later, many farmers and planters believed that schooling spoiled a good field hand. They preferred laborers to be illiterate or semiliterate. They wanted workers to continue with long-term dependence and high-poverty status.

Neither Blacks nor Latinos had the means or the institutional structures by which to bolster their education, as Jim Crow had destroyed highest hopes. A final nail to the coffin of desperation came with *Plessy v. Ferguson* (1896) before century's end. Whites refused to invest in the Black schooling structures, private or public. Also, unlike the North, no strong common schools movement had occurred in the Southern states. Very few of those with power ventured resources or energies to assist. As a result, efforts that were underway were mostly sporadic and disconnected, leading W.E.B. Du Bois to describe schooling during the period after Reconstruction through the end of the century thusly: "There were army schools, mission schools, and schools of the Freedman's Bureau in chaotic disarrangement, seeking system and cooperation."[10] Negro colleges were "hurriedly founded," but were "inadequately equipped, illogically distributed, and of varying efficiency and grade." Also, "The normal and high schools were doing little more than common school work, and the common schools were training but a third of the children who ought to be in them, and training these too often poorly."[11]

As it turned out, there arose a series of institutions designed to furnish teachers for the untaught, namely Black normal schools and colleges, though greatly limited in resources. Despite many detractors, extant systems were able to put "thirty thousand black" teachers in the South within one single generation in response to the crisis.[12] As a result, the work of education in the South began with Black higher education institutions doing most of the training, and with Black churches, associations, and institutions collaborating greatly.

It is interesting to note that some African American educators at the time strongly asserted that beyond practical concerns, education was to facilitate and develop individuals who could "agitate the existing social order," as Du Bois once proclaimed. But this proved to be a two-edged sword, as many Black teachers who pushed radical ideas were instantly fired by White principals as well as by most school boards and White superintendents. With White Supremacists forcing these voices to silence it was impossible for Blacks to fully address the issue of education. As a result, many of the Black bachelor degree graduates that arose were the more ideologically conservative leaders that did not assertively address Black racial injustice nor did their coursework well prepare them for the professions, as documented by certain Black authors at the time, including critiques leveled from African American schoolteachers turned scholars and advocates like Anna Julia Cooper. Among others, she adamantly refused to submit to a two-tiered educational system where an entire race of people was schooled for servitude and second-class citizenship.[13]

According to Vivian May (2015), Anna Julia Cooper also argued for a curriculum that confronted inequalities that minimized opportunities for greater educational access and success. In Cooper's talk about some of her contemporaries, Blacks and Whites alike, she asserted that those that were disenfranchised needed an education that fostered both intellectual curiosity as well as political consciousness and resilience, since a "neglected people ... must be fitted to make headway in the face of prejudice."¹⁴ As a most prescient thinker, she fervently believed that African Americans should expect equitable opportunities to an education, as the future of the race depended on it. Accordingly, Blacks would literally sink or swim according to the education they received.

The reality was that other racial groups such as Mexican Americans did not have it any better. They faced similar struggles of segregation and inaccessibility to public high schools, but with more *de facto* than *de jure* enforcement; while Native Americans were literally confined to the reservation. Limited by great odds, the few improvements that came about for other racial minorities were principally due to the efforts of the groups themselves, limited as they were. Their conditions eerily echoed the Black experience. Minority populations survived, but facing great duress and with few resources. Greater in-depth analysis about the Latino experience during this period is more greatly detailed in the second part of this book.

For Blacks, *former oppression from slavery resulted in a small but valiant group of around five percent that could read and write among newly-freed Blacks.*¹⁵ According to Black historian James Anderson (1988), this group formed the "vanguard for a phenomenal surge toward education." This was in alignment with what Frederick Douglass (1845) and others had been proclaiming: "Knowledge will set you free." As he and other Black leaders asserted, freedom and liberty truly revolved around education, with education signaling liberation. As the federal government was not going to be very helpful, much less after President Grant and the ending of Reconstruction, the means by which to obtain education and employment independently became the new heart of the struggle.

The percentage of students enrolled in school after the war was about half (48%) among eligible White students in the South, but with considerably lower numbers for Blacks where nearly 9 out of every 10 (9.9%) children remained out of school in 1870.¹⁶ Anderson's excellent documentation of Black education in the South adds to these census figures the Sabbath schools. These were Black church-operated schools during that period. Anderson's data goes beyond the official data as such figures were unaccounted in government counts. In 1868, for example, the African Methodist Episcopal (AME) church enrolled 40,000 pupils in its Sabbath schools; but this was augmented the subsequent generation, when by 1885 the AME reported an increased enrollment of 200,000 children.[17] Other church-run schools and alternative forms of education went unreported, at times operating under the radar. According to Anderson, the self-reliance of the Black community and its churches was critically important to the alternative systems that local Black communities created in their quest to ensure education for their children, sometimes independent from the faith community. While both types of efforts increased total numbers slightly, they still paled in comparison to population parity and overall need. The literacy rate for Blacks, as a result, remained substantially diminished after the war.

As it was, the Freedman's Bureau had very minor effects in the transition to high literacy, as resistance to Black emancipation was thwarted from *both* the North and the South.[18] What happened was that while major strides occurred a decade after the Civil War, dominant thinking among many Whites was that too much help had already been provided. In addition, White resistance intensified with the knowledge that Blacks were not going to relocate to Africa or leave the country after all. While a naïve expectation (or wishful hope), it was one that caused Whites to rethink their strategy of assistance. In giving up hope of returning Blacks to Africa, Whites became hell-bent on getting the upper hand once again. As a result, the few advances that had started after the Civil War were rapidly and most strongly restrained.

Outcome was that by the end of Reconstruction, the move for Blacks to obtain education redoubled in opposition by Whites. For Blacks, the need for literacy had obviously increased after full emancipation toward self-determination. For Whites, the fear was that if Blacks learned to read and write they would become more self-reliant and likely demand full independence with greater ability and newer rights to compete with lower-class Whites.

After much effort and many lives sacrificed after the war, Blacks were not allowed to advance to equitable educational status, as if the Civil War had never occurred. As was the case, tribulations afflicting the Black community would have been much harsher had it not been checked by their own efforts and the assistance obtained from charitable organizations, missionary societies, and certain philanthropic funders.

By *the end of the 19th century, most (80%) White children were attending elementary schools, yet barely 1-in-4 (28%) African Americans were enrolled in any public school whatsoever.*[19] By then, a number of initiatives had worked together to increase and provide support for public school education, absent facilities and resources for nonwhites. For example, the common schools movement had become widespread, even among pioneer schools, yet most still prohibited teaching to Black or Mexican students.[20] The number of HBCUs across the country had also increased by 1900, but it meant Blacks were not going to other institutions of higher education (IHEs) except in rare instances, as it also was very expensive to move out of the South to study.[21]

For Mexican Americans, it was worse. Lacking equivalent educational institutions and with one-tenth the population of Blacks, they were mostly left out of the educational process altogether, with rare exceptions until the following century.[22]

The "high school movement" was coming onto its own by end of the century, and educational progress had been much augmented and supported by the rise of educational associations that provided major endorsements to the public schools.[23] Yet it was rare for these schools to accept Black students. In the Southwest, all but several barred Latinos entirely from entering, regardless of aptitude or qualification.

While impressive advances had been achieved in education, these had virtually no effect on racial populations, as students of color with few exceptions were excluded from the mainstream educational process. As a result, no initiatives, reforms or educational advancements, other than HBCUs, impacted Black students; with the lack of special policies also affecting the Mexican American community. That which related to Puerto Rico was the land-grant legislation that affected one public institution of higher education, namely the University of Puerto Rico (UPR), and only applicable to islanders, away from the states. Also, these were not enacted until the early 1900s, within a decade after Puerto Rico had become a U.S. possession, still with an undefined political status, as U.S. citizenship was not granted until 1917.

Meanwhile, the U.S. educational system had grown substantially for Whites, as it had achieved a higher rate of student enrollment by 1900 that surpassed all European countries. It also represented a higher percentage of "freely" enrolled institutions than other nations worldwide.[24]

At the high school level soon after the turn of the century, when White students started enrolling in larger numbers, a division occurred among educators. Some believed education was to be offered to all students in contradistinction to those that wanted high school education only for the college-bound. As it was, the latter group sought alternatives to the academic curriculum for the non-college bound, namely vocational skills for the poor and the disenfranchised. This introduced controversies that continued long-term. Policies for the "dispossessed," as it was labeled, were accompanied by rhetoric espousing democracy, interpreted to mean class stratification through the public schools.

At this time, the country was also *en route* to a world-class university system, reaping the fruits of earlier public investments in land-grant colleges. With private funds, especially the fruits of Gilded Age wealth such as the Carnegie and Rockefeller Foundations, research institutions of higher learning like Johns Hopkins University in 1876, became well-endowed and took the lead in modeling itself after the German research university. Here "research" and "graduate studies" were unified as a new, holistic approach to higher education. German influence also introduced the concept of dedicated lectures, special seminars, and research laboratories.

However, conditions were different for HBCUs, despite funding from the federal government and charitable organizations. According to Goldin & Katz (2008), these "other" higher education institutions were greatly under-funded, with smaller HBCUs largely excluded from the "university revolution" that swept through much of public higher education the first part of the 20th century. As an example, less than 5% of the HBCUs had received accreditation by the Association of American Universities.[25]

The end of the 19th century marked a period of major change, as the nation had become a world power, having gone through major industrialization, several wars, and in the midst of major European immigration. In spite of the many factors confronted, the country had expanded quickly and had created an educational system that was not as structurally rigid as its European counterparts. In the U.S., these had become free, public, and compulsory for everyone, but with the major difference in excluding nonwhites.

The Stain of *Plessy*

AS BACKDROP, AN IMPORTANT BUT CONTROVERSIAL DECISION THAT PRECEDED *PLESSY* WAS *ROBERTS V. THE CITY OF BOSTON* (1850). Although the seat of abolitionism midcentury, Bostonians were still unwilling to permit Black children sit alongside a White child in the developing public school system a decade before the Civil War. This resulted in the State of Massachusetts earning the ironic distinction of becoming the first state to legally establish segregation. The two key attorneys in *Roberts* were Charles Sumner and Robert Morris[26] who represented Plaintiff Benjamin Roberts on behalf of his five-year-old daughter, Sarah Roberts. The case was lost and Sarah had to attend a segregated school far from home. Ironically, Massachusetts after becoming the first state to adopt segregation also became the first state to abolish segregation almost immediately thereafter—five years later in 1855. State legislation had overridden the legal decision, a rare occurrence. Despite this gain, many of the same arguments from the *Roberts* case were used in *Plessy*, nearly half a century later, when the entire nation was thrust into segregation.

Under the mandate of Plessy (1896), the single most important case of the 19th century involving civil rights, racial progress was not only halted, but greatly harmed. This was truly when institutions strongly harkened back to Jim Crow, without major restraint. *Plessy*, albeit a transportation case, had formalized the separation of Blacks from Whites by assuming a system of equal justice through a doctrine of "separate but equal." This held for transportation, accommodation, housing, health, welfare and education. It also permitted the segregated use of "public" facilities such as bathrooms and restaurants as well as access to better-funded public institutions, including public schools, colleges, and universities. Over time, it would be obvious that separate but equal would be equated to separate but *unequal*.

By 1900, with *Plessy* in full force, Jim Crowism flourished. During the first third of the 20th century, being a member of a racial group was like branding a scarlet letter of banishment. It was worse than wearing a "dunce" cap, as the latter was temporal. With denigrating labels for nonwhites, White supremacy was again legal. This was when race and intelligence melded into scientific racism, each supporting the other, as racial superiority and IQ were determined to be highly correlated, endorsed by the eugenics[†] movement. Such thinking had gained a major foothold in the U.S., a decade after social Darwinism had swept through Europe in the 1890s. This was followed by two decades that denoted a critical period of resurging racism across the country.

The limited progress that now could be attained by Blacks was limited to local court decisions or by legislative action that was quite unlikely, and certainly not by educational reform from the public schools. For their defense, the National Association for the Advancement of Colored People (NAACP) was founded in 1909 and two decades later a Latino counterpart, the League

---

[†] This is a movement that purports to improve the genetic composition of a race, oftentimes by advocating selective breeding to achieve such goals, among other methods.

of United Latin American Citizens (LULAC) came to the defense of Latinos in 1929. At the time, conditions for the education of racial minorities were deplorable. In contrast to normative education data for Whites, only 45% of Black children were enrolled in school in 1910. This expanded to 65% by 1940.[27] Comparable Latino data was unavailable for that period, though major indicators point to lower figures, as documented in the next chapters.

During this "age of segregation," it must be remembered that racial prejudice, discrimination, and stigma did not solely affect Blacks. Other nonwhites were subject to similar racialized conditions. All minorities were victims of unfettered atrocities and brazen injustice. This period, as it turned out, was less about Reconstruction and more about "reestablishing" the past by any means necessary. Initial *de facto* had now become *de jure*. As Latinos were but a small population, barely one-tenth the total of all African Americans in the continental U.S. at the turn of the century, they were virtually invisible except for pockets in the Southwest.‡ Regardless of size, racial groups were strongly subjected to high segregation and major discrimination that heightened as their numbers increased during the 20th century.

Through the aid of the Black church and with some foundation and charitable funds at the end of the Civil War, advancement in Black literacy was slow but cumulative. In 1890, illiteracy for Blacks stood at 61%. Estimates provided by the research on census data together with data from the Jones reports from the Bureau of Education a decade later indicates that the literacy "gap" between Whites and Blacks in the South was around 36% by the turn of the century.[28] By 1920, the gap was down to 25%. By the time of *Brown*, thirty-four years later, illiteracy for Blacks was still four times greater compared to Whites living in the South, irrespective of age.[29]

Both Black and White children suffered in educational achievement relative to their Northern brethren, as financially strapped Southern states were barely able to afford schools for one race, much less garner political will and funds to duplicate resources for a second set of schools, no matter how minimally funded and no matter how much money was taken from starving Black schools to fund White schools. University of Chicago educated Black scholar Dr. Horace Mann Bond laid bare the appalling racial disparities in educational funding in two books, *The Education of the Negro in the American Social Order* (1934) and *Negro Education in Alabama* (1939) that was used by

---

‡ It was one-fifth by the turn of the century if Puerto Rico's population is included.

legal teams and others to document and build equalization for desegregation cases.

Public school attendance was also very limited between the *Plessy* and *Brown* era, especially in rural areas. In 1890, it was around 30% for Blacks, increasing to around 55% in 1930, including one-third of all African American children in Southern schools that attended the public schools aided by the Rosenwald funds during the early 1930s.§ By the time of *Brown*, enrollment among public schools had increased, but with a great majority (70%) of African American students still attending fully-segregated schools throughout the country.[30]

For the financing of education, it was the per pupil expenditure that most greatly exacerbated after *Plessy*, greatly widening each decade, reaching highly unbalanced margins just before *Brown*—between 1940 and 1954. Ironically, it was also a period when the Deep South was pushing measures to "ante-up" greater funds for segregated schools, as NAACP was already conducting equalization suits showing that separate was not equal. With Southern states knowing that their Black schools were not equal to the White ones, they poured money feverishly to build the virtually extant public high schools in areas serving Blacks to ensure that these schools were not so drastically inferior to White schools and consequently not meeting separate but equal requirements. An example of the wide disparity was in Mississippi, where as late as 1950 Black schools received "$32.55 in education funding" for each child as compared to White schools that received $122.93."[31]

Dual Systems

IT IS ALWAYS EASIER TO UNDERSTAND THE SUBJECT OF EDUCATION WHEN ITS HISTORY IS UNDERSTOOD IN CONTEXT. THIS IS MOST ASSUREDLY THE CASE FOR RACIAL MINORITIES AND EDUCATION DURING THE *PLESSY* ERA. It is difficult to generalize about dual systems over the span of 58 years between *Plessy* and

---

§ Rosenwald Schools constituted nearly five thousand schools, shops, and teachers' homes that were used to expand the number of public schools for the education of Blacks in the South during early 20th century. Funds provided matching grants to build schoolhouses once a community/school district came up with sufficient resources in language, materials, money or labor to show their investment and commitment. Financing came from the partnering of Julius Rosenwald, an American clothier and later part-owner and president of Sears, Roebuck and Company, and the African American leader Booker T. Washington, among other sources.

Brown, with each racial group undergoing different experiences and with conditions varying over time. In actuality, every "outsider" group operated as best it could, fully independent of the traditional system of education for at least half a century. As American expansionism brought even more racial groups into the country at different times—involuntarily—many of these new school children did not attend school, as the majority were not accepted into all-White schools.

Survival for each group developed by fiat, each fending for itself independently, but also as "undesirable." For both Asians and Latinos, segregation was a common practice of exclusion, with the Chinese Schools in the Bay area of California suffering great disparities, not unlike Mexican schools of the Southwest. When segregated facilities were not available, which was often, some of the Chinese merchants were able to form their own schools, but more often students of color just stayed home or worked in the fields.

With schooling and society closely related, it is important to understand the relationship between the two, especially when racial groups were mostly hidden from view in ghetto-like enclaves, unseen by the general public, with each group receiving a particularized type of educational experience and exposure. During the late 19th and early 20th century, as American education sped along a trajectory of progress and international acclaim, a subdominant but parallel educational system had developed. While largely invisible, as if occult, this second-tiered level of schooling represented an altogether different context, as it was replete with troubling histories, where nonwhite students seldom succeeded, unable to receive quality instruction, and with schools stripped of basic resources and with all but few graduating from eighth grade, at best.

Whites and nonwhites, rich and poor, were nowhere similar in their educational experience or academic progress. Nonwhites developed differentially, as unique groups, tribes, races, ethnicities, nationalities; an amalgam of mixes that never entered into the melting pot of society. They did not mingle with the mainstream. They were excluded from view and seldom appeared in national statistics. They were mostly isolated and highly poor. This second-class society fell into an educational and social abyss, ignored and unattended, as if untouchable outcasts.

Altogether, this class of student was defined by what it was not—a "not White" stock—as "nonwhite" and "not majority." While today they form part of the American milieu, they were initially not perceived to be a part of America's initial founding or original conception. They were kept apart as if slaves, indentured servants, conquered peoples, spoils of war, relegated to a caste-like system, as throw-away people. Yet many were citizens—at least most of them and most of the time—but treated as if a lesser type, educated to be subservient, as not-quite deserving of the same treatment.

We know about "those" people today principally because many survived through the grace of God, and because some of their descendants became distinguished Americans and prominent leaders. These offspring together with other nonwhite students represent the major proportion of today's 50 million students. As such, this new crop now forms a critical part of the educational tapestry of the nation which cannot continue to be undereducated by denying their constitutionally-protected rights under the 14th amendment, now half a century after civil rights.

Dual systems of education do not grow overnight. They develop over long periods of time, slowly and incrementally. As such, they reflect and align with the standards of the dominant society.[32] Once formalized, such systems do not disappear easily without equally powerful forces that countermand. Changing the public schools after *Brown* has taken decades, with certain elements still lingering, seemingly interminably.

To combat oppression, subgroups must develop interpersonal mechanisms and methods for survival, self-preservation, and sustenance. The process is about basic survival. These methods are needed to help create and maintain a healthy outlook to withstand hardship. When broken, survival is threatened. Educational attainment, as an example, can play pivotal even countervailing roles, as it can combat subjugation or otherwise fall into conformity. These are difficult options. For Frederick Douglass, knowledge of reading was able to guide him toward freedom; but such an asset, though well developed and critical for survival, was oftentimes hidden as it was always conflictual for him, even during good times.

Viewed historically, education operates compliant to the values and beliefs of the dominant group. During the *Plessy* era, it aimed to reinforce and support social dominance and assure control by reinforcing the dominant ethos. For racial groups, both the negation and control of educational opportunity became the process for measured dominance and strict control. This was how schooling distorted and constrained racial progress. The process of education was that of "subtractive education," as educational scholar Angela Valenzuela (1999) calls it. In presuming to lead the way, education truly thwarted freedom; hence the reason why some minority leaders viewed education with concern and suspicion. Here education became a two-edged sword.

Education for domestication was that which prepared students for servitude rather than service. As such, whenever education is led by the dominant class, its message is contrary to critical learning and understanding. This is why educators like Paulo Freire (1970) talked about "liberatory" education, with liberation rising above cognition among the "oppressed," upholding the belief that it is the former that aids the latter.

Within this framework the American educational system persisted during the first half of the 20th century, fully enabling racial stratification. Its purpose was not to serve the needs of a full and equitable society but to reflect stratified ideals, usurping the intellectual capacity of certain students by subjugating their personal drive.

As *the nation grew, it sought refuge from its educational system in support of healthy families.* For a variety of reasons, slavery, indentured servitude, and colonization also became embedded parts of the system, as complementary entities to the American experience. While not new in concept, these structures slowly developed their own brand of uniqueness, differing slowly from the European models of the day—some good and others quite bad. Over time, measured dosages bred social inequality. For economic reasons, racial stratification was needed in certain sectors more than others, with the South and the Southwest more strongly agrarian-based and servitude-dependent, exhibiting strongest forces against nonwhites.

While educational expertise expanded, it was not the same for Blacks, Latinos, and other racial groups. Over time, criticism came from abroad about how the new nation was dealing with freedom and liberty. Phrases like "all men are created equal and endowed with inalienable rights" came back to haunt. "Liberty and justice for all" had been differentially employed. While racial minorities viewed it literally as an inclusive phrase about equality, Whites saw it figuratively, as a phrase that meant freedom for the nation, but not all citizens from within. To justify and look good before envious Europeans, as leaders boasted about their new society, it was the non-slave holders of the North that began institutionalizing systems of minimal education for Blacks and other nonwhites, assuaging guilt and rationalizing to clergy—and to each other—that they were contributing their fair share in adherence to the ideals of the republic, albeit still differentially applied.

Government had literally developed two contradictory systems of education—one for liberation, the other for domination; one for Whites and the other for nonwhites. *Plessy* represented a fusion where the remnants of pre-Civil War days would be protected in the freedom-loving spirit of the 20th century. Court rulings were legally sanctioning an apartheid system of education, one that had been informally in place, but now officially recognized, with the good housekeeping seal of federal approval.

With the Treaty of Guadalupe Hidalgo in 1848 concluding the Mexican-American War and the acquisition of much of today's Southwest preceding the Civil War, questions already had arisen about how the Mexican would fit into the American landscape. Confusion continued unresolved and the matter remained dormant, greatly undoing the spirit of the Treaty that granted both citizenship and "whiteness" in 1848. This created ambivalence as it also heightened injustice. Both Latinos and Blacks had been robbed from prior agreements, one which disregarded a Treaty and the other with disregard to the Civil War and the 14th Amendment.

These issues compounded with the entry of the Chinese mid-19th century on the West Coast, nearly coincident in time with the Treaty of Guadalupe Hidalgo. In short order, the category of racial groups that were deemed "not White" but also "not Black" had become confusing—Mongolian, Indian, Mexican, Black slave, free Black. Decades later, it got more convoluted with the entrance of more Hispanics and Asians, especially after the 1898 Spanish-American War, when Puerto Rico, Guam, and the Philippines were acquired as territories and Cuba as a protectorate. As such, racial designations had become largely undefined, but "not White." The *Plessy* decision presumably resolved the "Black problem," as conceived—*de jure*—but left fully undefined the fate of other racial groups—*de facto*. For Puerto Ricans, further conflicts of identity and belongingness arose when they were declared citizens in 1917 primarily to enlist in a war, though not quite White, but where they fought with other Hispanics in segregated units as did Blacks. This occurred during both world wars.

With *Plessy* legally establishing "separate but equal," a dual system assured a massive, second-class, tiered system that was to operate alongside a White system that would dominate long-term. Over time, this proved to be an incredibly staunch stance that would undermine and dictate the fate of education, as it worked in permanent contradiction to valid educational progress and social improvement. Interestingly, the economic leap the nation had taken after the Civil War slowed down gradually after *Plessy*, with the fallout not fully evident until several decades later, as immigration partly masked economic declines temporarily.

By 1920, the country had revamped its secondary schools, as it was becoming the premier elementary and secondary educational system, reaching the highest high school enrollment rates among industrial nations, but still adhering to a racialized, multi-tiered system of education. Up until then, there were few high schools that minorities could attend. Notwithstanding, advancements in education continued through the 1930s, for Whites, despite the Great Depression, so that by the start of WWII the U.S. boasted having created a very strong K–12 system, with high school attendance also now blossoming.

During this whirlwind, one of the most oppressive features of Black and Latino secondary education ironically came during the increased construction of high school facilities and the expansion of schools nationwide. This was precisely when most Southern and Southwestern state governments together with local districts ironically refused to provide ample non-segregated high school facilities for minority children.[33] The combined machinations of *de facto* and *de jure* exclusion was powerful, with few Latino and Black children able to attend high school, curtailing their higher learning altogether. In her review of the data, Ravitch reports that "As late as 1930, nearly 40 percent of black youths in the South lived in counties that did not have a four-year secondary school for blacks."[34] Later in 1940, while 80 percent of the Black population still lived in the South, "41.8 percent over the age of twenty–five had less than five years of elementary education compared to 10.9 percent of Whites."[35] By then, differences had become notable to all onlookers.

In review of the history of education for the African American during this period it is important to indicate that this process did not occur within a Black-controlled schooling environment. Blacks had very limited control over the process. This was deliberate as it was intentional on the part of the educational system. It was the African American teacher that was strictly hired to work in all-Black schools, but at lower salaries, with less school resources, under the threat of firing, and only at times, as it was a hand-picked and highly-watched group.

This was "the logical outgrowth of a societal ideology designed to adjust Black southerners to racially qualified forms of political and economic subordination."[36] Blacks had control so long as the parameters were defined and delimited by Whites. Confined emancipation and break from this process came about when former slaves "persisted in their crusade" to develop systems of education that "were compatible with their resistance to racial and class subordination."[37] But this was accomplished in solo and in defiance, not because of the system. This occurred despite systemic hurdles. It was different for Hispanics, however, as there were many fewer Latino teachers at the time, and with a much smaller population.

Conditions set the stage for pushback from Black professionals. In a sense, it was a group within a system and a struggle within a struggle. Historians assert that for as small and insignificant a difference as this resistance may have seemed, Black empowerment efforts yielded huge results decades later. It was "politics, power and ideology," as Anderson concludes that shaped the framework and opportunity to structure needed educational means in response to the needs of Blacks and other children of color.

The educational system was binary as it separated Whites from all others, but rather complex among nonwhites themselves, as multiple groups were in play in different subsystems and in different ways. Hence, these structures in the society operated loosely, haphazardly, without guidance; and over time, rather independently. They had become quite confusing and unmanageable. With indecision prevailing, guidance was sought through the courts, but with legal decisions merely reflecting social inconsistencies that were already contradictory. For Latinos, for example, many rulings passed the legal buck, but leaving too much discretion to the states and local authorities. In actuality, the period between *Plessy* and *Brown* was one of mayhem and non-resolution for the nonwhite.

It became obvious that a dual system could not long endure for moral, international, and practical reasons. As racial groups had grown in number, it had become even more highly embarrassing for the country not to have resolved its anachronistic system of education. Not only had the condition of apartheid become duplicitous in racial policy across the nation, but so was it most highly reflected in its educational system at large. Education had become disparate and in some quarters tripartite, often operating as mini-systems for three racial groups—Black, Brown and White—with additional tribal schools in reservations and great restrictions for Chinese schools isolated in the West.

As too much effort, oversight, and expense was needed to maintain multiple systems, education became the medium by which disparity would be tackled, as it was evident that schools had become highly segregated, disjointed, and truly unequal. Equally important, differentiated schooling systems had become rather costly in addition to being inefficient and unmanageable. As schooling had become a set of loosely connected and disparate systems spread across the country with limited coordination and oversight, it was only through the Supreme Court that such a dual system could be dismantled nationally. No other branch of government could tackle this difficult task openly. In 1954 it was the *Brown* decision that came with great expectations, but also with unanticipated consequences.

Reformers Miss the Point

IT WAS INITIALLY ENCOURAGING THEN DISAPPOINTING THAT WHILE EGALITARIANISM WAS FAR FROM REALITY AT THE START OF THE 20TH CENTURY, REFORMERS TALKED ABOUT "EQUALITY," BUT SELDOM AGREED ON ITS MEANING AND OFTEN WORKED AT CROSS PURPOSES FOR ITS IMPLEMENTATION. A breath of fresh air and rather distinct from peers was Lester Frank Ward, as both educator and sociologist. As the first president of the American Sociological Society founded in 1905 (later the American Sociological Association, ASA), his voice was one of few against White Supremacy.[38]

Ward reasoned that the major contributor to inequality was the "unequal distribution of knowledge." He said, "I know no other problem of applied sociology that society can solve until this one is solved." Far-sighted in vision, he literally ascribed to Francis Bacon's statement centuries earlier that knowledge was power, as he also advocated that talent and ability was more powerful, as it "was everywhere." When he asserted that what was rare was "opportunity, not ability," [39] he was decades ahead of the claim that "talent is overrated" and that the educational gap is more a "lack of opportunity." Echoing Horace Mann from half a century earlier, he boldly asserted that there was no greater purpose for education than to equalize society.

In contradistinction, contemporary "reformers" like William Torrey Harris, U.S. Commissioner of Education at the turn of the twentieth century, also believed that American education would go awry if it was to provide one type of education for the laboring class and a different kind for children of the rich and powerful. But this was more lip service, as he and Ward could not have been more distant on how they both approached and applied educational policy and practice. There were also critical disconnects in what they proclaimed and vast differences on how they acted.

Harris had been a member of the Committee of Ten and former NEA President. However, it is important to indicate that even reformers like him had gotten so caught up in American jingoism and imperialist thinking that their educational policies suffered from internal contradictions. While maybe well intended, his views were too greatly hampered by an ideology of Anglo superiority.

As it turned out, Harris was the same person that confirmed the appointment of Victor S. Clark, as President of the newly-established Puerto Rico Board of Education in 1899. Soon after taking office, Clark proclaimed that the medium of instruction for Puerto Rico was to be English and pushed for this to occur immediately, installing the infamous Clark Policy in Puerto Rico.[40] As a reformer, Harris never took issue with Clark's jingoistic and anti-pedagogical policies that later choked education across the island.

While the Clark Policy was seemingly for instructional purposes in Puerto Rico, it was, in reality, for the express purpose of "Americanizing" islanders. The idea of educational achievement was patent nonsense. Ideology trumped education, with education transforming into colonization. It was worse than ideological football or misapplication of knowledge acquisition and academic advancement. Devastatingly for Puerto Rico, this approach occurred at an inappropriate time, amazingly when no one knew English. As it happened, without the development of linguistic expertise, this ill-founded decision literally froze the entire process of education for the island. This flawed and racist policy which endured for decades resulted in major disruption of formal instruction for islanders, causing massive dropout rates and major language confusion for nearly five decades.

One researcher carefully documented that between 1900 and late 1940 "seven different language policies were implemented with none accomplishing English-speaking and/or bilingualism in the island."[41] This has been chronicled as the most major educational catastrophe in island history, with remnants still affecting current English language instruction.[42] Astonishingly and most disappointedly, Harris was later lauded as one of the major stalwarts in education policy alongside Horace Mann.[43] While an odious and shameful acknowledgement, it was rather indicative of the period.

Another education reformer hailed as a progressive voice and "champion" of egalitarianism was Charles W. Eliot—a scion of wealth and cousin to T.S. Eliot—serving four decades as Harvard President until 1909. Beyond many contributions to higher education, including catapulting Harvard University as leader in prestigious graduate studies internationally, he was also quite active in pre-collegiate education reform.[44] In 1903, he became NEA President, after chairing the "Committee of Ten" in 1892 that led to the standardization of college preparation and admissions as well as subsequent high school reform. He also later helped with the College Entrance Examination Board (CEEB) in 1906 and assisted with a series of other reforms. In addition, he later compiled and edited the *Harvard Classics* in 1910, producing a wealth of publications on liberal education through a series of classics on world literature for a total of 51 volumes. He was known to have challenged educators to obtain a liberal education by reading the classics for 15 minutes each day.

Liberalism aside, Eliot proved to be highly enigmatic and controversial. On one end, he fiercely opposed American imperialism, staunchly supported W.E.B. Du Bois' entry into Harvard University (class of 1890), conferred an honorary doctorate on Booker T. Washington (1896), and was against blocking the admission of Jews and Catholics into Harvard. At the other end, he was controversial in his opposition to the education of women as well as a strong defender and later collaborator of the American eugenics movement in the 1920s to the great disappointment of many colleagues.[45]

In totality, the vast majority of so-called "reformers" during this period were proponents of stratified education, where the poor went through a different track and racial minorities remained as a permanent underclass. Among them, Ellwood P. Cubberley, initially a schoolteacher and later dean, wrote what was then considered to be an important book for school administrators in 1916, as it became a basic text guiding educational administration for years. He also later wrote a book on the history of American education, *Public Education in the United States* (1919) and authored several additional books on the history of education, but where the education of nonwhites was neglected in each of the publications. While his books became best sellers, highly influencing thinking among new generations of teachers, a dual system of education was assumed, as he never addressed its shortcomings.

Cubberley's impact in shaping the lives of educators during this period and on overall educational reform was enormous, as he played a major role in the professionalization of both teaching and administration. His view that there was not to be just one curriculum, as a "one size fits all" model might convey, is quite lucid and on target, much ahead of his time. But among his astounding pronouncements, the following provides discriminatory and perturbing insights: "Our city schools will soon be forced to *give up* the exceedingly democratic idea that all are equal and that our society is devoid of classes" [emphasis added].[46] While quite prodigious in his writings, lest he be dismissed, he also was Superintendent of Schools in San Diego, CA (1896) near the turn of the century, and soon thereafter Dean of the School of Education at Stanford University, among other positions of influence. Nonetheless, his opinions about race and class as well as eugenics are typical for his time for educators at senior levels of leadership.[47]

Applauding similar ideologies was John Franklin Bobbitt, who was highly influential with his book, *The Curriculum* (1918), based on scientific management theory (principles taken from an industrial model), with the belief that the purpose of education was to prepare youth for specific work they were to later attain in the workplace, including factory work. As such, "The curriculum was to adapt to the needs ... of the industrial society."[48] Curricular differentiation was the euphemistic word for this type of instruction. In effect, this approach was epitomized by the "social efficiency" movement in education, prominent through midcentury. As promoter of the social efficiency movement, he also was an active member of the eugenics movement.[49] As an educational leader, he reflected these types of beliefs during the first third of the twentieth century.

In upholding social efficiency, many school practitioners had strong ideologies about race, but suffered from considerable ignorance about the plight of the disenfranchised. Up until WWII, dominant thinking among many key educators was to focus less on the academic curriculum for those not going to college because they were eventually to occupy low-skilled jobs. At the same time for K–12 education, progress was greatly hampered as leadership was incapable of advancing the goals of equity and liberatory education.

Before the term egalitarianism confuses further, somehow the term could not have meant equality for all. It had a different meaning, reserved for only one sector of society. This is not unlike many of the pronouncements from founding fathers like Thomas Jefferson, another believer in education for all as well as equality for some. Such escapes from reason were so deeply seated that attention to race was far from these leaders' mindsets, as if unconsciously unaware.

Much debate and talk around reform seldom confronted the contradictions of racial inequality. This occurred despite continual admonition from contemporary statesmen and educators like W.E.B. Du Bois in *The Crisis*; from Carter Woodson who founded *The Journal of Negro History* in 1915; the work of Alaín Locke in his publication, *The New Negro* (1925) on the Harlem Renaissance; the writings of Ana Julia Cooper at the turn of the century; among many Black scholars of that era that clearly and quite artfully espoused contrary evidence and held opposing views. Worse, these educators were barely referenced, if at all. Seemingly reasonable and prominent White educators could not see the plank before their eyes. They were obviously not highly versatile academically. They were also rather smug in their "liberal" thinking and White "ideological" framework of superiority to consider any minority scholar as equal.

Seemingly "progressive" educators, as the label might infer, were not all that progressive after all. Inconsistencies and contradictions often came from the very top, trickling later to sycophants, high-level practitioners, and lay people alike. Let's add Woodrow Wilson to that list, the only education-related President during this time, as he was prior Governor of New Jersey and President of Princeton from 1902 to 1910, coinciding with the last decade of Charles Eliot's reign at Harvard. Wilson, son of a Presbyterian minister, although appointing the first Catholic and Jewish faculty at Princeton, held repugnant views toward Blacks and strove to keep them out of Princeton. He was also most forceful in assuring a segregated workforce and held a private viewing at the White House of *The Birth of a Nation*, celebrating the repugnant achievements of the KKK that were once again coming into prominence in American politics. This was a time when scientific thinking fused with pre-existing racism to provide credibility to eugenics and racial superiority which he forcefully championed.

During this period, key policymakers and educational theorists bypassed the issue of a dual system of education, never addressing gross inequities among racial groups, even when segregation was constitutionally unequal. John Dewey, principal founder and leader of the Progressive Movement in education, and its most prolific writer, was one of the exceptions to these trends. In contrast to most peers, he set a different tone regarding prominent views on social heredity when he insisted in 1909, for example, that "there is no 'inferior race.'"[50] Regarding racial intolerance, he responded to efforts that aimed to limit immigration and the nativist intolerance towards foreigners when he tackled the issue of racial discrimination in a paper presented to the Chinese Social and Political Science Association in 1922 that "Race prejudice is a deep-seated and widespread social disease."[51]

His views about inequality came from a societal perspective and he was strong that the masses cannot attain this well until there has been a change in education.[52] Later, near the start of the U.S. involvement in WWII he contributed strong sentiments regarding racial hatred and on one occasion vehemently stated: "There are still many, too many, who feel free to cultivate and express racial prejudices as if they were within their personal rights, not recognizing how the attitude of intolerance infects, perhaps fatally as the example of Germany surely proves, the basic humanities without which democracy is but a name."[53]

His was a refreshing change, as the era was a distinct period that blemished the country's attitudes about race while muddying educational thinking. More detrimentally and to the point, such attitudes did little to advance the lives of millions of nonwhite children. It was a time of vicious outcries against diversity, even open violence, as witnessed by lynching and atrocities launched against nonwhites and the founding of racist organizations, with lasting animosity through the civil rights era and beyond. It was as if the sting of *Plessy* atrophied the minds of educational leaders. By contrast, Dewey represented the Horace Mann of the 20th century.

On an equally positive tone, this period also produced publications from scholars like Du Bois (1903; 1935) and Carter Woodson (1933), where considerable evidence was being exposed about how damage to the African American was being conducted in the very classrooms they attended. Books like the *Mis-education of the Negro American*, as Woodson titled one of his books, to the internal damage to the "soul" and the "spirit" of the Black man, as Du Bois immortalized in his 1903 book using the term in *The Souls of Black Folks*, came as inestimable additions to the literature.

There were also the writings of John Hope Franklin, Anna J. Cooper, E. Franklin Frazier, and Kenneth Clark that were contemporaries to many of the White men of distinction just referenced, but never cited as equals nor very well known by White reformers for any hope of balanced scholarship. While this may be forgiven for the average reader, it is inexcusable among scholars and eminent educators, most especially when they claimed to have "researched" and greatly "studied" education literature and the presumed heritability of intelligence and represented the scions of scholarship and liberalism. In looking back, it was these White reformers that gave education a "bad rap," as some would say, not to mention revealing poor scholarship and intellectual negligence, laying racism aside.

Among the valiant writers that described the ill effects of segregation and deprivation that resulted from deprecatory and dualistic systems of education, the work of Kenneth Clark and his wife, Mamie, rank high among them. They documented the psychological effects of racial isolation and how it impacted the social-emotional state of Black children, most especially self-concept. Their "doll study" was later cited as evidence by Thurgood Marshall from the NAACP in his arguments before the High Court during *Brown*. Certain research and related documentation that was produced also lent credibility to the condition of education and the general state of Blacks in America. Psychologist Gordon Allport in his book, *The Nature of Prejudice* (1954), for example, analyzed the effects of racial discrimination at the time of *Brown* and represents another eminent researcher that was an exception to typical and standardized, White scholarship.

As WWII drew to a close, the Carnegie Foundation chose Swedish economist, Gunnar Myrdal as a voice with authority that would be "fair and impartial" in his assessment of American progress mid-century. In *An American Dilemma* (1944) he described the state of Black public education in the South as marked by "miserably poor standards all around." He described schools in some rural areas as suffering from major lack of equipment, lax enforcement of truancy, inferior teaching, poor teacher training, and differential payment to teachers, among many other injustices. His conclusion was unquestionable and most definitive: "Negro children come out of their school system—elementary and secondary—very poorly educated,"[54] as they are also highly "neglected."

B*y now, national policy in education seemed to descend into a pit, as much disdain toward racial groups spread like a plague nationwide.* While this had been the case from colonial times to mid-20th century, affecting even Presidents that spoke in derogatory tones about race, it was dismaying to have this continue, especially in the face of contrary evidence and by "eminent" leaders. Why then the charade of objectivity and the claim of scientific rigor?

It would be difficult to quote many prominent educators or major American leaders that spoke kindly about racial groups in egalitarian terms prior to Presidents Kennedy and Johnson, or the efforts of Truman in creating the Civil Rights Commission in 1947 and enacting the presidential order to desegregate the U.S. military. The list of distinguished Americans that fall into this bandwagon is short and narrow. Highly disappointingly, those times were highly unfavorable to racial minorities. Meantime, racist policies not only endured, but had become ever more brazen.

For Blacks and other nonwhite Americans, all suffering from grave discrimination and inattention, there were few educational advocates during this period of so-called educational reform. Predominant educators represented a silent generation about the most important issue facing education—the total exclusion and abandonment of racial groups. Was the elephant in the room not big enough? How is it that they failed to see these deficiencies? How is it that so many embraced eugenics? What does it mean when we talk about educational advances from reformers? Good questions all, many relevant today.

We must mind the source and the subtleties of racism behind the lectern. Much has been said (or omitted) in the name of reform that turns out to be another version that is disparaging to nontraditional populations. Reform or otherwise, individual and institutional racism has no place in educational theory or practice, as it will not work for anyone. A word to the wise is that educators must be ever critical and mindful of such egregious errors in judgment, no matter how erudite or well-schooled they may seem. Educators must hold the feet of colleagues of this ilk close to the fire and demand personal and professional accountability from every direction and at every instance, as such thinking is still dominant in many of today's leaders and among its most hallowed institutions.

Testing and Profiling

IN LOCKSTEP WITH FLOUNDERING REFORM, ADVANCEMENT IN STATISTICAL MEASUREMENT BROUGHT SCIENCE FULLY INTO THE ERA OF BIASED EDUCATIONAL ASSESSMENT AT THE START OF THE 20TH CENTURY. This had been propelled by the works of Sir Francis Galton in advanced statistical techniques, including his prescient work in England on the "bell-shaped" curve (normal distribution curve) that integrated science with racialization. He later expanded his statistical justification, piggybacking on the pioneering work of statistician Karl Pearson on regression and correlation, including the Chi-squared test (1900) for the measurement of differences among groups. In later joint ventures with Pearson, both scientists linked their findings with the work of biologist and population geneticist Ronald Fisher, creator of the analysis of variance (ANOVA) and designer of the experimental design and his simplified analyses of large data sets. It is both noteworthy but disheartening to acknowledge that all three were active members and proponents of the eugenics movement, hence the emphasis on statistical differences rather than similarities, a much more common occurrence.[55]

Most astoundingly, this occurred during the era of "progressivism," with both movements reaching major heights during the early decades of the 20th century, surprisingly coincident with U.S. government regulations disallowing corporate monopolies, condemning labor exploitation, challenging rising poverty, proposing anti-child labor laws, and eventually culminating in women's suffrage. This is ironic, as if two different planes were co-occurring, but in schizoid parallels. It was not a left-right hand mis-coordination, but a left-right hand bifurcation, split-brain. While these various events were often at odds, they strangely struck a common chord when thwarting the advancement of people of color. While progressivism cannot be confused with liberalism, as we must also be careful in not superimposing too much anachronistic thinking in judging the past, it is powerful to think that regardless of dominant political party, religious persuasion, or social strata, racism seemed to dominate nearly every range and level of thinking, obscuring logic and basic humanity.

With *Plessy*, the turn of the century became a time when education experts and school psychologists utilized "scientific measurement" and "statistical methods" to delimit racial groups as "social problems," like pariahs to the system. Given high competition for efficiency and control, with scarce resources, students that were presumably tainted by race were left outside the school system so as not to infect the education of others.

In schooling, while contradictory movements co-existed, continuing trends in racial subjugation painted a foundational pattern. Apart from educational reform, these were the processes of deeply-rooted racism that were deeply engrained in the psyche of the country and its various institutions as they also reflected public school practices in banishment. In actuality, it was a deliberate perpetuation of a dual system that was reflected in tripartite conditions when multiple races were at play.

Despite evidence that IQ testing could be highly biased, it was utilized for subjugation in the name of scientific and educational progress. It provided the excuse by which racism could be justified and excused. Test scores were used in deprecatory ways for the placement of unschooled and low-literate racial populations, presumably endowed with inferior intelligence. While the use of IQ tests was greatly flawed, it was fodder for scientific racism, infecting school districts in the hundreds of thousands by the 1920s.

With increasing immigrant numbers at the turn of the century, together with rising modernization and corporate expansion, the popularization of education was a logical outgrowth, as education grew into a behemoth, but lacked needed control for greater efficiency and accuracy in judgment. During this shift, millions of Black and Mexican American children became outliers in a racialized system of exclusion, both by design and by default.[56] The irony was that when America needed to boost its labor and utilization of grey matter the most, it was also a time when racism prevented participation of these workers the most. Surprisingly, they were not even close competitors as is the case today. It was no accident that even the labor unions played a significant role on both sides of the argument at that time. Along a similar route, equally racist thinking also dominated the administration and control of outlier populations among colonial island territories like Hawaii, Guam, the Philippines, and Puerto Rico.

During this period of "bogus science," as David Tyack (1974) of old once described it, the IQ craze came into prominence as "the" presumed leveler for the schools. Simply put, it was an easy way to categorize students quickly, efficiently, and cheaply, as if counting down from an assembly line. Albeit a European import, the utility of the IQ test spread like a virus, quickly becoming the standard by which student placement was soundly justified, as was the forfeiture of certain children. It seemingly came just in time to respond to the dilemma of the minority. It helped place (or displace) "defective students" into special classes.[57]

After WWI, bogus practices overtook the public schools, rapidly changing the state-of-the-art so that within five years (by 1923) IQ testing had become the norm.[58] This was when millions of students started taking IQ tests in droves. As claimed by many then (and since), it was unbelievable how common, yet "misunderstood," the use of testing had become. It seemed like teachers were satisfied to make serious decisions based on one single test—though disastrous to millions. Despite admonitions from some experts about potential misuse, it is astounding how even the most respectable in the field allowed such disservice to run amuck. For racial groups, as they were deemed most dispensable, few would question their test results. Even high scores were perceived as anomalies, as cheating, as part of the 5% statistical chance factor, not representative of brilliant outliers. Astoundingly, this conveys eerie echoes today.

It was at this time that Virgil Dickson (1923), director of research and guidance at both the Oakland and Berkeley school districts in California wrote a major-selling textbook for teachers about the importance of the IQ test in the placement and assessment of children. This was part of an edited series of books by Lewis M. Terman, leading expert on testing and measurement that specifically highlighted the IQ test. Intelligence had become a convenient label, defined as the "ability to learn" or the power "to judge well, to comprehend, to reason well."[59] As a result, mental tests were used everywhere as an aid in classifying children "into effective working groups,"[60] not to mention the exclusion of minorities from entering *bona fide* classrooms. With the IQ accepted as a constant and permanently reliable measure of intelligence, its preponderance dwarfed evidence to the contrary.

As utilized, mental tests became invaluable in determining the grade level in which a child could perform satisfactory school work as it also predicted the progress they would likely make. Reasoning was that there existed a positive correlation between high IQ scores and school as success, as this was what truly mattered most to teachers. Simply put, it was truly believed that since inferior mental ability was "largely responsible for school failure" and since all studies showed that "IQ remained relatively constant," it was logical that "the chief cause of school failure in the elementary schools cannot be removed under present curriculum requirements."[61] Logically and without question, it was assumed that "average failure was not due to poor teachers, to poor health, or to poor attendance, but to lack of ability."[62] It was further thought that 20% of the children that entered first grade could not under the most variable conditions be carried through the first seven grades of the standard curriculum before age sixteen.

Answering the question of what to do with children of "inferior" intelligence was simple. They needed to take a "different course of study," with a "small amount of academics" and "a "large amount of the manual [skills]."[63] The adage depicting a "clumsy brain but skillful hand" became the destiny for many pupils, most especially for the limited number of racial minorities that attended the public schools. The answer to the question, "Does the inferior child gain interest when segregated?" came back unequivocably as "yes" because "school children do better school work and have greater interest when segregated into classes of their own."[64] For Latinos and Blacks, this was the destiny for the bulk of their population.

The relationship between IQ testing and special placement was significant for Blacks and Latinos. As an example for the Los Angeles public schools in 1929, some 2,800 children had been assigned to ten developmental centers with a total of thirty development rooms located primarily in working-class sections amidst the city. According to district reports, an estimate of the flow was that these centers and their accommodations could "only serve one-quarter" of the "subnormals" at the schools, as many more had to wait for a transfer out of the normal classes.[65] This was as anti-pedagogical as it was discriminatory and self-fulfilling.

Alfred Binet, father of the IQ test in Europe, believed that education when properly implemented had unlimited power to create, promote, and even accelerate intelligence,[66] as its exposure had the power to increase IQ scores, but the *opposite* was held by American educators, mid-1920s. When Binet died in 1911, much ahead of his time, thinking had become so entrenched nationwide that his words were insufficient to later refute fallaciously new concepts based on his work.[67] Incredibly contrary to Binet's thinking was that children were born with different innate abilities so that treating them as if they were alike would be against sound educational practice, especially since IQ was perceived to be the most credible measure that also represented a fixed imprint. IQ scores were believed to be fully heritable and unalterable. By extension, the best way to diagnose school potential was through testing, forgetting this could be self-prophesied. While far from the truth, this had become the norm, miseducation at its best. Most distressing, such practices ran against Binet's original thesis, the father of IQ testing.

Equally powerful at that time, it was also believed that "democracy does not mean equality of achievement, but rather equality of opportunities for achievement."[68] Great! While an accurate platitude, such thinking was turned on its head. One would think that opportunities for children with low IQ would be equally different by providing "greater" opportunity for the child to advance, especially if IQ was a result of environmental factors rather than nature to dismiss predetermination. It was also the case that many of the questions were class-biased, as nontraditional students would not know the meaning of words like regatta or the number of presidents preceding Lincoln among typical questions being asked, as if these were aptitude oriented. But this was not to be. Dominant thinking was that advanced study (opportunity for success) for low-IQ children would place unjust burdens on the child that would be inherently unfair, therefore exposure to more difficult material or higher-order thinking had to be limited. Such tautological and circular reasoning dominated this period, becoming the stopgap to minority achievement and creating a climate of continual failure and self-fulfilling results.

The use of intelligence tests did not greatly wane until after mid-century, as attitudes about school failure for racial groups persisted long-term. Not surprisingly, this resurfaced during the 1960s. An example was when a Boston school official defended the reason public schools were not yielding expected results. Reasoning was: "We do not have inferior schools; we have been getting an inferior type of student."[69] School systems defended themselves in the 1960s much like earlier decades, as the compensatory education philosophy was to overcome the "cultural deficits" of the child. Despite *Brown* and later educational reforms, educational philosophy and practice did not always change, as it defended existing structures that aimed to teach and socialize the nontraditional child relying on former logic in much the same way. Results blamed the victim, though with different arguments later, as William Ryan well documented in *Blaming the Victim* (1971; 1976). Thinking aligned with what Cubberley and earlier reformers would have expected at the start of the century. Progress sometimes stifles even when positively, corroborating evidence is indisputable.

As evident, the color line in schooling disingenuously misapplied the process of sorting students into categories of aptitude by whatever justifiable criteria possible, merely to indicate that the status of "difference" was equivalent to "lesser than." Such mislabeling placed racial students in a continual position of inferiority and permanent defensiveness, causing considerable psychological damage to their mindset and self-concept, research results about which psychologist Kenneth Clark and wife Mamie conducted extensively midcentury with Black students as most damaging. Disappointingly, inferior schooling practices did not end there nor did they stop with *Brown*. In point of fact, similar practices continue today. Much research indicates that low expectations can yield low performance, as research on the Pygmalion effect concluded decades later.[70] Further research on student tracking and academic profiling continues to this day, as Gilda Ochoa (2013) has recently documented. Many of these findings and their effects are documented in her book, appropriately titled: *Academic Profiling*.

The Fallacy of Reform

EDUCATION HAD MORPHED FROM AN INSTITUTION THAT WAS A GATEWAY FOR THE SUCCESS OF THE WELL-TO-DO TO A SYSTEM THAT WAS NOW PROVIDING OPPORTUNITY FOR THE MORE TYPICAL, MODAL STUDENT, BUT STILL HANDICAPPING THE DISPOSSESSED AND VIRTUALLY ELIMINATING THE ENTRY OF RACIAL MINORITIES. Reform was for White schools, unfocused on balance, not about equality of access or opportunity for all. Equity had not entered the formula for success. Minorities were still barred from typical classrooms. Even the Horatio Alger rags-to-riches stories remained elusive and devoid of minorities. There was seemingly no way out of the morass.

Du Bois, as per his initial writings in *The Crisis* magazine which he helped found in 1910 for the newly-formed NAACP (1909), was a strong defender of more balanced opportunities and denounced the impact of the dual system affecting Blacks. He saw this dichotomy as a major contradiction and one that was splitting America from within, while also placing it distinct and apart from the rest of the world, as it underutilized its citizenry.[71] Quite pointedly in *The Souls of Black Folks* (1903), he made a prescient pronouncement in the first paragraph of his foreword stating unequivocally: "The problem of the Twentieth Century is the problem of the color-line."[72] Without misspeaking, he had predicted the 21st century, as it is dividing socially along the lines of caste and segregation, based on race and color, one for the "White" student and another for the "nonwhite."

Cornel West's book alludes to similar sentiments in his 25th anniversary edition of *Race Matters* (1993) when he said: "Race is the most explosive issue in American life precisely because it forces us to confront the tragic facts of poverty and paranoia, despair and distrust. In short, a candid examination of race matters takes us to the core of American democracy."[73] In retrospect, it seems that the color-line is what has both divided and defined America, as has been depicted by many minority scholars during that period as well as for today.

In his analysis of race in America, Myrdal had appropriately labeled the issue of race as a national dilemma. By the end of the century, we may be more inclined to label it an American calamity. Andrew Hacker in his review of racial progress in America came to similar conclusions in *Two Nations: Black and White, Separate, Hostile and Unequal* (1992). By now, the persistence of race and color and its depression on achievement have become an American obsession as well as its major challenge, as race fully correlates with achievement nationwide. But we are getting ahead of the story with battles in between.

In defense of the African American, nearly 100 court cases from 20 states and the District of Columbia challenged segregation, racial discrimination and education-related cases during the era of Plessy. Nearly all dealt with race, access, and social justice, according to eminent scholar, J. Morgan Kousser, former editor of the journal *Historical Methods* and author of various books and publications on American jurisprudence. A fair number of these cases also pertain to Mexican American civil rights and social justice, though still lacking high reference in much of the extant literature, as there remain considerable gaps in much of the cited literature.[74]

Going back to the statistical report on *Negro Education* (1917), led by Thomas Jesse Jones, an African American statistical compiler for the Bureau of Education at the time, for Black children ages 6-to-14 during the first decade of the 20th century, barely half attended any school whatsoever, with very few remaining in school beyond the fifth grade.[75] His report, later called the

Jones Report, also confirmed that as a result of bifurcated and polarized educational systems there was a heavy economic burden placed on the maintenance of multiple school systems, different for each race and varying in cost across the country. According to his report, nearly all were differentiated by race and color, where race was the factor whereby school systems incurred greater expense in maintaining dual and tripartite systems.

Notwithstanding, as Jones further reported, these segregated institutions were still "grossly inadequate," and "heavily underfunded." The situation at the high school level was worse as such schools were quite "rare" and "fully segregated," prohibiting entry of any type. Jones further documented that more than half the schools that allowed entrance to Blacks were sponsored by foundations or religious organizations as seldom were local school system funds or federal dollars allowed to be utilized.[76] This was an astonishing pronouncement by an authorized agent of the Bureau of Education. In higher education, the situation was similarly dismal. As late as 1940, barely 1% of college graduates were Black, including those from HBCUs.[77]

For Latinos, the situation was more complex, as entrance into any high school in the Southwest was largely prohibited except for the privileged few. There was inability to attend even the few segregated schools that catered to Hispanics. Other than race, this was also strongly due to the non-completion of 8th grade. Unable to rely on any system of education—segregated or otherwise—many Latinos were not admitted into high school. Many remained hidden away in Mexican Schools where 8th grade was the highest possible level. It is estimated that barely 1-in-10 Mexican Americans ever enrolled in high school during this time, let alone graduated.[78] This condition lasted decades, easing little between the 1930s and the 1950s. As a result, educational attainment for Latinos was lower than for the African American at every level of the educational ladder, exacerbating even more greatly at the postsecondary and university level.

Segregation as Disenfranchisement

THE ERA OF SEGREGATION WAS RATHER DELIBERATE IN ITS STANCE TO KEEP RACES PERMANENTLY SEPARATED AND APART AS WELL AS FULLY DISENFRANCHISED. When it came to assimilation, the stance was not to use the school to redress racism and imbalance, but rather "adjust" the minority child to White middle-class norms that were socially acceptable. Trust in the scientific method was such that statistics on "retardation" in school and reliance on intelligence tests was sacrosanct in explaining the causes of school failure in the child or on the family and neighborhood. For example, when renowned school administrator Ellwood Cubberley wrote about the schools in the early 1900s it was to defend schools in accommodating to societal norms, not the other way around. According to Cubberley, students were to "adapt" to existing school practices and structures. In fact, tracking was the proper placement of dullard students into vocational education as such practices were embodied in his type of reform.[79]

Not to be outdone, it was Charles W. Eliot who told the Teachers' Association in 1911 that our society "is divided, and is going to be divided into layers whose borders blend, whose limits are easily passed by individuals, but which, nevertheless, have distinct characteristics and distinct educational needs." More to the point, "Freedom produces inequalities and it is foolish to educate each child to be President of the United States." The belief was that there were "four layers in civilized society which are indispensable … and so far as we can see, eternal." [80] After the top layers of the management, leadership and guiding class was that of the skilled workers followed by the commercial class, with the bottom layer consisting of household workers and persons working "in agriculture, mining, quarrying and forest work."[81] With such thinking, Blacks and Mexican Americans were easily destined to fail. The educational system that was to homogenize other Americans was not meant for them.

Lacking substantial political power to affect change in the schools, the tactics available to minority communities were limited. These were the courts, boycotts, marches, sit-ins, community petitions and lobbying, most of which were desperate but the only seemingly available options against entrenched power structures. It is important to gauge the context during the first third of the century by carefully tuning in to what sage elders were concluding about the system of education at the time. Du Bois, as a leading voice, explained that the ideal was not to have segregated schools, but that under the circumstances there was no choice. Schooling, by demanding total assimilation and Anglo-conformity assaulted all forms of cultural differences, creating a sense of shame at being "foreign," "different," and "unique." Obviously, schooling to be "White" was detrimental if one was "Black" or "not White."

> There are all too many schools where Negroes are admitted… but they are not educated; they are crucified … I have repeatedly seen wise and loving colored parents take infinite pains to force their little children into schools where the White chil-

dren, White teachers, and White parents despised and resented the dark child, make mock of it, neglected or bullied it, and literally render its life a living hell. Such parents may want their child to "fight" this thing out—but, dear God, at what a cost! ... [And if the battle is won] The cost may be high, and the child's whole life ... an effort to win cheap applause at the expense of healthy individuality.[82]

Distressing trends were becoming evident in the research literature for racial groups, especially between education and opportunity. As more students entered high school, research was unearthing major fault lines between schooling and employment. For example, in a major study of about 20,000 Black high school students, a U.S. Office of Education senior expert on Negro education, Ambrose Caliver (1950), found that "the more schooling a black person achieved, the more dissatisfied he was with his job."[83] As an African American researcher, Caliver[84] well documented that Black literacy had increased substantially, from 42.9% in 1890 to nearly 80% in 1940, as Negro high school enrollment also zoomed by the 1940s, increasing from 1.6% of the total Black enrollment in 1890 to 10.5% in 1940.[85] Black college attendance had also increased substantially to almost 30,000 by 1939.[86] Yet, dissatisfaction with employment was higher. Point was that by midcentury, though schooling had increased, employment had not caught up with schooling, as Blacks were overqualified for leftover and undesirable jobs.

Caliver had also previously (1940) reported for that period that "Study after study showed that Black students aspired to professor or other white-collar occupations that were closed to all but a small number who could make a living serving the needs of the Black community or who could find one of the relatively few jobs available in the civil service."[87] Jim Crowism had flourished and education, even when well attained, was not yielding expected results.

When education began to finally help Black students get ahead, the job market was not sufficient or ready to overcome decades-old inequities in hiring. As a result, there came to be an over-qualification of workers for existing openings that did not require high skills. This was a Catch-22 dilemma for racial minorities. One of the exceptional occupations interestingly enough was the job of schoolteacher for Blacks, where it was found that they were hired in greater numbers to work in urban schools. But the major reason this worked out was because they were being hired to work *exclusively* in highly-segregated schools, in a ghettoized professional manner and at lower wages. This circumstance, deplorable as it was, became far worse for Latinos, as even fewer could yet enter the teaching profession because only a small fraction had completed college,[88] but also because certain school districts like Tucson, AZ put limits on the number of Mexican teachers they could hire. However, this varied by region, as in the border districts of Texas like Brownsville, where there was a higher concentration of Mexican Americans, it was easier for Hispanic teachers to be hired.[89] Regardless, the combination of ghettoized markets coupled with insufficient numbers of prepared teachers limited the number of Mexican Americans that would enter the profession.

Given the great disparity between aspirations and actual career opportunities, another downfall was guidance counselors that further thwarted curricular options. They were an especially crucial influence, with few minorities filling those jobs. Here counselors reinforced the social mores rather than overcoming them through education. For racial students, two conditions prevailed: teachers lowered their expectations for minority students, while guidance counselors also lowered the student potential by suggesting they seek more realistic careers. This coupled trend persisted for decades, much beyond the years of civil rights. In the autobiography, *Malcolm X* (1965), Malcolm Little explained how he was greatly hurt by his "most admired" high school teacher when counseled not to seek his career of choice, creating the reason why as an honor student he dropped out of high school to live with his aunt elsewhere. He never forgot or forgave his favorite teacher for his lack of confidence, causing Malcolm to later rebel and eventually take-on the system head-on.

Separateness was strongly entrenched against racial minorities, enforced by structural differentiation across the country midcentury. The nation was divided structurally as it was divided in a hierarchically-tiered educational system that produced a state of inequality that was so palpable it had become notoriously obvious. This had been predicted by an African American scholar, Newton Edwards. In commenting about the state of education during this period, he reflected some of the contradictions in American schooling in a far-reaching report in 1939 ironically called *Equal Educational Opportunity for Youth* which suggested that far from being the "bulwark of democracy" schools had come to represent the very process that "created the inequalities they were presumably designed to prevent."[90] Historian David Tyack agreed with this analysis when he later wrote: "Schools have sometimes helped to destroy family and community cultures that met human needs and values more fully than did the culture they sought to instill."[91]

The push for Anglo conformity had been arising for over a century, as expressed by educators like Julia Richman (1905) at the start of the century.[92] In plain fact, the more successful the school was in Americanizing the child, the more the student was weaned away from the standards and traditions of the home culture, creating a wedge and eventual separation between child and parent. Over time, especially if the child went away to school—like for Native Americans—the child would likely separate from the family and its customs altogether. As a result, it was Richman and colleagues that argued long and hard for the creation of bridges between parents and their severed children at that time.[93] As she saw it, Anglo conformity did not work for racial groups, as it inevitably split families apart and resulted in the further division of communities.

Sometime later, Doxey A. Wilkerson (1940), an African American educator and researcher in describing the educational system in her time, observed that "the degree of such separateness tends to be most pronounced in areas" where the population is "most heavily concentrated" and where "social statistics is lower than in the North as a whole."[94] Such institutional separation became massive as racial populations expanded in the central cities.

During the late 1940s, as the nation settled down in respite after the war, educators frantically scrambled to catch up with new demands for greater schooling. By the 1950s, large crops of students seemed to enroll everywhere, as a baby boom mushroomed, but once again excluding minorities from full participation with Whites. However, the decade was soon to be shaken up by the McCarthy era and then by *Brown*, both followed by the Russian Sputnik in 1957 and the inevitable start of a long march towards civil rights 1960s onward.

At the time, minority migrations were in full swing, with the Great Migration of Blacks coming from the South, Mexican American migrants entering from the Southwest, and northern migrations from Puerto Rico, each adjusting to rather different schooling conditions, with schools now growing with disproportionate numbers of minority students. In high school, to make the process easier to organize, students were routinely assigned to one of three tracks—academic, vocational and general—but based primarily on intelligence testing. Inevitably, many Black and Latino students wrestled with new placements and accreditation processes, with tracking singling them out with rampant demotions.

As this suppression was felt more greatly in the South, and as the majority of Blacks resided in the South, there had arisen a movement to migrate, at first to the Midwest in the 1880s, especially the states of Ohio, Missouri and Kansas. Migrations later increased reaching heights of half a million around 1920 and 1.6 million by 1940, the peak of the "Great Migration"[95] into other central cities of the North. It is interesting to note that these patterns reversed around the 1980s, with net migrations heading South this time, with more affluent and retiring Blacks starting a return back South.[96]

Notes

1. Zinn, 2003.
2. Schlesinger, 1941.
3. This is not necessarily complementary, as this period (1877–1900) was also one of ruthlessness, high corruption, and industrial monopolies.
4. Billingsley, p. 117.
5. Ibid.
6. According to Tuskegee Institute 4743 people were lynched between 1882 and 1968, most frequently from 1890 to the 1920s, with 73% being African American. https://en.wikipedia.org/wiki/Lynching_in_the_United_States
7. Margo, 1990, p. 8.
8. Taylor, 1976.
9. Anderson, 1988, p. 149.
10. Du Bois, 1902, p. 290.
11. Ibid., p. 291.
12. Ibid.
13. May, 2015, p. 203.
14. Ibid.
15. Billingsley, 1992.
16. Snyder, 1993, *120 Years of American Education*.
17. Anderson, 1988, p. 13.
18. Ibid.
19. Margo, 1990.
20. There are 106 land-grant colleges and universities nationwide, including the University of Puerto Rico (UPR).
21. Drawn from the historical list of HBCUs.
22. Data show very few exceptions, with lower participation rates than African Americans.
23. The NEA represents one of the largest labor unions in the country, with an estimated 3 million members.
24. Nagdy & Roser, 2016.
25. Goldin & Katz, 2008.
26. Robert Morris was one of the country's first African American attorneys, and Charles Sumner later became a U.S. Senator, as an abolitionist. This was the same Sen. Sumner that later became infamous for having been beaten nearly to death with a cane by U.S. Repr. Preston Brooks from South Carolina in 1856, when Sumner was writing at his desk in an almost empty Senate chamber.
27. Billingsley, p. 172.
28. Ibid.
29. Data come from the Jones reports at the Bureau of Education, from 1910 to around 1920 as well as from census documentation during that period.
30. Despite the Great Migration, the number of Blacks in the North was still very few, as the vast majority resided in the South. Most figures take this into account, as they are not inflated by figures from the North.

31. Herbold, p. 107.
32. This is not much different from dual systems in other countries. India's caste system, illegal since 1949, had different educational systems, by caste. South Africa had an apartheid system, now abolished since 1994, where nineteen separate departments of education were officially established for each ethnic group.
33. Anderson, 1988, p. 186.
34. Ravitch, 2000, p. 374.
35. Ibid., p. 374.
36. Anderson, 1988.
37. Ibid.
38. Ward was a champion of civil rights, strongly asserting the rights of women, and a strong critic of Herbert Spencer who sided with the eugenics movement and his theories of *laissez-faire* and the survival of the fittest.
39. This view was known as "egalitarian intellectualism."
40. Together with other island territories, Puerto Rico was ceded to the U.S. by Spain in 1898 under the Treaty of Paris, as war booty from the Spanish-American War of 1898. In 1900, Congress passed the Foraker Act that set up civil government in the island.
41. Rodríguez-Arroyo, 2013, p. 79.
42. This policy was not fully resolved until 1948, when the island was granted some measure of autonomy, further affirmed in 1952 when the Commonwealth of Puerto Rico was enacted.
43. Tyack, p. 43.
44. Adam Cohen, 2016; Eliot, 1911.
45. Ibid.
46. Ravitch, 2000, p. 96.
47. Winfield, 2007.
48. Ravitch, 2000.
49. Winfield, 2007.
50. Cohan & Howlett, 2017, p. 17.
51. Ibid., p. 18.
52. Ibid.
53. Dewey quoted in Boydston (Ed.), p. 277.
54. Myrdal, 1944.
55. Karl Pearson greatly influenced the origins of modern statistics and Ronald A. Fisher was the fountainhead for modern statistical science and experimental design. A highly-readable analysis of this period and its connection with eugenics can be found in the first chapter of *Statistics for the Helping Professions* by Besag & Besag (1985).
56. Tyack, 1974, p. 217.
57. Dickson, p. iii.
58. Ibid.
59. Ibid., p. 30.
60. Ibid., p. 65.
61. Ibid., p. 130.
62. Ibid.
63. Ibid., p. 139.

90 THE STORY OF LATINOS AND EDUCATION IN AMERICAN HISTORY

64. Ibid., p. 147.
65. González, p. 65.
66. Alfred Binet was a French psychologist that created the first practical IQ test in France. In 1905, the Binet-Simon scale was first introduced, with its first revision published in 1908.
67. Carol Dweck (2006) well analyzes the IQ and its history in a subsection of her first chapter.
68. Dickson, p. 171.
69. Tyack, p. 282.
70. Rosenthal & Jacobson, 1992; Ochoa, 2013.
71. Du Bois was founder and editor of *The Crisis* which started in 1910 as an official publication of the NAACP, one year after the official founding of the NAACP in 1909.
72. Du Bois, 1903, p. v.
73. West, 1993, p. xiv.
74. Kousser, 1986.
75. Note that this figure has since been revised by Billingsley (1992) to 45%.
76. Ravitch, 2010, p. 108.
77. Herbold, p. 107.
78. MacDonald, 2016.
79. Tyack, p. 188.
80. Ibid., p. 110.
81. Ibid., p. 111.
82. Du Bois, 1935, pp. 329, 331.
83. Tyack, p. 222.
84. As the first African American doctoral recipient in education at Columbia University in 1930, Ambrose Caliver was selected by President Hoover several years later as Sr. Specialist in the U.S. Office of Education where he compiled some of the most comprehensive data on African American educational achievement since the days of the Jones Report during the decade of 1910.
85. Tyack, p. 222.
86. Caliver, 1950, p. 114.
87. Ambrose Caliver quoted in Tyack, 1974, p. 222.
88. Anderson, 1988.
89. MacDonald, 2006.
90. Edwards, 1939, p. 152.
91. Tyack, 249.
92. Julia Richman was the first successful woman district superintendent of the New York City schools.
93. Richman, p. 119.
94. Doxey Wilkerson, 1936, p. 344.
95. Taylor, 1976.
96. U.S. Bureau of the Census (1980), *The Social and Economic Status of Black Populations in the U.S., 1790–1978*.

· 3 ·

BROWN AND BEYOND

Beware of false knowledge; it is more dangerous than ignorance.
George Bernard Shaw

IT WAS THE MID-TWENTIETH CENTURY THAT SIGNALED A NEW EPOCH FOR AMERICA. THIS WAS WHEN MIDDLE-CLASS AMERICA BEGAN TO FLOURISH LIKE AN EPISODE FROM TWILIGHT ZONE. It was a calm period. It was a pleasant repose. It was a time of new prosperity. This was when everyone was going back to work. It was a Levittown period of serenity, when suburban America began growing by leaps and bounds once again. Everything was coming up roses after the war. Without doubt, everyone was seemingly settling down to raise a family, huddled around a new TV, sitting back and enjoying life. But Pleasantville was not without its challenges.

With conformism as the new culture, it was difficult for those that did not fit in, as "they" were coming from the "outside," either the South or somewhere else. They were strangers much before neighbors. They did not belong with the entitled. They were not to become masters of the universe, and not all had served in the war. This was the time when Black families continued with their migration, with second-generation Mexican Americans coming up from the Southwest and Puerto Ricans flying from the island. All were reshuffling life, many into large cities, with the majority in *barrios* and a select few in the suburbs. Yet nearly all found it hard to rent, even into neighborhoods from which others had just fled.

Calamitous Times

FOR MINORITIES, THIS WAS A TIME TO PUSH BACK AND CLAIM THEIR OWN. This was most especially the case as GIs had now experienced the country from afar, with a different lens, kindling an explosion of high hopes and greater success. Oftentimes cultures clashed. Over a million Blacks and half a million Latinos had served in the war, but no matter. They still were different from the others. Prosperity would be harder for them. Hope was pushing the concept of fairness and equality to the brink of eruption, as Black and Latino GIs returned only to find that vast numbers together with their families were being dismissed, unattended, and excluded.[1] This led to frustration, discontent, and the reclaiming of rights. Conditions were not only intolerable, but led to few of the avenues available for equity and justice, back to the streets and the court system; with few getting needed attention and many eventually altering schooling altogether.

For Latinos, this was a different add-on to the previous decade, when gangs of "White" hoodlums had attacked "newcomers," like the Zoot-Suit riots of servicemen attacking Mexican Americans in Los Angeles during the middle of World War II.[2] What were these newcomers doing? Why were they here? The assumption was that "they" had entered yesterday and illegally, forgetting their original rights, whether through squatter's rights from centuries earlier, citizenship rights fought and gained, Bracero rights as *bona fide* foreign agricultural workers, or as GIs returning from the war.

It was the mid-fifties that ushered in a truly different kind of survival for racial minorities. During this period, racial migrants were beginning to discover larger cities after the war, as the nation was beginning to boom once again. But new migrants were finding Northern cities to be cold and distant, ghettoized, almost inhospitable. For self-preservation and for economic survival, not unlike what had occurred in the South and the Southwest decades earlier, many formed mutual-aid societies that provided safety, referral, and security, with assistance from civic societies, nonprofits, self-help groups, resettlement houses, and religious groups to make ends meet. For many Latino families, "SAMS" and other similar home-banking systems were established. This was where families pitched in with monthly allowances to create larger pots of money that could then be distributed to kinship and friends in larger amounts periodically, as needed, with everyone having an equal chance to obtain large pockets of money through a quasi-revolving account a during time of need. Operating as a beneficiary society and bank all at once, these systems helped families save, exchange, and survive. I remember well when it was my dad's turn to receive his SAMS, as this was the time to buy new clothes and school supplies, even a time for ice cream and celebration.

As states were enforcing compulsory schooling once again, there was an explosion in school attendance soon after the Second World War. For a variety of reasons, schooling conditions were creating a dropout problem for Latinos and Blacks, where nearly 8-in-10 dropped out of high school, assuming viable enrollment in the first place.[3] Schools weren't ready for them and they weren't ready for school. With large numbers dropping out, gang warfare rumbled throughout.

Gang formation was depicted in movies like *Blackboard Jungle* (1955), then *West Side Story* as a play in 1957 and later as a movie in 1961, depicting New York City gangs during the mid-1950s, with Puerto Rican first-generation newcomers fighting the more established Polish and Italian immigrants for rights to turf. This was also when sociological books like *The Shook-Up Generation* (1958) and *The Violent Gang* (1962) started coming out, both describing problems with gang warfare and juvenile delinquency. In Chicago, the Latin Kings were established in 1954 then expanded to New York City, as a self-protecting Puerto Rican gang. Soon after, the Blackstone Rangers among African Americans came into its own in Chicago, with brotherly gangs mushrooming across the country in self-protection.

During *this time, the nation was caught in transition, fully unaware of its racial cover, one that would impact the very core of its foundation, that which was hidden deeply underneath.* This was about a dual but not so parallel system of education, raising its head from oblivion, seeking resolution. While the problem centered on education, its solution transcended education, as it was basic to the American creed, permeating all institutions. Here, education and society strongly melded, but differently for each group. Much had been learned after a world war, a hundred years after a Civil War between the states. While the universe of knowledge and diversity was expanding, and the seeds for later globalization were being sown, not enough was occurring in the housing and employment sector, let alone education.

A major issue was greatly about educational access sprouting from inequality. A major war had been fought precisely on the principles of democracy, freedom, equality, and social justice. Schooling for children was now just as important as schooling for the returning GI. Also, new lawsuits were in the front burner for justice not yet settled, with charges of discrimination that included race as a critical factor.

In 1950, the setting was that African American students were highly segregated, and where seventeen states sanctioned the process by decree. Just over fifteen million students were enrolled in 1950,[4] for roughly 83% of all 5 to 17-year-old White students in the country, but only with a 69% enrollment among Blacks,[5] and barely 28% for disabled school-aged children.[6] The level of literacy for Black students had been estimated around 89% in 1950,[7] with the average number of years in school for Whites at 11.3 years, with a comparable median of 7.8 years of schooling for Blacks and 5.4 years of schooling for Latinos.[8] After half a century of *Plessy*, education had become highly polarized, racially divided, and very uneven.

As a major war was now over, it was time to refocus on the essentials of education back home. The *Méndez v. Westminster* (1947) decision by the California Supreme Court was a case in point, where it was established that separate schools on the basis of race violated the 14th Amendment. This was important because it was at the aftermath of WWII that it laid the groundwork for *Brown* (1954), but initially focusing on Mexican American and Puerto Rican children discriminated on the basis of race.[9] It is interesting that it was this decision that caused California to immediately change its laws on segregation signed by then Governor Earl Warren, who ironically later served as Chief Justice for the High Court when it presided over *Brown*.

It had become obvious that dual systems of education could not be long-supported for the growing number of Blacks and other racial groups, as segregation was still the law for Blacks and for racial groups like Latinos. The demand for equality in the schools eventually turned into a push for integration which forced the issue that eventually led to *Brown*. Though many public arguments were moral and pedagogically-based, behind-the-scenes discussions were more strongly centered on politics and economics, not morality and justice.

By spring of 1954, within a period of two weeks, two Supreme Court cases were adjudicated,[10] both obtaining unanimous decisions, and both written by Chief Justice Earl Warren. *Hernández v. Texas* (1954) ruled that Mexican Americans (and all other racial or national groups) had equal protection under the Fourteenth Amendment for representation in court. *Brown v. Board of Education* (1954) ruled two weeks later that "in the field of public education the doctrine of 'Separate but equal' has no place," reasoning that "separate educational facilities" were "inherently unequal."[11] Both cases became landmark decisions, and both had been led by a minority team of attorneys—one team Black and the other team Mexican American. These represented turning points in American history as well as new educational policy.

These decisions eventually opened the floodgates that eventually led to civil rights in the mid-1960s, becoming one of the most calamitous decades in U.S. history. Nothing was to be the same afterwards. Many Americans have minimal understanding about how radically different the first half of the 20th century was from the second half, with the century's midpoint (and near breaking point) focused on *Brown*, as every septuagenarian can well testify.

The Era of *Brown*

IT WAS MIDCENTURY WHEN *BROWN* IN 1954 OVERTURNED *PLESSY* FROM 1896, ENDING 58 LONG AND ARDUOUS YEARS. The decision forced the dismantling of a racially-divided and separately-held school system, declaring it was unconstitutional and requiring it to proceed with "all deliberate speed," a phrase that pleased one justice, with the calculated knowledge that "deliberate" as then understood was a euphemism for "slow."[12]

Despite good intentions and the force of law, it did not go smoothly afterwards, as the subsequent ten years proved a barren decade for social change. What followed became flooded with ardent struggles, with few improvements in education despite multitudinous marches, protests, sit-ins, and further litigation. Even President Eisenhower bucked the integration of a high school in Little Rock, as he also lamented his nomination of Chief Justice Earl Warren, viewing it as the "most unfortunate decision" of his life.[13] Racism had been so deeply entrenched that the country was caught in an impasse. Accordingly, even after Kennedy's election, not one single piece of legislation dealing with civil rights was pushed during his first 100 days, to the great surprise and major disappointment of civil rights leaders. Little seemed as easy as many liberals had thought. Impasse was severe.

Lamentably for education, politics like flies often get in the way of schooling, with educators inept at swatting them away. An example at that time, where strength won out, was the heated controversy that *Brown* had brought about in Little Rock in 1957 when then Governor Orval Faubus tried to block the continuance of integration at Central High—with admittance of the Little Rock Nine—when violence escalated to thwart integration. In refusing to honor the ruling to enforce *Brown*, Faubus argued, similar to Governor Wallace years later, that this would "destroy the public school system." As a result, an extraordinary summer session was called, where all Supreme Court justices gathered to hear the case in *Cooper v. Aaron* (1958) and the High Court made vehemently clear its previous verdict in another historic and unanimous decision. Somewhat prophetically it clarified: "Law and order are not here to be preserved by depriving Negro children of their Constitutional rights."[14] This gave new definition to "law and order," a phrase now often misused, seemingly innocuous, but highly incongruous to what it meant at that time.

For the first time in American history, the country was coming to terms—after *Brown*—that all students needed to be schooled together within one single, unified school system. This was ground-breaking, as it unmasked a dual and sometimes tripartite system, ending nearly six decades of *de jure* and much of *de facto* segregation. It signaled the end of an era. By dismantling an old institution, the process took much more than a decade after *Brown* to reconstruct, as it was not until the mid-sixties, several years after Kennedy's memorable speech on the American Negro, that definitive plans were first framed as a starting point, with educators and policymakers finally working together in an arduous partnership that is still wrenching to this day.

Kennedy had learned from Eisenhower and from the Montgomery bus boycott of 1955 as well as the integration of the Little Rock Nine at Central High in Arkansas in 1957 that decisive action had to be taken in the admittance of a Black Air Force veteran, James Meredith, into the University of Mississippi on October 1, 1962, but not without struggle. As it turned out, it took some 30,000 U.S. troops, federal Marshalls, and national guardsmen to get Meredith to class that day, after a high-stakes showdown with Ross Barnett, Governor of Mississippi, in the struggle to admit a Black student into the university. There had been considerable rioting by students the previous days.[15] Then less than a year later on June 11, 1963, once again after pressure from many political fronts, Kennedy authorized the Alabama National Guard to carry out an order from a federal district court in the admission of two qualified Black youngsters from Alabama to enter the University of Alabama against Gov. George Wallace's orders not to integrate. It was that evening before a televised audience that Kennedy gave a most memorable civil rights speech when he said, in part:

> One hundred years of delay have passed since President Lincoln freed the slaves, yet their heirs, their grandsons, are not fully free. They are not yet freed from the bonds of injustice. They are not yet freed from social and economic oppression. And this Nation, for all its hopes and all its boasts, will not be fully free until all its citizens are free.
>
> We preach freedom around the world, and we mean it, and we cherish our freedom here at home, but are we to say to the world, and much more importantly, to each other that this is a land of the free except for the Negroes; that we have no second-class citizens except Negroes; that we have no class or caste system, no ghettoes, no master race except with respect to Negroes?
>
> The Negro baby born in America today, regardless of the section of the Nation in which he is born, has about one-half as much chance of completing high school as a White baby born in the same place on the same day, one-third as much chance of completing college, one-third as much chance of becoming a professional man, twice as much chance of becoming unemployed, about one-seventh as much chance of earning $10,000 a year, a life expectancy which is 7 years shorter, and the prospects of earning only half as much.
>
> We cannot say to 10 percent of the population that you can't have that right; that your children can't have the chance to develop whatever talents they have ... Not every child has an equal talent or an equal ability or an equal motivation, but they should have the equal right to develop their talent and their ability and their motivation, to make something of themselves.[16]

This courageous speech set into motion a major wave of activity. It laid the seeds for massive legislation for later civil rights, this time with education both as cornerstone and as a human right. In looking back, more than half a century later, similar conditions continue to haunt some educators today. The difference today is that students of color have grown immensely large, facing yet troubling waters, where high percentages continue severely undereducated with all too many performing below grade level.

Even President Kennedy had failed to realize the importance that civil rights had become and the impatience many were experiencing years after WWII. With continued frustration at the slowness of "deliberate speed" and a scarcity of accomplishments for civil rights, a march for jobs and freedom was held in front of the Lincoln Memorial in Washington, DC on August of 1963 where MLK, Jr. delivered his "I have a dream speech." It was Robert Kennedy who later understood that the fight for freedom and full entrée into American society had become as important as the freedom drives against Britain had become for colonists centuries earlier. This was serious. It was for justice. But Whites and eminent power groups did not see it that way. As one author put it, for Blacks it was the equivalent of the "same Give-me-liberty-or-give-me-death absolutism around freedom for racial minorities that had once driven White Americans to revolution."[17] Yet for Whites it was another agitation. Much of the country remained clueless. Yes, there was concern in some parts of the country, but no urgency from White America.

By the time Johnson took over the White House, the nation was ripe for a Second Reconstruction. Distinct from any predecessor, this President was a former schoolteacher and principal at a Mexican School in South Texas, so he was highly acquainted with the plight of the Latino as well as the Black student. From humble beginnings, he was for the little people and very much oriented toward social justice. Rising to Speaker of the House and later President of the Senate, he knew everyone's secrets and boldly used that information to his advantage in advocating for civil rights. As such, he was probably more intimately acquainted with skeletons in everyone's closet than any previously elected president. With knowledge and conviction, he acted vigorously and decisively, though eventually dissolving southern friendships and ultimately losing every state in the Deep South by the next election, while carrying the rest of the country by landslide. As father of the Second Reconstruction, as he came to be known, he arguably did more for civil rights than any single president in American history, save Lincoln himself.

We tend to forget that the reason why President Johnson signed the original Elementary and Secondary Education Act (ESEA) in 1965 was because of the shameful inequities in state and local education services and many remaining barriers for the provision of access for equal school funding. It was also because little had happened ten years after *Brown* and also because a centennial had passed since a Civil War with insufficient improvement. It was further because Johnson represented the South and he wanted to make a difference. The ESEA was in partial response to some of the residue of embarrassment that a century after the Civil War and a decade after *Brown*, the vast majority (98%) of Black students were still in all-Black schools, with hardly any Southern White student attending a Black school.[18]

As intended, educational processes began to reinforce needed systems of support and legislation that also aimed to dismantle anti-discriminatory practices against persons of color in all domains that were impacting the general society. When equity begins to blossom its effects also positively influence many other practices as well as long-established institutional policies that denigrate.

Upon signing the most sweeping legislation in the history of education, Johnson reminisced about his former students out loud: "I wonder how many of these [Mexican American] children ever made it." He never forgot his earlier experience as a teacher, going out of his way to sign historic education legislation back at the one-room Mexican Schoolhouse where he began his career as a teacher and served as principal. The twin education acts—the ESEA of 1965 and the Higher Education Act of 1965, its counterpart—were not only illustrative of a national change in direction, but also sowed the seeds for subsequent amendments ongoing today, keeping its intent vibrant, alive, and quite relevant. The key to enforcement ended up being the threat to take away federal funding to school districts that did not have a plan for integration of the schools. It was the "carrot-and-stick" approach to educational policy.

As a result, President Johnson aimed to give *additional* funding to high-poverty schools to force districts to turn around. For all the uproar during that time and since, it is significant to note that this legislation *did* increase educational progress, as research has subsequently documented. Disappointingly, however, increased performance was short-lived, as much of the original legislation was quickly whittled down, slowly dismantled and overturned piece by piece through court-ordered decisions which moved the nation back to where it was mid-1960s, as minority achievement plateaued within a decade after its passage. During this downturn, having learned the lessons coming from the U.S., other countries were influenced to start working on their educational improvement rather differently, but greatly copycatting the U.S. on its achievements. It is interesting to note that by the end of the century, a good number of them had surpassed U.S. educational achievement.

In reviewing the history of educational progress, we tend to forget that great progress was achieved between the start of the Civil Rights movement and the end of that decade (1965–1970). As alluded, both racial and economic progress began to substantially reduce by the middle of the 1970s, despite later rhetoric to the contrary. But during that short hiatus, real wages rose, with the proportion of total income received by the bottom 60 percent increasing from around 16 percent to just over 18 percent, with the relative income received by top earners declining slightly.[19] Another gain was the increase in average family income rising faster than corporation profits during that ten-year period.

Between the mid-1960s until around the late-1970s, another phenomenon had developed. Poverty began to decrease as educational achievement steadily increased.[20] While this was good, it fizzled by the early 1980s, with increases in educational improvement already dormant, as the K–12 achievement gap began to also widen and high school graduation rates plateaued among Blacks and Latinos. Poverty also again skyrocketed. While differences in the relative economic position and educational gap between Blacks and Whites had reduced significantly during that period, they were short-lived. While substantial progress had been achieved in a very short period of time, it had rapidly dwindled. Hereon it was back to the past.

Despite later downturns, education statistics had started to turn around. By 1975, 87% of Blacks were enrolled in school.[21] That year, the high school graduation rate for Blacks jumped to 43%, with 12% attaining four or more years of college.[22] The enrollment of Blacks in all types of colleges also increased more than five times between 1960 and 1980.[23] However, by the end of that period college readiness had begun to falter, as remediation had become commonplace for Black and Latino students entering colleges by then, with too many institutions of higher learning offering remedial courses and too many students not completing degrees.

As *the decade of the 1960s progressed, the country, together with its schools, underwent a major cultural revolution.* During this time, the nation's complexion started to change, as new rules from the 1965 legislation on immigration quotas began to allow entry and citizenship to previously excluded immigrant groups from Africa and Asia. Thus began the second phase of the sixties, transitioning from the swinging sixties to later being dubbed as the cultural decade and the decade of civil rights.

Regrettably, this trajectory crashed when two iconic leaders—Martin Luther King, Jr. and Robert F. Kennedy—were assassinated in April and May, respectively, both in that incredibly historic year 1968. These events tore the nation apart and possibly derailed its course forever. By the Democratic Convention that August the country had become a tinder box. Writers like Norman Mailer penned *Miami and the Siege of Chicago* (1968) chronicling the events. The nation had spun around, as national unrest spilled into the streets, dominated by turbulence and unrest.

It was the year that shook the nation as it "rocked the world."²⁴ It not only sparked urban riots in major cities across the U.S., but was also pivotal in witnessing the Soviet invasion of Czechoslovakia, with tanks rolling down its main streets in August, and an event in October where Mexican college students from the University of Mexico were massacred by police for protesting just before the summer Olympics opened in Mexico City, first-time ever on Latin American soil.

Back in the U.S., it was also the year that Mexican American students staged a coordinated walkout of East L.A. public high schools, later inspiring the HBO film, *Walkout* (2006), with the major role of Sal Castro, the teacher who inspired the students. Students walked out demanding among other key items equity in facilities, advanced placement courses, bilingual/multicultural programming, and non-biased, non-racist teachers and administrators. It was an event that later motivated other school protests like the Tuley High School boycott in 1971 of Puerto Ricans in Chicago in tandem with the Bowen High School boycott on the other side of the City by Mexican Americans, both led by Latino high school students, with support from two major Hispanic educational organizations in the city.

For other parts of Chicago, it was enough to start the movement of the Urban Progress Centers citywide at the urging of local leaders, as Richard J. Daley's machine followed up on charges of not being able to quell Chicago's unrest in 1968. It is interesting to note that just previously (1966), the largest U.S. Latino riot had broken out in the Division Street neighborhood, in the heart of the Puerto Rican community, protesting police brutality against Puerto Ricans.

For New York City during infamous 1968, the Columbia University protests were among many other student demonstrations around the country and the world. Columbia's protests erupted with over seven thousand residents from Columbia-controlled properties (85% of whom were African American and Puerto Rican).

A series of Latino student protests by mostly public high schools between 1969 and 1972 ricocheted among Latino communities in New York City, Newark, Philadelphia, Boston, and Los Angeles, among other cities. This was parallel to what was also occurring among Black communities nationwide. But for Latino students, it was the first time they had demonstrated their concerns openly and in large numbers, rippling throughout major urban centers. At the time, the Latino high school dropout rate was in excess of 70% in many large urban centers such as New York City, Chicago, and Los Angeles.²⁵

Other links between the university and the institutional apparatus that supported the U.S. involvement in the Vietnam War sparked further unrest when fuel was added to the fire by Blacks and Latinos that felt they had been disproportionately drafted into the war. Multiple racial confrontations rippled through a polarized country, as fury reeled almost in adolescent rebellion, not fully settling down until after Nixon's resignation in 1974.

*A*nalysis for this period shows that the Kennedy-Johnson Administrations emphasized a two-pronged approach on domestic problems.[26] They conjoined policies promoting economic growth and general prosperity with social welfare programs targeted to the most recalcitrant pockets of poverty.[27] It is important to indicate that Johnson was never convinced that economic growth *alone* could reduce systemic forms of poverty without the relief of *social welfare* and concerted *educational initiatives* working jointly. Subsequent research now firmly supports that persisting educational disparity is a major reason for persisting economic inequality.[28] Both poverty and education must be broached concurrently. Johnson's multi-pronged approach seems to be forgotten nowadays, and even less appreciated. Comprehensive remedies require more than one approach working in tandem.

During this period, given the disastrous war in Vietnam, the second other war was the "War on Poverty" which may have been arguably a bit more successful, as arguments between education and poverty became a tug of war. The politics of education, though short-lived, became the politics of the nation, when not focused on Vietnam. Given emerging trends in racial composition, rising demographics began pushing issues never before encountered. As a result, education and poverty became inevitable twins, though each blamed the other for the "American problem" by asking if inadequate education was feeding poverty or if poverty, from the other end, was limiting educational achievement via a "culture of poverty." Battle positions were drawn and lasted through the century, now reemerging in recent debates.

*W*hile the 1960s was *"good for civil rights,"* it was also a period of *"revolt,"* as society was shaken up by *"cultural"* and *"political changes"* greatly prompted by educational movements.[29] The civil rights era brought forth huge changes in society at all levels, but much fell in disarray for education during subsequent administrations. While Humpty-Dumpty had shattered, it had been set free and the egg could not be put back together again. For education, pockets of innovation and hard work came from community-based action and hard-fought, local school takeovers; yet school reform became shambles afterwards, as accountability was fully absent and subsequent educational leadership non-responsive. Over time, a resurgence of racism crept back into school leadership.

Diane Ravitch (2000) informs that there was a mismatch between children and the schools, with poorest schools lacking basic resources and representing the least experienced teachers, where children that needed instruction the most were least likely to obtain it.[30] In fact, children from all classes were poorly educated, except that wealthy children had the advantage that parents could help make up the difference. One contemporary African American educator put it this way, "Progressive White teachers thought they were freeing Black students from a racist educational system."[31] But it was not "pity" they needed. It was "basic teaching."[32] It was precisely such lackadaisical approaches that put kids in jeopardy at the start, as they had not received needed skills to put them on the road to success or hurl them into college in the first place. Patronizing attitudes claimed that minority students should not be challenged, as little was expected of them. Such attitudes reverted back to the start of the century, fully backwards.

While civil rights mid-1960s had brought "relevance" back into education, this turned *laissez faire* mid-1970s, after the era of Johnson. Minimal requisites reaped low expectations for all. The following decade tried to bring more structured curricula, increased standards, and more formidable graduation requisites, but it was botched by unevenness in implementation as it was further damaged by the political environment, whirling back to the late fifties.

The decade of the 1980s, touted as "the decade of the Hispanic," brought a heightened sense of cultural diversity, where diversity and cultural competence was now more openly discussed and seemingly valued. While many of these advances were cosmetic and fanciful, lacking much rigor or consistency, it was replete with well-founded overtones of racial and ethnic diversity and minority reawakening.

In her comprehensive review of educational history, Ravitch (2000) encapsulates how education and diversity was a missed opportunity for that time:

> A society that is racially and ethnically diverse requires, more than other societies, a conscious effort to build shared values and ideals among its citizenry. The society that allows large numbers of its citizens to remain uneducated, ignorant, or semiliterate, squanders its greatest asset, the intelligence of its people. A society that tolerates anti-intellectualism in its schools can expect to have a dumbed-down culture that honors celebrity and sensation rather than knowledge and wisdom.[33]

With achievement scores already leveling by the end of the 1970s, as earlier documented, there arose a major concern about the quality of the nation's schools. For some observers, it seemed that the sustained "assault on the academic curriculum" from the late 1960s and early 1970s had taken its toll.[34] In 1985, Bill Honig who had been state superintendent of instruction for California, published a book that provided important data on what education was not doing. This mine of information had formed part of the documentation used in the seminal report, A Nation at Risk in 1983. Honig's account cited investigations where reporters were sent to scores of schools across multiple districts only to discover that academic credit was being offered for courses with little substance such as cheerleading, student government, and mass media.[35] Bottom line was that bright students were not being challenged, but neither were minority or low-income students. He concluded that many of those that were dropping out were "scoring better" on achievement tests of reading and math "than those who stuck it out for their diplomas."[36] In fact, "20 percent of today's dropouts," he asserted, had "IQs over 120." While the credibility of his findings was severely diminished by a personal conviction in 1992, his conclusions were likely on target.

Quite pointedly and along similar lines, nearly half the White students and about two-thirds of Black and Latino students left college without earning a degree between 1984 and 1987.[37] Altogether, while progress was being made in that Black and Latino students were now entering college, they were not yet graduating at levels close to their White peers. As change did not occur overnight, progress had to be regained through cumulative programs that would reinforce one another. This led to comprehensive higher education efforts.

Looking back, impetus for minority students had most especially emanated from four principal federal initiatives within a period of several decades:

1. Starting in 1944, the GI Bill had assisted many Black students with costs for higher education and related needs for veterans of the Second World War and for scores of others that later entered the Korean War and subsequent military deployments. This was further reinforced in the 1980s, with a resurgence of programs that took advantage of this resource, with back-to-college initiatives taking the lead.
2. The National Defense Student Loan (NDSL) programs that provided scholarship and loan aid soon after Sputnik (1957) was refortified and later supplemented by other scholarship opportunities, aided by

economic assistance of various types. Latino students benefited from this legislation as high school entrance and graduation rates had finally begun to rise.
3. With the further desegregation of higher education institutions, Black enrollment increased proportionately, similar to desegregation of the University of Mississippi in 1962 and the University of Alabama a year later, when the first Black students entered these universities.
4. Population growth among HBCUs also added a considerable number of minority students into higher education, with a greater percent going onto graduate studies than from traditional "other" universities, a surprisingly, refreshing statistic.[38] At a later date, however, some HBCUs then lost enrollment among Blacks as opportunities opened up at the newly desegregating and higher resourced White colleges and universities.

It is noteworthy that each of these programs was first sponsored by the federal government, creating the template for later private sponsorship that followed these government efforts in lockstep. In retrospect, the momentum was not kept up nor did the states piggyback on these opportunities. Since then, many of these initial efforts have all but disappeared, leaving all but lip service behind.

The System Flounders

AS MENTIONED, WARNINGS ABOUT HARMFUL TRENDS IN EDUCATION WERE CLEARLY ELABORATED IN A PROFOUNDLY DEVASTATING FEDERAL GOVERNMENT REPORT RELEASED AT THE START OF THE EIGHTH DECADE OF THE 20TH CENTURY, *A Nation at Risk* (1983). The report strongly indicated that as education went so would the nation. Results elevated major concerns about education to a national discourse as it also created a head storm. It hit home with three major conclusions: (1) American education had not kept pace with changes in society and the economy; (2) the nation would suffer if education was not dramatically improved; and (3) some children were benefitting more than others, as the system was not egalitarian, with education remaining stagnant in its advancement toward minority and low-income groups. In its conclusion, the report placed blame squarely on lax academic standards that highly correlated with *laissez faire* behavioral expectations. It also lambasted the lack of attention to equity. As a result, both *quality* and *equity* entered the national forum of discussion and debate.

Conclusions from the report were sobering. It indicated that learning was a critical investment the country was ignoring, yet required for the new information age. It strongly underscored that the internal strength of the nation's social and economic wellbeing was highly dependent on the improvement of education. After years of educational meandering and wavering, the report forced a needed focus and urgency about the educational enterprise, as it critiqued the previous decade of mediocrity, low expectations, and unacceptable standards for teaching and instruction.

The report well indicated that by ignoring basic signposts and bypassing the needs of significant population groups, public education had reached a troublesome condition, with vast numbers undereducated and where minority and low-income populations were not performing better than several decades earlier. With *A Nation at Risk* heightening the angst among many smug educational groups and associations, responses to the report became highly defensive, as if new posturing would resolve dire conditions. It has been estimated that this one report spawned some 400 other reports by the end of the century, taking issue with different sections of the federal report, with a good number defending the status quo from one corner of the country to the other, as if problems resided within the report rather than the system of education under critique.

In brief, the report unequivocally summarized a stockpile of data warning that educational mediocrity had put the nation at risk, with little time to lose. While many students were already at risk—a known fact—the report poignantly posited that this was now also putting the nation at considerable risk, a more sobering reality. Its bottom-line conclusion pointed to a state of affairs that was unacceptable, intolerable, and even shameful.

Needless to say, the report set off a hornet's nest, causing a flurry of activity in education reminiscent of the mid-1960s, when educators wrestled an earlier panic that propelled an avalanche of legislation. Uproar was so great that then President Reagan whose agenda was to eliminate the Department of Education was forced to not only reconsider the decision, but to work at reforming the entire educational enterprise. For the field, it forced going back to the drawing board to reflect more profoundly about the process of education to answer questions like: What is causing poor results? Who is getting taught and how? What is yielding differential effects? What else must be done?

Among its recommendations, the report cautiously suggested there had to be "a strong public commitment to the equitable treatment of diverse populations" as "the twin goals of equity and high-quality schooling have profound and practical meaning for our economy and society, and we cannot permit one to yield to the other either in principle or in practice."[39] In reflecting back, it is ironic that what resonated most strongly with policymakers was the need for "more rigorous and measurable standards," with the emphasis on "equity" ranking low,[40] and with the latter remaining absent from the educational focus that followed, as it continues to be missing today. This has been disappointing. This omission was a major oversight, as racial minorities are now paying a heavy price. Now nearing four decades since *A Nation at Risk*, the needle has barely moved on educational progress for minorities, with international test data also reflecting how U.S. students are now gradually falling behind other nations.

Major Warts

SIX YEARS AFTER *A NATION AT RISK*, PRESIDENT GEORGE H. BUSH CONVENED A NATIONAL SUMMIT ON EDUCATION WITH STATE GOVERNORS IN 1989. It was the first such meeting among states since the days of the Great Depression. The purpose was to establish benchmarks to be achieved by the year 2000, later referenced as "National Performance Goals."[41] The conference opened with the President affirming: "There are real problems right now in our educational system, but there is no one Federal solution." He later refined his statement by underscoring: "And we're going to work with you to help find answers, but I firmly believe that the key will be found at the State and local levels." In response to the charge, the summit established six national goals.

1. All children in America will start school ready to learn.
2. The high school graduation rate will increase to at least 90 percent.
3. American students will leave grades four, eight, and twelve having demonstrated competency in challenging subject matter including English, mathematics, science, history, and geography; and every school in America will ensure that all students learn to use their minds well, so they may be prepared for responsible citizenship, further learning, and productive employment in our modern economy.
4. U.S. students will be first in the world in science and mathematics achievement.

5. Every adult American will be literate and possess the knowledge and skills necessary to compete in a global economy and exercise the rights and responsibilities of citizenship.
6. Every school in America will be free of drugs and violence and will offer a safe, disciplined environment conducive to learning.

Given these laudable goals, the conference was an impressive start to a rather important set of initiatives, except that key players—teachers, professional educators, school administrators, key researchers, among others—were conspicuously absent.[42] With this highly strategic blunder, suggested solutions to cure the educational ills of the nation (patient) did not come from the educator (physician), but from politicians whose political futures were vested. The fact that many governors themselves later partnered with vulture corporations and venture capitalists made the matter worse, if not disingenuous and if not for its serious intent.

Not only were the goals out of range, but structures were not contemplated to carry out the goals. This resulted in a process that was more like a charade, making a mockery of the education establishment at the hands of government itself. A break between government and the educational system was imminent. It was not that big government could not get the job done, as this missed the point, but that it did not seriously focus on fixing the problem. It was merely a show with little urgency, lacking depth and without teeth, with little if any reference to critical suggestions from *A Nation at Risk*.

In 1994, the National Educational Goals known as Goals 2000 were set by the U.S. Congress and signed by President Clinton to set goals for standards-based education reform. These updated President Bush's earlier goals, as it also added two more to the list, bringing the total to eight goals. These were to be met by the millennium (2000). *Goals 2000* established a framework by which to identify world-class academic standards, to measure student progress, and to provide the support that students would need to help meet the standards.[43] However, by fiscal year 2002, *Goals 2000* was no longer authorized or funded by Congress.

To date, now completing the second decade of a new century, none of the national goals for education proposed by either George H. Bush or Bill Clinton have been met. Teacher quality and school safety evaluated in 2000 had actually gone backward, as per a national review panel.[44] The closest since then have been the high school graduation goals, with latest data (2018) at 84%, not yet the 90% expected rate by 2000.[45] The process was unrealistic, as few resources had been assigned to attain the goals, whether local, state, or national. For much of the talk and hype echoed in the corridors of power, public education has seldom been good about allocation, reinvention, reform or change, as history now well attests, even worse at continuing initiatives of this type.

Lacking are viable paradigms about what works in education. Mere platitudes do not fix problems. Initiatives of these types are designed with inherently faulty structures, devoid of strong leadership and absent any capital. Other than lofty pronouncements at the expense of education—as if needed—the dialogue cannot be taken seriously, with the urgency of time and commitment greatly lacking. Over and again, national leadership has played with education, seldom handling it seriously.

Several decades since the initial summit and its latter goals in 1994, education is still waiting at "go," with half the nation's students now facing greater risks. As it turned out, many educators saw *Goals 2000* as the predecessor to the NCLB which mandated measurable goals for schools and students focused on the calibration of achievement test scores for all groups.

A New Century

AFTER MUCH FLURRY FOR NEARLY TWO DECADES AND A BARRAGE OF STUDIES, THE FEDERAL GOVERNMENT EVENTUALLY LAUNCHED A COMPROMISE EDUCATIONAL INITIATIVE AS NEW LEGISLATION. In 2001, the No Child Left Behind (NCLB) Act was enacted, and a new movement of reform through measured accountability was born. NCLB introduced a confusing period of education reform at the start of a new century. According to many teachers, this seemed to set back the clock to a punitive and reactive system of weights and measures, formerly dehumanizing students and now adding teachers to the block. Diane Ravitch in her recent book, *Reign of Error* (2013), documents this initiative well, as she summarizes the dangers of slipshod reform for America's public schools.

Under the guise of accountability, NCLB elevated test results through test-driven instruction at the expense of teacher-led initiatives. The new legislation led teachers to posit that if content is not important enough to be tested, it will not be important enough to be taught. As a result, its stress on math and science upended art, music, humanities, social science, civics, and P.E. Instructional emphasis was also at the expense of social and emotional development; at times even curtailing recess and social recreation. While accountability is needed to rev up the system, its actions were punitive and its measures quite faulty.

One very favorable outcome was the disaggregation of data, as it forced school districts to report achievement and graduation data for minority and low-income students for the first time, making transparent key weaknesses among overall school data that masked inequities. Yet ESSA, its successor, has now taken a step back by leaving key educational decisions of this type to the states, with many states now balking to report disaggregated data.[*]

Implementation of NCLB had also assumed that the closure of schools was good, under the guise of accountability and rigor, but with worse options for replacement, forgetting about the damage to children left unattended and shuttled between schools, disproportionately affecting minority and low-income children, the very students it meant to rescue. With impatience to assess teacher competence, it also implemented flawed measures of teacher effectiveness and promoted unbalanced standards for school success.[46] Worse, it aborted the provision of needed funds to failing schools, while turning around to fault these same schools for poor performance. This spun a Catch-22 scenario the better part of two decades, with millions of students caught in the crosshairs.

Lacking the resources to "fix" the problem and the moxie to fight the battles, school districts have been grossly negligent in their efforts to combat "failure." The movement was more about testing and less about true accountability, even more about blaming and not fixing, as if greater documentation was needed to dramatize student deficits that exonerate the system. Thinking that changing principals and firing teachers by itself would repair a faulty system has been wishful at best, and poorly conceived at worst. While we know that Black and Latino children are not doing well in school, there is a limit to the number of times and intensity of assessment before focusing on the more important remedies needed to enhance learning. It is the latter that counts.

Schools spend far more time and effort diagnosing than in repairing. That is akin to a recent dental TV ad that features a mock dentist examining a patient's teeth merely to "diagnose" the problem, but unqualified to fill cavities or repair dental deficiencies. As per the commercial, the patient is left bewildered, with loose prosthetics evident while strapped to a chair, with the caption: "Why monitor a problem if you can't fix it." As tests circulate wildly

---

[*] The ESSA, Every Student Succeeds Act, was enacted in December 2015 to continue the work of the NCLB, No Child Left Behind.

and test developers flourish, schools swim in debt, absent of needed resources or any assistance to combat its ills. Altogether, it has been a mindless operation, botching reform once again.

With bottom-line thinking and the business model pummeling schools, many reformers actually thought schools could be run like factories, with teachers as technicians on an assembly line and kids as products performing to specifications. As Lily Eskelsen García, NEA President, accurately pointed out during our interview, "This fully distorts the process of education."[47] From the standpoint of policymakers, the only thing that was targeted was "a score that had to be produced," she articulated. All that mattered was "efficiency in hitting the numbers," like Powerball lottery; and "When teachers don't make the numbers, God help them." No doubt about it, "It is a punitive system." As a result, another generation of students—13 years of schooling—are lost. "We stopped focusing on equity and stopped asking the really important questions such as whether students could get AP classes or whether they are advancing in the arts and music or connecting high schools with early community college credits," she affirmed.

After many painful setbacks, NCLB expired in 2015, without greatly changing the status quo, while also greatly ignoring equity. Arguably, it may have pushed the clock back. Unsurprisingly but maybe worse, NCLB was replaced by the Every Student Succeeds Act (ESSA). The day after, most interestingly, test developer Pearson Learning stocks took a hit,[48] though it has recovered slowly, as little has changed since then.

With the ESSA law now promising to address educational conditions, major policy decisions are back in the hands of the states for implementation and redirection, with critics signaling "here we go again." ESSA lacks important equity provisions. As one scholar commented, "Giving the states control can be a two-edged sword."[49] Remaining questions are: "Will ESSA do the job better than NCLB?" and "Are we moving in the right direction?" Evidence is still lacking. But we must remain hopeful, for every law must be made important for the success of the educational enterprise for the country and the future of its children.

The Other Education

THROUGHOUT THE HISTORY OF AMERICAN EDUCATION MANY EVENTS HAVE BEEN UNFAIR TO HISPANICS, AS THEY ALSO HAVE BEEN UNFAIR FOR BLACKS AND OTHER RACIAL MINORITIES. For Hispanics in particular, past events continue to have long-lasting results, with residues still present. This history penetrates deeply into the soul of Latino culture. As a result, education continues to represent a most serious challenge for the cultural enrichment, maximum intellectual development, and personal empowerment of every Latino in the U.S.

For this trajectory to be effective, it is important to focus on what has happened in the past so as to improve on this history and ensure better options are available for every Latino nationwide. To more fully understand important portions of this story, we must gain knowledge from the experience of Latinos in this narrative and round out the story to create a fuller picture for this racial group, as it differs from the African American experience in critical ways.

Different from prevailing thought, Latino Americans are uniquely different from that of other demographic groups. Such a story is best understood when viewed from a different vantage point. Otherwise, too much will be assumed and lumped with that of other racial groups, resulting in continual misunderstandings and arriving at the typical conclusion that all minorities are more or less the same, with emphasis on "more or less." Myths of these types need to be dispelled.

Notes

1. Migration from the island of Puerto Rico to the Northeast and the Midwest started soon after WWII.
2. This alludes to racist attacks on Mexican Americans by White servicemen that spread into a riot in June 1943, despite many Mexican Americans serving with honor and courage during the Second World War.
3. Margolis, 1968.
4. Census data, 1950 population reports.
5. Billingsley, 1992.
6. Mondale & Patton, p. 133.
7. Billingsley, 1992.
8. Census Bureau, 1950; Latino data is based on 1950 select sample of Hispanics. This was a limited sample from the Southwest, as full Latino census counts were still not available.
9. The *Méndez* case, for example, involved parentage that was Mexican American and Puerto Rican.
10. *Brown v. Board of Education* (1954); and *Hernández v. Texas* (1954).
11. Nine years earlier, a Texas court in *Méndez v. Westminster* (1947), argued a nearly identical case based on the 14th Amendment, with the defendant being of Mexican American and Puerto Rican parentage. This set the precedent for *Brown*.
12. *Brown II*, issued in 1955, was to define the process by which *Brown I* was to be carried out and enforced in areas that still had segregated schools—the vast majority.
13. O'Donnell, 2018.
14. Williams, 1989, p. 271.

15. https://www.npr.org/2012/10/01/161573289/integrating-ole-miss-a-transformative-deadly-riot
16. John F. Kennedy, Civil Rights Speech, June 11, 1963.
17. Steele, 2015, p. 150.
18. Mondale & Patton, p. 144.
19. Ryan, 1976, p. xii [2nd edition].
20. Kim, et al., 2001, p. 1.
21. *Ibid*.
22. Billingsley, pp. 177–178.
23. *Ibid*., p. 180.
24. Kurlansky, 2005.
25. Margolis, 1968; Lucas, 1971.
26. Danzinger & Gottschalk, 1993.
27. Kim, et al, 2001.
28. Danzinger & Gottschalk, 1993.
29. Ravitch, 2000.
30. *Ibid*.
31. Lisa Delpit, 1995, p. 16.
32. *Ibid*.
33. Ravitch, 2000, p. 466.
34. *Ibid*., p. 408.
35. Honig, 1985.
36. *Ibid*., p. 25.
37. Ravitch, 2000, p. 410.
38. The Great Society programs included a host of legislative initiatives undertaken by the Johnson administration such as the Civil Rights Acts of 1964, the ESEA, the Higher Education amendments, and Head Start.
39. *A Nation at Risk*, 1983, p. 13.
40. *Ibid*., p. 27.
41. Forty-nine governors attended the conference held in September 1989 in Charlottesville, Virginia.
42. Surgenor, 2014.
43. https://en.wikipedia.org/wiki/Goals_2000.
44. *Ibid*.
45. NCES, updated December 2018.
46. Ravitch, 2013.
47. Taken from interview author held with Lily Eskelsen-García, 2017.
48. Pearson is known as one of the largest test developers and publishers in the business.
49. Taken from stocks trading, December 2015.

PART II

LATINO EDUCATION

The further a society drifts from the truth, the more it will hate those that speak it.
George Orwell

LATINO EDUCATION ROUNDS OUT THE HISTORICAL PORTRAIT OF LATINOS AND EDUCATION AS IT ALSO PORTRAYS CURRENT ISSUES THAT FULLY CHALLENGE THE EDUCATION OF HISPANICS TODAY. Historical knowledge becomes well-grounded on past events when it is strongly substantiated by documentary evidence. A rich understanding of this past greatly contributes to a fuller knowledge of the present, as both interrelate. This is important because much of what should occur in the education of Latinos must fully relate to that which has yet to be corrected and redressed from the past. With the earlier chapters as backdrop, the Latino story can now be more fully retold, examined, and appreciated in the context of what we have learned about American education.

· 4 ·

THE MISEDUCATION OF LATINOS

THE EDUCATION OF LATINOS IS INDIVISIBLE FROM THAT OF AMERICAN EDUCATION. YET, IT DEVELOPED QUITE DISTINCTLY AND APART. It followed an altogether different path. Its route was like no other group before or since. Until the Second World War, Latinos were literally invisible in American society and discourse, as they were much smaller in number, poorly counted, and greatly isolated from most other groups. Living primarily in the Southwest and predominantly in highly-segregated sectors, they struggled in isolation and developed almost independently from all other groups.[1] Puerto Ricans in the island were also remote and inaccessible. For both groups, navigating rather differently and away from nearly all other racial groups before civil rights, it was not until after the First World War[2] that the Latino diaspora began to interface visible.

While migration north had started with the Mexican American movement out of the Southwest, it was propelled by the northern push from the *Mejicano* escaping Mexico during the late 1920s through the 1940s, as a result of the Mexican Revolution. Northern migration increased more rapidly after WWII with larger influxes from the Southwest coupled with continual movement out of Mexico due to the Bracero agreement and accompanied by the flow of migrants from Puerto Rico, primarily to northern urban centers, and to parts of the Midwest and Florida. Although much of the country had started moving to the suburbs by then, Latinos were moving somewhat differently, up North to large urban centers, similar to the Great Migration of Blacks to the North. The Latino diaspora increases more strongly during the second half of the century, with added immigrants coming from Cuba during the late 1950s and from other Latin American countries 1965 onward.

As a result, Latinos charted a rather unique path in quite distinct ways in the American crossroads of survival. This path is worth understanding, not only because it has ramifications for learning about today's educational challenges, but also because it reflects how the country responded to people of color that eventually impacted the Latino community. It is within these social conditions that education played a fundamental role in the Latino story, as public schools operated strongly within this maelstrom.

Despite additional migratory shifts among Hispanics midcentury onward, *Latino students were still attending highly segregated public schools.* According to Gary Orfield, et al. (2016), public school enrollment increased in size and transformed in racial composition quite dramatically since the mid-1990s. According to his report from the UCLA Civil Rights Project, "Intensely segregated nonwhite schools with zero to 10% White enrollment have more than tripled in this most recent 25-year period."[3] As racial segregation has been most intense among Latino and Black students, it has also been accompanied by striking rises in the "double segregation" of race and economic status. Most recently (2017), according to NCES, Latinos have become the most segregated racial group in America, as they now attend schools that are predominantly Hispanic (57%) as compared to the average Black student that attends schools that are 49% Black. Hispanic segregation trends now reflect considerably large pockets of racial isolation across the country.

At the same time, Latino enrollment has been increasing dramatically. Data now (2017) indicate that nearly half (49%) of all students from the fifteen largest school districts are Latino. They represent the largest racial group in 12 of the 15 districts. Growth has been phenomenal. One district (e.g., Gwinnett in GA), for example, has had such rapid growth in enrollment that Hispanic students have increased more than seven times since the mid-1990s.[4]

During the 1960s, Latinos were a much smaller number than Blacks, about 43% of the total African American population,[5] yet by the end of the 20th century its numbers had surpassed African Americans in both the public schools as well as in the general population. Today, public school enrollment indicates that Latinos outnumber African Americans by nearly 50%, while also now attending the most highly-segregated schools. This not only represents significant shifts, but massive cultural changes that are occurring among the nation's school districts.

For the 68 largest districts that constitute the Council of Great City Schools (CGCS), as another example, Latinos represent the single largest demographic group across these districts at 40% compared to 29% for African Americans, 8% for Asian/Pacific Islanders, and 3% other, with Whites representing barely 20% of all students across these districts (2017).[6] Given that this condition is of recent vintage, implications for both the context and culture of America's public schools are enormous.

Education for Latinos has been greatly contingent on their zip code, income, and language group. While this may be changing somewhat, school achievement continues to strongly correlate with zip code. Achievement also correlates highly with generational status, with second-generation Latino students not faring much better than first-generation counterparts. In many respects the education story is parallel to that depicted by Carter Woodson about Blacks in *The Mis-Education of the Negro* (1933). Yet, the Latino narrative represents a different *kind* of miseducation, albeit highly "mis-educated" nonetheless. These different factors relate primarily to language, history, culture, geography, and racial blends. These will be explored in greater detail to more fully understand what has transpired for the Latino.

As history is always prologue, a substantial part of the current experience by Latinos in education is indelibly blended with the past. Try as they may, cultures can never divorce themselves from their past, as both past and present intermix in shaping the future. From a cultural lens, quite the case for Latinos, the past has always had great meaning, even veneration, as culture and history greatly meld and reinforce. History is also at the heart from where pride in heritage strongly emanates.

It was during civil rights that Latinos started relating alongside African Americans and other racial communities in a common struggle with common bonds, while before America's era of civil rights the struggle for each was fully and indelibly independent and nearly solitary from the other. Turns out, many racial groups across the land have also lived in isolated enclaves, unacquainted with each other and seldom working together until just recently.

The story of education for Latinos is also the story of Hispanic nations and how its citizens came to this country. This did not begin with a desire to immigrate. It was much more about transnational relations at the start, even about war and colonization. While what is occurring today is quite different from the antecedents of a century ago, it also relates to a unique past long ago, prior to the founding of the U.S. Suffice it to say, education, nationality, and current life in the U.S. have all fully interrelated in dramatic ways for the Latino population in U.S. history, but in a largely forgotten past. Here it would be helpful to backtrack into history and reconstruct.

A Glimpse of the Past

AFTER SEVERAL CENTURIES OF NEAR CONSTANT WARFARE, MANY LATINO NATIONS ESTABLISHED THEIR IMPRINT IN THE NEW WORLD BY OVERCOMING A SUFFOCATING STRANGLEHOLD FROM SPAIN. This occurred soon after Napoleon's invasion of Spain during the Peninsular War, at the start of the 19th century.[7] This was the time when multiple movements of national independence against the Spanish swept through most South American countries, each declaring their full independence from Spain.

Not long afterwards, some of the countries got caught in an American web. As a result, citizens got trapped without crossing borders, as they became enmeshed with the U.S., principally through war and conquest. Paralyzed in the mesh, the best hope for many was that the "American" [*norteamericano*] seizure would represent a safer and more trusted haven than former Spanish colonizers. Among the U.S. interventions that began the 19th century was that which occurred early with Spain for the acquisition of Florida in 1819 which brought Spanish people from *La Florida* into the U.S.

Several years later it was the "Monroe Doctrine" in 1823 that brought Latino nations under the aegis of an American protectionist banner. This doctrine warned European nations that the U.S. would not tolerate further colonization of Latin America from European powers. Yet it was the concept of "Manifest Destiny" that defined U.S. expansionism two decades later as a "divine right" which asserted U.S. dominion across the Americas. Strangely, while the U.S. was to protect Latino nations from European intervention through the Monroe Doctrine, it was Manifest Destiny shortly afterwards that declared the only country that could intervene was, in fact, the United States itself—most enigmatic.

The concept of Manifest Destiny was first introduced in 1845 when a newspaper editor first coined the phrase when calling for the annexation of Texas which had become a Republic in 1836, foreshadowing the war with

Mexico. In reference to the "Spanish-Indian-American" populations of Mexico and Latin America, the author used disparaging terms to denote Hispanic people as a race of "mixed and confused blood."⁸ In viewing the territories of Mexico, depictions from the northeastern press were unkind to Mexicans.* Racist attitudes like these set the stage for conquest and dominion, well formulated by mid-19th century and ready-set for the Mexican-American War.

Later, the territory gained by the Mexican-American War (1846–1848) forced Mexico to cede nearly half its territory in the Treaty of Guadalupe Hidalgo (1848). By the end of the century, American expansionism crept farther with the Spanish-American War (1898), this time capturing war booty that included Puerto Rico, the Philippines, and Guam, with Cuba as a protectorate, all falling under the U.S. flag. As spoils of war, millions of Latinos and other nonwhites became U.S. citizens nearly overnight, excluding Cuba. It was war and the accumulation of distant territories that increased U.S. diversity through the acquisition of sovereign nations through war with these countries and even within their native populations. Such acquisitions reshaped U.S. racial composition, unwittingly or otherwise.

By the end of the 19th century, with increased U.S. international strength, additional interference continued in the affairs of independent nations, as it exerted influence over their internal politics. In brief, major incidents of interference became common. By the start of the 20th century the U.S. had already been intervening with Latin American countries. This had represented a new type of control over the southern Hemisphere. Some conflicts led to exploitation, others to the subjugation of peoples and nations, and still others to later Latino immigration. While this was exemplified by the defense of Cuba against Spain, eventually leading to the Spanish-American War, interference grew considerably afterwards with other nations.

In the aftermath of the Spanish-American War, for example, the Philippine Republic resisted colonization from the U.S. leading to the American-Philippine War (1899–1902), with Filipinos eventually succumbing to colonization. Other effects from the Spanish-American War also resulted. According to the State Department, the U.S. was "Spurred by the nationalism aroused by the Spanish-American War"⁹ and as a result "the U.S. annexed

---

* Note that colonial thinking from Britain had prohibited intermarriage with Native Americans, calling it miscegenation. By contrast, Spanish Royal Government encouraged intermarriage that resulted in racial mixtures of Spanish Europeans. Spain did *not* view this as "mixed and confused blood" (MacDonald & Rivera, 2015).

Hawaii in 1898 at the urging of President William McKinley." It is interesting to note that nearly coincident with the start of Manifest Destiny in 1842, then Secretary of State, Daniel Webster, had sent a letter to Hawaiian agents affirming U.S. interest in Hawaii and opposing annexation by any other nation. The Secretary also proposed to European powers "that no nation should seek special privilege or engage in further colonization of the islands [of Hawaii]."[10] Seemingly, Manifest Destiny had expanded beyond Latin America.

Back in Latin America, given these developments by the dawn of the 20th century, it is no surprise that over the next two decades the U.S. engaged in rather open conflict with Latin American countries. For example, in 1904 the U.S. approved and supported a rebellion in the country of Colombia that led to the creation of a U.S.-approved nation called Panamá which then quickly allowed the U.S. to build the Panamá Canal. On three other occasions U.S. troops occupied Nicaragua. This occurred in 1909, in 1912, and then again in 1926. In 1914, U.S. forces moved into Mexico during the Mexican Revolution. In 1915, the U.S. also occupied Haiti. Then in 1916, U.S. troops occupied the Dominican Republic. And in 1917 the U.S. entered World War I, having just granted Puerto Ricans U.S. citizenship that year, but also as cannon fodder, as draftees into the war. Over time, these engagements together with others at later dates began to coax many Hispanic groups into the U.S. mainland.

While Mexicans received citizenship by Treaty in 1848, Puerto Ricans attained citizenship in 1917. Meanwhile, Blacks had become citizens by legislation in 1866, but Native Americans had to wait until 1924.[11] Subsequently, varying by country and event, Latino refugees began entering the U.S. at different times during the 20th century, oftentimes as a direct result from U.S. intervention with the country. Cuba serves as a prime example, but Honduras, Nicaragua, Panamá, and El Salvador represent other examples, with refugees later entering the U.S. Regardless of citizenship or national rights, each group coming from a Latino nation was eventually treated as nonwhite. This meant facing segregation and other discriminatory laws, as had been the case with Mexicans and then with Puerto Ricans.

Issues of racial identity became complex for countries that represented war booty like Guam and Puerto Rico, and for many others that entered into conflict with the U.S., as it meant restricting their freedom when landing in the U.S. and guided by Jim Crow laws before middle of the next century and its vestiges afterwards. While much was to have changed after the Civil War, in actuality little fully changed for the nonwhite subsequently. Slavery had been partly recaptured by Jim Crow, as high segregation and separate but equal doctrines dominated. Former Latin American citizens residing in the U.S. had to succumb to these laws. With the acquisition of half of Mexico and all of Puerto Rico, for example, the U.S. controlled Hispanic citizens from two key Latino nations, with their rights and futures in American hands, and with guaranteed citizenship for members of both groups, but treated as nonwhite.

In education, ostracism against nonwhites was ruled by prejudice and discrimination. This set the stage for racial minorities, with non-acceptance in schools dominating. For Blacks, for example, education grappled along peculiar circumstances after the Civil War, with the American Methodist Episcopal (AME) church playing significant roles in the 1880s and other charitable donors (e.g., Rosenwald) later the next century. For Native Americans, education was greatly aided by missionaries, but remained primarily under government control. Both the African American and the Native American also obtained federal assistance, with set-aside funds for educational purposes. For the Mexican American, it was principally the Catholic Church that helped bridge the educational divide. Former *Mejicanos* never received federal aid of any sort.[12] Other than through refugee acts, there has not been any legislative or executive order to assist the transition of Latino newcomers into the American society, less so for the establishment of any schools that have been federally earmarked for Hispanics.[13]

Mexicans, as an example, and as new American citizens annexed by war and bound by treaty, entered the country unwillingly, virtually without consent. Facing a turbulent change in status, citizenship, and language usage, they were stripped from their cultural base. Abruptly separated from their native lands, many ironically became strangers in lands that had been formerly theirs. While some returned to their native country at some risk, most had little choice to remain but later found themselves in a massive web of confusion with questionable rights. The majority that owned homes, lands or businesses, for example, lost their belongings and assets by the 1900s after the loss of multiple court decisions and costly proceedings.[14] These "newcomers" were to start anew in their former lands, nearly vanquished. Loss of land, employment, language, and property had occurred outside their control. Different from other entrants, they never underwent an Ellis Island-experience.[15] For them it was overnight, with chaos and trauma and loss of rights.

Also, theirs was not the type of acculturation like that of the White European, since newcomers from Spanish lands carried the stigma of color, never to be accepted like Whites. As it was, they never became full-fledged citizens the same as Whites, not even for their grandchildren. Mostly brown and of darker complexion, many continued with native language accents so as not to be confused with American Blacks or Native Americans, as they desperately wanted to retain their brand of identity. In fact, many remained close to their community for protection, while holding onto anything they could claim as their own. Over time, they worked among the agricultural fields and cattle-grazing farmlands across the country. Some migrated to urban centers to survive, seeking better living conditions. Others traveled farther north, moving from farms to *colonias* and *barrios* in search of big-city jobs and housing that would accept them. Finding unsatisfactory shelters, they often settled in highly-segregated and unacceptable housing by default.

While some conditions echoed the African American experience, the history of Latinos contrasts, with many distinctions outweighing similarities. As already stated, Latinos lived in geographic and cultural enclaves, isolated and greatly distant from their African American counterparts during 19th century expansionism; but with unique variances of difference in climate, language, geography, history of colonialism, religion, family values, and culture. Even the story of Mexicans is considerably different from that for Puerto Ricans, Cubans and other Latinos.

In general, while lacking the full benefits of citizenship, Latinos were "legally White but socially Mexican," as Donato & Hanson (2012) have labeled and well documented.[16] As a result, much of Mexican American history went undocumented, as "White," but "not White," as an invisible group for counting, lost in the White census counts and unidentified as a special group. Yet, they were visible for unabated racism with extreme discrimination, never fully accepted as Whites.[17] Whenever historical records traced their travail, they were not found to have escaped the wrath of prejudice and persecution, including lynching and killings, ironically because they were lost as "White."[18] For Mexicans, everywhere traversed was littered with posted signs reading all too commonly, "No Mexicans or dogs allowed."[19] In short, the story of Latino populations at the time—Mexicans and later Puerto Ricans—was quite different from other newcomers. This made for confusing times, great misunderstandings, deplorable living conditions, and very limited formal education, if any.

For all practical purposes, the new Latino existed outside the mainstream, living between shadows and borders, many encountering extreme prejudice and ultimate exclusion.[20] Vast numbers suffered under agonizing and difficult circumstances. Many events occurred almost in silence over a century, between the Treaty of Guadalupe Hidalgo and *Brown* (1848 to 1954). This was a different life from the Native American who was confined to live in reservations or from Asian Americans (primarily Chinese) highly concentrated in few regions during the 19th century, with both of these latter groups considerably fewer in number.

As Latinos increased in high proportions midway through the 20th century, their sheer numbers prohibited being long ignored.[21] This state of affairs, coupled with their enigmatic "White" status, led them to suffer through rather brutal and contradictory sets of laws. Albeit primarily by *de facto*, conditions were quite oppressive, akin to that for Blacks, despite legalistic jargon to the contrary.

To a great extent, Mexican Americans were significantly battered and bruised along with other racial groups during this period, with no group winning the Olympics of tribulation. Compared specifically to Blacks, Latinos had certain advantages, but also considerable disadvantages, each outweighing the other, with major trials and tribulations in between. The story for Puerto Ricans was also devastating, though altogether distinct, with considerable tales relayed in other books, as the majority was initially fully isolated in the island of Puerto Rico.[22]

Differences in the Latino journey along tortuous routes are important to highlight not so much for griping and least of all for boasting "woe is me" or even to compare wounds, but for knowing that history need not repeat itself when missteps are learned. It is important to once again underscore that Hispanics are not all alike. Each group brought a different history before their incorporation into the maelstrom, bearing different experiences and living under different habitats and regions.

These personal encounters and experiences helped build needed resilience. Over time, Latinos added further to their cultural memory. Raw experiences fueled the need to survive and overcome. But history, as always, is difficult to reconstruct and interpret, with much recall accompanied by painful and controversial memories. Latinos suffered long-term agony and oftentimes harbored much resentment. In the long run, what worked for the Mexican American was different from what was applicable to the Puerto Rican. But both endured difficult conditions of alienation and racism. As this preview provides the broader context, more detailed documentation better uncovers a fuller Latino story and its educational legacy.

Latino Beginnings

THE START OF THE LATINO STORY IS BEST UNDERSTOOD WITH THE BEGINNINGS OF THE SPANISH AND PORTUGUESE CONQUESTS OF THE NEW WORLD. While the initial encounter produced the biggest transfer and exchange of food and other goods in world history, it also commenced with brutal and disjointed colonization processes that crushed indigenous peoples. This likely became the greatest clash among civilizations in world history, ushering a most traumatic period of genocide. The encounter is likely not comparable to any other global event.[23] Such conquests and colonization later paved the road—or provided excuse—for subsequent atrocities in the New World, including later American colonization and imperialism. History at times unfolds through unusual epicycles of events.

The period of conquest began with Columbus confronting the Taino,[24] *Arawak and Carib Indian tribes of the Caribbean during his first journey (1492) and three subsequent voyages (1493–1502).* This opened the floodgates for later *conquistadores* that fought the Aztecs in Mexico (1519), the Calusa warriors in what is today Florida (1513–1528), the Incas in Peru (1532), and later the Pueblos in New Mexico (1598). By conquering tribal groups, Spanish explorers also expanded their ancestry through *mestizo* (Spanish and Indian) and *mulato*† (Spanish and African) blends. Lineages such as that of Cortés with *La Malinche* who bore his first son, Martín Cortés el Mestizo (1523), was among the first *mestizos* of the New World.[25]

With each Spanish landing being different, every settlement charted its own course and created its own history, hardships, and legends. In rapid time, Spanish-led invasions during the next century grew to overtake South America, Central America, the Caribbean and parts of North America, distinguishing itself as the fastest and most expansive spread of European civilization across any continent worldwide, with Spaniards vastly dominating the Americas—north and south—by late 16th century.

The *conquistadores* divided much of the New World into conquered territories. Its presence became ubiquitous in rapid order. With much of the Western Hemisphere quickly populated by the Spaniard (and some Portuguese),

---

† For consistency, the Spanish spelling of *mulato* is used rather than the English spelling as *mulatto*.

descendants quickly became nation states across the hemisphere. As gold and silver deposits exceeding expectations, new riches helped Spain dominate Europe, contributing to its Golden Era mid-16th century.

The Hispanic/Latino that sprung from the New World developed independently of the blue-blooded Spaniard, the *peninsular*, and its second generation, the *criollo*. For the latter, as original descendants from Spanish *conquistadores*, these were the original designations prior to racial intermixing, as many were without mates in the New World. Progeny was eventually through *mestizaje* with the natives. Soon after, African slaves were brought to replace native *indios* to work in the mines as early as 1517, as many indigenous *indios* became afflicted with European diseases like smallpox and measles. Rather quickly *mulato* blends also became prominent throughout the Caribbean.[26] As Nelson Díaz (2018) illuminates, Columbus brought pestilence along with colonization.

Such racial mixes were quite different from their English counterpart years later, when both Pilgrims and Puritans fled from European persecution with intact families, barring any mix with indigenous natives. The Spanish invasion was different. Spaniards came in droves to conquer, not settle. But as they came without families, many eventually stayed behind when *peninsulares* returned with bountiful riches. It was this layover group that adjusted to New World conditions that introduced *mestizaje* into the new continent together with *mulato* descendants from coastal shores and Caribbean islands. It was these populations that swiftly marbleized the New World, eventually generating a unique *Latino* composite as a New World descendent.

Over time, internecine revolts against the Spaniards themselves rose in great numbers eventually resulting in the wars of independence between 1808 and 1826, after which nearly all Latin American countries became independent. Other than disputes over boundaries such as between Argentina and Chile, there have been relatively few disputes. During the 20th century there were no interstate wars except in 1995 when Ecuador and Peru went to war.[27] For the most part, Latin American countries did not fear their neighbors.

Today the Latino population represents over half a billion people across the Americas, nearly all descendants from the Spaniards with minor Portuguese stock, mixed with *Indio* and *Negro*, dependent on geographic sector. This "Cosmic Race" (*la Raza Cósmica*), as some would later call it, is a rich tapestry, a veritable blend of races, cultures, colors, and tribes throughout the map of today's kaleidoscopic Western Hemisphere.[28]

This newly formed Latino population came to represent a new phenomenon, as a veritably different amalgam globally, while expanding exponentially in the continents. The resulting "population" among these nations now represents one of the sleeping giants of the 21st century. The formation of Latino cultures and societies from within this polyglot has made Latino nations (at large) a large numerical presence to contend with. Each of these nations is fully Latino, flowing with mixed blood, the Spanish tongue and, at times, intermixed with indigenous languages. As different nations from one another, they once were united in despising the Spanish blue-bloods, in strong enmity against Spain, with some derogatory terms lasting to this day, most especially from Mexico.[29]

Nobel Prize laureate Gabriel García-Márquez described the Latino American world quite vividly when accepting his prize for Literature in 1982. As per his acceptance speech and as depicted in many of his novels, populations emerged from "fantastic" and "surreal" historical events that combined to create a "magical realism" which partially explains the Latino reality. Yet, it does not fully capture the essence of today's Latino that has become a global phenomenon. It is nothing like the Old World that gave it birth. By contrast, it is so different from "older" European worlds that it is seldom understood and quite likely one that *tampoco el Americano* [neither the American] fully comprehends.

The past two centuries witnessed this Latino mix added to the American experience as another layer of an evolving Latino onion. This has become complex. Here the table has turned upside down. In the U.S., Latinos have become another colonized group, but also a unique Latino reality. Having beaten former Spanish lords through centuries of struggle, the U.S. Latino became a newly-minted, American-made version of second-class existence. Having escaped one master, U.S. Latinos fell into the hands of another. After obtaining relative freedom abroad, new masters utilized different methods in a different country, in different ways, though reminiscent to former years of Spanish domination. This new American phenomenon put the Hispanic in a limbo-like status, as remnants from past oppression was not fully shed.

The Latino label is an incredible mix of dynamics with great diversity from within a macro-Latinized nation. *Latinizmo* conveys an altogether different blend from either the American or European type. This Latino entity defies simple categorization. It arose out of cataclysmic events spurred initially by Spanish greed across the hemisphere and later by American expansionism, while creating its own version of reality to survive. This offspring now brings an added and altogether different ingredient to Americanism. As part of a new history, Latinos have undergone considerable changes and crises over the years, each time battling another nemesis to survive another day and overcome another hurdle. The result has embedded in the Latino culture a stubbornness to resist and the will to overcome and beat the odds. Today, representatives from eighteen Latino countries from the Americas and many of their offspring are residents of this country as is Puerto Rico. Then there are citizens from Spain that are also residents. Altogether it forms quite an assemblage of Hispanics/Latinos.[30]

The Latino culture is not a *tabula rasa*, as each national culture is replete with a mosaic of historical precedents and antecedents. This is important to acknowledge in the provision of culturally-responsive educational approaches for today's Latino students. As such, Latinos form a rich array of cultures and legacies, with great diversity within each national group, altogether with greater diversity from which English stock generated in America. Latinos have emanated from a multiplicity of indigenous people, blended races, and immigrants worldwide. As a result, they represent unique mixes. These are difficult to define and even harder to categorize. This has created a rather formidable fusion that represents a most diverse and veritable "panethnic" society globally, as Cristina Mora (2014) defines it.

Education Began in Spanish

THE FIRST SPANISH SCHOOL IN THE AMERICAS WAS LA ESCUELA DE GRAMÁTICA (GRAMMAR SCHOOL) FOUNDED IN MODERN-DAY SAN JUAN, PUERTO RICO IN 1513.[31] The school depicted a rather advanced institution, where Spanish, Latin, literature, science, history, math, the humanities and the arts were taught.[32] It was founded by the first Bishop of Puerto Rico, Alonso Manso, who had arrived in the island the year before (1512).[33] As the first inquisitor of the New World, he later became the island's eighth governor. Under his command, the first grammar school of the New World was established and became the model for sister schools across the Caribbean and later throughout the hemisphere as a prototypical Spanish school.

Education was highly valued by the Catholic Church and quickly spread throughout the New World. According to historian Hugh Thomas (2010), in addition to excellent schools formalized by Franciscan monks as early as the mid-1550s near the vicinity of Lima, Peru, certain *criollo* families in that vicinity hired tutors for the education of their children, using a template much like the *peninsulares* had practiced in their initial settlements. The practice of hiring tutors spread among certain Inca families during this period. This occurred similarly in parts north of the hemisphere.

In general, the level of literacy was rather high among Spanish settlements. Major works of literature, for example, were taught at the new schools that incorporated highly-developed grammar books. Among the mission schools, for example, historian David Weber documents that by 1572 Franciscans had produced "at least eighty literary works in the native languages."[34] These included catechisms, grammars, and dictionaries that were usually copied by hand rather than printed, including bilingual catechisms in multiple languages, indicating advanced literacy. Such literacy further accelerated in the New World with the printing press.

Before 1600, two printing presses were already operating in the continent, one in Mexico City (1539) and the other in Lima, Peru (1561).[35] It is important to recall that during the "common schools" period in the U.S., literacy had been guided strongly by McGuffey's Readers (grades 1–6) starting around year 1836 and lasting until 1960 in U.S. public schools.[36] Centuries earlier by contrast, Spanish literacy in the New World had advanced considerably, but strictly under the Catholic Church. This included high levels of Spanish literature that were being provided to indigenous populations.

During this period, but in still other regions, the first Spanish colonial schools were also being developed by Franciscans. This began in 1606 in the area of today's St. Augustine, Florida which was first settled in 1565.[37] Colonial schools of this type later flourished, as Florida remained a Spanish Territory until 1819. By distinction, in the California region, a spurt of settlers' schools were founded in Baja California around 1697, with others a century later in Alta California[38] among the settlements of San Diego (1796) and Santa Barbara (1796); then later in San Francisco (1797), San José and Monterrey (1795), among others.[39] By then, these new settlers' schools had begun to reflect a more secular orientation as these were some of the first public schools of the later Southwestern United States. Interestingly, this growth was parallel but not independent from the spread of missions that also flourished in Alta California during the period.

The Society of Jesus, more commonly known as the Jesuits, established over twenty-one missions from San Diego to the north of San Francisco Bay. Flourishing missions and schools were eventual casualties of the European jealousies and conflicts, known as the Bourbon Reforms, as King Charles III had ordered the expulsion of Jesuits from New Spain (Mexico) in 1767. Their vast properties throughout today's Latin America were sold off to benefit the Spanish coffers, with Franciscans replacing Jesuits in the schools and missions. Most were established before the U.S. Declaration of Independence, with several missions founded precisely that same year such as San Juan Capistrano near Newport Beach and San Francisco de Assisi near San Francisco (1776).[40] Many Spanish missions and well-established schools flourished throughout the Southwest at the time the thirteen colonies were becoming states of the Union.

In Texas, settlers' schools were first established in the San Antonio valley by 1746, though settlements had started earlier, such as one from modern-day New Mexico and another from California. These settlements began when the first wave of settlers came into the Santa Fé area during the early 1600s, as they had started in 1598 by the first *conquistador* born in the New World, Don Juan de Oñate. After a Pueblo uprising, it was not until a century later around 1717 that a second wave occurred more formally.[41]

From contemporary chronicles, literacy seems to have remained fairly stable throughout the period, where about one-third of male settlers and soldiers in colonial New Mexico (1692 to 1821) could sign their name, a strong indicator of literacy.[42] More formal schools were created during the last decades of Spanish rule in northern Mexico, though uneven in quality and at various stages of formation during the turbulent Mexican Era soon after independence from Spain in 1821. According to MacDonald (2004) who well documents this period, literacy served the colonial era's rudimentary needs to communicate with Spanish officials fairly well, as it also helped conduct trade and formalize the documentation of baptisms, marriages, and deaths, as such primary needs were being taught at the schools.[43] Throughout, the acquisition of the Spanish language among Indian tribes required high levels of literacy, as this was a principal objective of the Spanish Crown. This had been strongly reinforced by Spanish decree in "domesticating" the natives through mission schools.

As education flourished, the Spanish system also became well organized and self-reliant, as the Catholic Church lent support for highly-educated teachers, including well-prepared priests that were also charged with teaching. Schooling and the spread of Catholicism occurred in tandem, as there was no separation between religion and schools. By 1600, there were about 1,100 friars throughout the New World.[44] As a result, educational knowledge was rather advanced, as learned schooling among the friars was formidable and Catholic catechism strongly adhered. This well affirms that Spanish schools, however envisaged, were fairly structured, highly disciplined, and of high literacy. Spanish schooling in the New World had incorporated the highest levels of literary knowledge, fully transplanted from the European Model via the Spanish Empire which by the mid-1600s ruled most of Europe.

Latinos in the U.S.

WHILE THE LATINO PRESENCE WAS VIRTUALLY EVERYWHERE IN THE AMERICAS, ITS OFFICIAL ENTRANCE INTO U.S. HISTORY CAME THROUGH THE ACQUISITION OF TERRITORIES AT THE START OF THE 19TH CENTURY. The Louisiana Purchase came in 1803 with Jefferson's presidency. It is interesting to note that Spain had just sold that territory to France three years earlier. As a result, it had been strongly Spanish in orientation. So, it is important to indicate that about 200,000 Hispanics already resided in the region.[45] It was this new land acquisition that hastened the Lewis and Clark expeditions of the Northwest (1803–1806) which later propelled the Westward Movement.

Another acquisition that brought Hispanics into the country was the Spanish territory of "La Florida" in 1819, previously referenced. This came after a series of battles and land transactions for ownership that eventually ceded "La Florida" to the U.S., with Florida becoming an incorporated territory in 1822.[46] The territory of Florida together with the Louisiana Purchase and the later addition of the Republic of Texas (1836), soon after the Battle of the Alamo, more than doubled the country's land mass by the first third of the century, as it also played a major role in subsequent sprawl and the national expansion of Latinos in American soil, with lands greatly inhabited by Spanish descendants.

Expansion was so rapid that by midcentury the U.S. had increased considerably in size once again, reaching farther into both the Northwest and the Southwest. This included the recent Mexican territories of the Southwest due to the Mexican-American War and the Oregon Territory—both in 1848—and soon thereafter the Gadsden Purchase of 1853. With nearly half of Mexico's land territory ceded to the U.S. from the war with Mexico,[47] many Mexican-owned mineral rights came under U.S. possession, as determined by the Treaty of Guadalupe Hidalgo (1848), not to mention the many Mexican businesses that were taken over soon after as well as the large *haciendas* that were confiscated.[48] Under the Treaty, however, it was decidedly agreed by the standards of international law that Mexican nationals residing within that jurisdiction were to become U.S. citizens, with full rights accorded to such citizenship for all Mexicans living within the territory.

These *Mejicanos* formally entered the U.S. in a rather dramatic and hurried manner after the war, as *bona fide* but overnight citizens. Being nonwhite, former *Mejicanos* were put at great risk if not carefully monitored, as the status for people of color was under debate and highly controversial, and as Manifest Destiny and concomitant attitudes toward nonwhites was in formation. Timing was unfavorable, as citizenship and property rights for the Mexican instantly clashed with land-seeking and money-grubbing miners and others from the 1849 gold rush the following year, and as the 1850 Homestead Act also encouraged squatting of lands that had been owned by *Mejicanos* for centuries. For *Mejicanos*, this included the difficulty of finding titles and the exorbitant payment of legal fees. With the U.S. representing the largest slave society in the world at the time, American patience with race was slim, with razor-thin tolerance for differences at a breaking point.

With nearly 4 million Black slaves by then, the country had become so wrapped up with slavery and the Indian "problem" that it seemed to lack the time or temperament to struggle with yet another nonwhite population. Temperament also exacerbated back East, fed by rage from the "Know-Nothing Party" that was highly anti-immigrant and anti-Catholic. Mexicans were denoted as representing immigrants as well as Catholics. Added to that, the average American was ill-prepared to deal with a another racial type, one that was now perceived to be "mixed" or "mongrel," let alone not speak English. These were already four strikes against the Mexican newcomer. As a result, the role of a "foreigner" from the newly conquered Southwest was perceived to be troublesome.

For the newly-christened Mexican American, this new status resulted in a quilt-like hodgepodge of local laws that were strung together by default, woefully inadequate, and fully contradictory. It thrust the Mexican in a state of panic and constant fear, fully confused about "rights" and acceptance in a totally new and foreign situation. *Socially*, Americans did not know how to respond to this new category of person. *Racially*, Americans disliked the Mexican. *Legally*, they were stumped. Are they White? By law, "yes." Should they be segregated? How? No one knew what to do about people of Mexican origin as to their "race" or their "kind," much less regarding their "strange" and "foreign" tongue and newly-claimed citizenship rights that typical Americans disregarded altogether.

Lacking equal rights and treated socially as both a "Mexican" and as a "foreigner," the Mexican American was placed in "another" category of citizenship, and in a totally "different" class, almost as if "a colony in a nation," echoing the title of Chris Hayes' recent (2017) book, but based on Du Bois' phrase (1935) when depicting the African American condition. The phrase was equally descriptive of Puerto Ricans that would find themselves in similar straitjackets at the end of the 19th century.

Presumption quickly became that "Mexicans" would be "unassimilable" unless strongly "Americanized," otherwise their acceptance would not be possible. With the added concern about the lack of English language skills, it was quickly surmised that the educational process could only be implemented through racially separate and linguistically-segregated learning. This became the presumed goal of teaching *them* English and accommodating *them* to a new environment. Turns out, it also became the stratagem to keep *them* isolated, never mind academic development.

According to Donato & Hanson, such informal racist beliefs led to convert Mexican students into permanent learners of the English language, forcing the few that were enrolled to attend segregated schools, but truly to remain in the same grade for multiple years. Later, a new type of school was branded as a "Mexican school." This confined the Mexican American to the long-term, if not permanent, teaching of American values and ways. This became the practice, as a convenient way (or excuse) by which to effectively keep Mexicans at bay and their children away from any education.

A major obstacle for the jingoist American was how to abide by a treaty that declared "Mexicans" as citizens when in fact they were not acceptable as "White." Such persons could not be confined to a reservation like the Native American,[49] as this would be an egregious rejection of Mexico's agreement and a violation of international law. Hence, resolution was delayed. In the meanwhile it relegated the former *Mejicano* to a "lesser than" status. Politically, the stance was to let states decide, passing the hot potato into the hands of the Southwest, away from the eyes of most Americans, including the Deep South. Postponement placed the Mexican American in an indeterminate "limbo" status that forced everyone to be in a paralyzed "wait and see" stance. Uncertainty delayed the pressing question of what to do with the Mexican.

It is important to understand that major portions of the Southwest were in a state of raw development after the treaty. Texas had just become a state in 1845. California, on the other hand, had barely been settled by any American. In 1846 there were hardly 8,000 settlers in California (not counting Native

Americans); yet the territory quickly entered the Union in 1850 because its population mushroomed overnight by roughly 100,000 as a result of the gold rush the previous year. This was phenomenal growth that set the Mexican as the villain that was obtrusively elbowing its way into virgin territory, as if not already there. Arizona and New Mexico, on the other hand, did not become states until the early 20th century, while Nevada became a state in 1864 and Colorado in 1876, as the centennial state.

With early belief in Manifest Destiny, the country had acquired new territories as it had also displaced hundreds of Native American tribes in its march across the West in the 1830s. In concluding the Civil War in 1865 and completing the Alaska Purchase of 1867 soon after, the United States had become a behemoth with a southwestern region that was fully disjointed and under extremely rapid development. In less than a century from independence, the nation had marched Native Americans across the West in the late 1830s, declared Manifest Destiny, and fought a Civil War. It had grown from thirteen colonies in 1776 to 38 states and many territories, increasing nearly nine times by its first centennial in 1876. The country had now spanned the full width of North America, literally "from sea to shining sea," by its first centennial.

Education in the U.S.

BY CONTRAST WITH EARLY SPANISH SETTLERS, EDUCATIONAL PROGRESS FOR LATINOS IN THE U.S. PROCEEDED ALONG AN ALTERNATE PATH FROM ENGLISH SETTLERS. Among American colonists, education for the general public was slow in development until the start of the 19th century. This early period was a time of building a strong agricultural economy. It was easy for everyone (White) that was able to work to rapidly find employment. During this period, the purpose of education was more to teach rural children sound values and vocational skills than academic excellence.[50] For the Latino, many had been well oriented in schooling, given their Catholic upbringing, so education was more common, but this was still for the very few and nearly everything changed midcentury with U.S. rule.

Meanwhile the nation was going through a major transition from its agrarian roots to urbanization. In 1820, for example, America was 90% rural, but within a century, by 1920, more than half the U.S. population was to live in cities.[51] More specifically, major urban growth occurred at the start of this period, between 1820 and 1860. Chicago, for example, was "a muddy small town in 1830" which grew to "over 109,000 by 1860."[52] With similar increases in urban centers, especially in the North, schools multiplied so quickly they could not keep pace with students required to fully meet the needs, with many pupils easily turned away for lack of space.[53]

After the Civil War, another urban growth spurt began hand-in-hand with industrialization. Growth was further heightened by large immigration flows toward the end of the century. These factors forced education to supply workers with stronger technical/manual skills, as these were mostly driven by industry. For example, by 1870 some 61% of students between the ages of five and eighteen enrolled in some type of schooling, and by 1898 the typical youngster (White) could boast having attained five years of schooling, with one percent attending college.[54] The downside was the application of the "factory model," with which the country had become enamored, as this was the way schools were being run, where everything was "standardized, modularized and predictable," with order as the guiding yardstick.[55]

During this haste, pluralism and attention to differences ranked least in the minds of reformers, even less for bureaucrats. Later in the century, this model of control became the way to run schools just as much as the "business model" is trying to elbow its way into 21st century schools, also boasting as the most efficient system. While both models suffer from inherent flaws, it is for vastly different reasons.

For Latinos toward the end of the 19th century, because rising institutions were demanding greater efficiency, higher schooling, and more effective institutions to manage social demands, they were elbowed out. Worse, their skills were truly unwanted. It was impossible for them to compete. In fact, it was up to social agencies and schools to find places for everyone except persons of color. It was almost like warehousing. Here Latinos and Blacks literally had no options. They were all too easily pushed out, without a place in the established order. For example, there were the asylums for the insane, as there were almshouses for the poor and prisons for criminals.[56] Likewise for nonwhites, lands were reserved for Native Americans, Mexican schools for Mexican Americans, and segregated institutions for the needs of Blacks. This frame of thinking literally spilled into the next century, made more easily after *Plessy*.

Unquestionably, the country was becoming segmented, divided, and split according to expected places in society for every type of citizen to "fit in." This brought order as it also introduced control for the management of social affairs. Conditions were worse for non-Black racial groups that already lacked access and were being denied basic rights, mostly Latinos. The forcing of more controlled environments and mechanical processes whereby greater watchfulness was introduced all worked to create a firm vigilance from which categorization and later subjugation was facilitated.

In retrospect, to understand why Latino students are treated the way they are nowadays, Luis Cruz, former principal and now a national trainer in education, made an important point during our interview when he reflected on Latinos and education history:

> The educational system we have inherited was one that was not designed for a majority of Latino students to be successful. In fact, the educational system we are part of today is doing exactly what it was designed to do years ago, as it hasn't changed much. It was not to ensure that a majority of Latino students would benefit academically. As a result, the system as we know it today psychologically brainwashes our students to believe academic excellence is not for them.[57]

So what is to be done?

> Our job then is to not only alter the system so that our children can benefit, but also to ensure our students begin to *embrace* a belief in themselves and their academic success. Otherwise, institutional racism and discrimination in our schools, willingly or otherwise, will severely damage our children.[58]

It was precisely this late 19th century attitude that filtered into the *Plessy* era, but with spillover into today's reality. Somehow over time, society became complacent with this former education model of domination through domestication via schooling that it has had a hard time snapping out of this mentality, most especially when dealing with the minority youngster, almost as a subservient class. It was as if schooling got caught in an interminable time warp from which it has had difficulty escaping. At the time, conditions to enter the economy were favorable without the need for much education, but the context for today is obviously quite different. Yet, in an anachronistic manner, if the model for today is that which presumably worked at the turn of the last century, then serious problems inevitably result. In reviewing this historical juxtaposition, professor Samuel Betances accurately projects this dilemma onto the educational challenges that have faced Latino students at two critical junctures in American history, in some ways uncannily similar:

> Latinos must do at the turn of the 21st century what White Europeans didn't have to do during the last turn of the century. It took many Europeans several generations to get into college, with several exceptions, as they also moved from a simple to a more complex economy gradually. At that time, there was a high dropout rate, but a

low dropout problem. Young people could easily enter the society with limited skills [except for the Latino in the 19th century]. For Latinos today, it is now a low dropout rate, but a much higher dropout problem. For them, it is no longer four generations to get into the complex economy. They must move from agriculture to computers in one generation. They are expected to catapult from poverty to the professions overnight and then confront the computer rather than the cow. That's a tall order![59]

Actually, conditions were worse at that time for a field hand or average worker. Latinos were not acceptable, as they had the stigma of color. Even when they could enter the local economy, given the right skills and experience, they were not desired as workers. The Mexican worker had to supersede certain class lines and pass manual skills, not to mention master minimal language knowledge, let alone be admitted as a foreigner and a Catholic with little education. But then they represented color differences as nonwhites. Here they were at a considerably greater disadvantage than any immigrant worker, as even when they crossed religious and language barriers, they could not pass the cultural, class or color line. In effect, they were workers of the last resort, nearly destitute.

Excluding Latinos from Public Education

ENTERING MIDCENTURY WITH THE TREATY IN 1848, MEXICAN AMERICANS TREADED A WANING PATH IN EDUCATION. THEY FACED AN ERA OF SEGREGATION WITH AN UNMISTAKABLE "DUAL" SYSTEM IN THE MAKING. As they did not fit either side of the equation—Black or White—they were literally placed by default into a third category of race, as "other White." As such, it became a label by which they could be ignored and cast aside, as it was difficult to bring legal suits as Whites, but also could not be categorized with Blacks, as emancipation had not yet occurred and dual systems were not truly formalized. This Catch-22 condition halted them from receiving assistance as a minority group, as they had very limited rights. For all practical purposes, they could not receive the benefits of Whites, as they were "other White," nor could they receive federal reparations for being Black [after the Civil War] or for entering a segregated "Black" school, as they were not really Black. So, they were greatly barred either way, losing both sides, with progress shelved.

Unattended, Latinos were unable to fully enter the educational mainstream due to non-inclusion; expelled by default. Though technically in the right, the Mexican American had few American allies and virtually no defenders, with the exception of the Mexican government itself, but even then in a highly limited manner. The group had become an outcast, confined to a "no man's land," lacking the full benefits of citizenship, truly a foreigner in their former land.

How did this happen? Let's return mid-19th century, denoting the period when considerable educational progress was afoot across the nation. This was when access to schools via the common schools was in full swing. Recall that this period marked the birth of public schools. Ironically, the time of expansion for American education was precisely when the doors of educational opportunity closed for the Mexican American that had just become a citizen. Most ironically, they could not benefit from the booming period of educational expansion. In fact, this was precisely when major discrimination and general subordination of Mexicans began, an extreme contradiction. Could they attend segregated schools? How? These were virtually nonexistent before the war. Hence, it was quite rare to attend any school whatsoever.

Soon after the Civil War, schools for Mexican-origin children started to become available,[60] albeit mostly in the context of de facto segregation designed to keep Mexican American students apart without providing meaningful education. Unlike Black Americans with segregated schools after the war, Mexican Americans in the Southwest experienced segregation based on local determination with little recourse to statutory mandates.[61]

It became a matter of course to send Mexican American children to segregated schools of their own, and much later to that which became known as the Mexican school, as these slowly increased across the Southwest by default, flourishing by early 20th century. Meanwhile, it was most difficult for them to attend segregated schools, let alone non-segregated schools. Even then, many of the officials that supported segregation on pedagogical grounds also recognized that too many educators were isolating Mexican children in order to give them "a short school year, inferior buildings and equipment, and poorly paid teachers."[62] For almost nearly every case under review, schools attended by Mexican Americans were considerably inferior to Anglo schools, even those recorded in official state reports.[63] At the same time, many *colonias* [communities] were deprived of having any schools whatsoever.

In the Territory of New Mexico, San Miguel and Valencia (1998) note that schools began to segregate between "Whites and Mexicans" as early as 1872 and that by the 1880s nearly half of the enrolled school children were in segregated schools.[64] For Texas, the first Mexican school was established in 1902. In rapid fashion by 1930 some 90% of south Texas schools were segregated.[65] For California which had state codes that prohibited the admission of

"Negroes, Mongolians and Indians" into regular public schools, "Mexicans" were never specifically mentioned, yet by the 1920's they were "the most segregated group in California's public education system."⁶⁶

Without question, the treatment of Mexican American students in new American schools [*escuelas Americanas*] was perceived by Mexicans with great fear, as these educational settings had become suspect and literally foreign. In the Southwest, only Texas mandated in its 1876 Constitution that public schools were to be racially separated (Black and White), from elementary school through college, but with Mexican schools established some two decades later. For California and the rest of the Southwest, segregation was encouraged with local districts deciding, resulting in few opening their doors.

As it unfolded, most districts opted for elementary schools to become highly-segregated institutions—mostly *de facto*. In short time, with the expansion of Jim Crowism, public schools converted into "tripartite" institutions of segregation in the Southwest, with most schools for Whites, some for Blacks, and many others for Mexicans, with each category viewed quite distinctly. Nonetheless, it is important to note that in cities like San Francisco special Chinese schools also had been established for Asian Americans, but for a much smaller and localized population at the time.

In general, for racial minorities, American schooling had transformed into a rather overt and debilitating process of "gradual internal colonization" and "Americanization," where it was more about acculturation than learning. In fact, much of the research references schools in the Southwest during this period "as an agency for the acculturation of the Mexican American."⁶⁷ One particular observer underscored that socialization had transformed the "3Rs" into "3Cs"—*cultural* norms, *civic* instruction, and *command* of the English tongue.⁶⁸ At the secondary level, there were no Mexican schools. For the rare Latino that may have attended a White high school, the curriculum included some doses of practical instruction, but with vocational education and acculturation as the major thrust for the Mexican student.

A*s it was, the process of Americanization in the schools became one of "subtractive schooling." This was a process whereby "dehumanization" worked to derail the purposes of schooling toward the subdominance of a culture.* The concept which Angela Valenzuela (1999) well defines in *Subtractive Schooling* is one where academic achievement is downplayed and hardly emphasized, with little learning taking place. Typical teaching in the core content subjects like math, science, and language arts were rarely taught.

As evident, by the end of the 19th century, schooling had assumed a rather specific role for Latinos. Schools had imprinted the message that the cultural identity of this group was "foreign," with the blemish of "outsider" in multiple connotations as "strangers" in their own land and unwanted in the new context of *Americano*. For entry into the mainstream, students had to be reshaped, basically "re-acculturalized." Education had become the facilitator of social goals towards acculturation. In actuality, it was about becoming "responsible American citizens of Mexican-origin,"[69] within their limits. This meant Anglo-centric curricula had become dominant for classroom instruction, at the expense of learning salient skills and achieving intellectual functioning. More specifically, "replacing habits of food and dress with American versions was paramount to the Americanization process."[70] Furthermore, textbooks had become an explicit handbook on how to normalize Anglo-centric history and culture at the expense of Latino heritage and culture. The process provided explicit and formulaic ways that helped reframe identity formation as it reshaped personal growth *a la versión Americana* [in the American version].

As English-only policies became dominant, these also enforced English usage, even in the playground. Officials further encouraged parents to "only" speak English at home. This pattern was even more strongly reinforced mid-1920s onward when the Mexican American migration began to move to the Midwest. Most of these public schools re-segregated only to serve Mexicans.[71] Over time, as public education became an important tool for economic development and upward mobility, the process had actually converted into repressive means for conformity; worse, they exemplified the expectancy that Mexicans were to become subservient to the needs of the dominant society and its growing working class. Schooling was subtractive mainly as subjugation.

The process of Americanization was gradual in implementation, but continual and progressive in duration and intensity. It did not happen overnight. In reviewing this history from the Treaty of Guadalupe Hidalgo onward, several distinct phases are clear, as per documentation from San Miguel & Valencia (1998). In essence, both the process of acculturation and education worked in tandem, with the former dominating the latter. From past studies, coupled with most recent scholarship, these principally fell into five distinct stages of increasing assimilation.

According to the authors, the *first stage* began during the 1850s, when Spanish was limited as a medium of instruction in the schools. By 1870, a *second stage* kicked in, when Spanish was prohibited altogether. This occurred when states like Texas and California passed English language laws prohibiting the use of native languages, later followed by similar laws in the Territory of New Mexico (1891) and elsewhere. During the *third stage*, around the 1880s, Mexican culture was slowly eliminated from public school curricula. For example, references pertaining to Catholic topics and Mexican history were systematically removed or taught in an anti-Mexican context. At the same time, many Mexican American children were beaten up or bullied to drop out of school. This was followed by a *fourth stage*, where the "imposition" of an Anglo-centric curriculum became common, as this shift also started being reflected in textbooks from the 1880s onward. The *fifth and subsequent stages* were those where, in fact, cultural references conveyed "disparaging" references about Mexicans in the Southwest together with denigrating statements about the culture. This latter stage strongly coincided with *Plessy*, as Mexican Americans now entered the new century. Thereon, practices accumulated by the degree of repression received through schooling. "Mexican schools" and dropping out of school altogether were accumulating and becoming more the case to control high numbers from entering school by the start of the 20th century. As the Mexican school became the minority version of the common schools and as the expected norm during the early 1900s, it came to be known considerably different from the more typical "common schools" known by Whites.

Educational progress for Latinos had some parallels to the African American experience after the Civil War. In reviewing this period, Carter Woodson (1933 [2005]) famously critiqued that the "Negro," once indoctrinated with Jim Crowism and segregation, had undergone the misadventure of a schooling process that had left him or her incapable of analyzing the condition of peers, as this form of education had sapped the ability to critically analyze the experience of one's own; basically, "too White" to exert critical analysis. Carter's analysis had concluded that this "mis-education" had created the conditions for the "educated Negro" to no longer be committed to the needs of Blacks or to be in a position to properly analyze social conditions as they [Negroes] had developed "contempt toward their own people" the more educated they became.[72] He concluded this as internalized self-deprecation and eventual self-hatred, one which Mamie and Kenneth Clark were to confirm decades later in their research.

Joel Spring (1997) well addressed a similar process in assertively using the term "deculturalization," referring to "the stripping away of a people's culture and replacing it with a new culture."[73] He further stated that for this model

"U.S. government leaders and educators rejected the concept of the United States as a multicultural society for a society unified around Protestant Anglo-American culture"[74] and conformity. As a result, programs for Americanization were designed to replace native cultures with the dominant White culture. In effect, schooling upheld a mindset to "civilize" students from seemingly backward cultures by changing their way of life, their cultural beliefs, their language, their names, and for some—like Native Americans—even challenging religious beliefs.

In a parallel manner in the South, one-third of which was Black at the turn of the century, African American educators like Anna Julia Cooper (1892) combated the concept of "debilitative education" by transcending negative self-formation to better concentrate on efforts toward the traditions of resistance. Her views of education were redemptive, as she addressed defeatism and marginalization among Blacks. This resulted in her adamantly fighting against the pathological characterization of Black people as mentally incapable and not valuing education.

Notwithstanding similarities across non-mainstream cultures, a major distinction for the Mexican American from any other group was that there were no formal mechanisms in place to help their adjustment after the impact of the Mexican-American War, whereas the Black community received federal assistance during Reconstruction and then subsequently, albeit rather limited and racially oppressive. The Freedman's Bureau, for example, helped with the training of Black schoolteachers as it assisted others in workforce development, though woefully underfunded and severely limited in duration. In addition, agrarian reform through land redistribution occurred during the war and continued for a brief period thereafter, where former enslaved Black farmers could own land, but short-lived. The program denoted as "forty acres and a mule" was to be put into operation, but then rescinded. Hardly any Blacks obtained new lands by homesteading. Other types of assistance were also short-lived, with few gains soon reversed with Jim Crow.[75] Nonetheless, even comparable reparations for Mexicans, however, were never at play.

Also by contrast, no similar promises had been made to Latinos as a result of or after the treaty. They had to adjust from one culture to another, confront an entirely new language, obtain new employment skills, and survive from one region to another, with many losing their lands and personal savings in the process. This period had become a hard time for conquered *Mejicanos*, as they were denied any federal assistance whatsoever.

In education, Reconstruction had been successful in partially bolstering the establishment of Black colleges and universities after the war with the intention of principally serving Black college entrants. This was further bolstered by the second Morrill Act of 1890 that required states to establish "separate" land-grant colleges for Blacks if they were excluded from extant land-grant colleges. But for the Mexican once again, there was no such consideration for either higher learning or employment training so that entry into higher education institutions was not available for them in the same way.

For the average Mexican American, what transpired in education was a highly "truncated" process, as too few attended high school. Consequently, opportunity for college was seldom available, as most White institutions would not welcome them, and where no Latino-oriented or Latino-sponsored university was available. For the most part, the Latino student had to make it exclusively in a "White world" or not make it at all, with few options for support or financial assistance. For them, it was a near total cultural surrender or bust.[76] In a most difficult manner, going through the process of postsecondary education principally meant working against culture, as that which was taught was fully antithetical to Mexican values, in parallel to what Woodson, Cooper, and Du Bois were documenting for Blacks during that period. For Blacks, it meant that graduates had to go outside the former confederate states for an integrated education or attend an all-Black institution. For the Mexican American, choices were quite stark, without the benefit of an Hispanic or Mexican university or any type of federal assistance.

The demographics for minority populations during this period are important to understand, as numbers often influence social policy. Going back to 1700, it is important to recall that there were barely 25,000 Blacks in the U.S. at that time. It was only as a result of rapid increases in agricultural production and trade soon afterwards that labor demands for workers increased and Blacks were brought in to alleviate shortages, but mainly as slaves. They were brought from the West Indies and directly from Africa, rapidly increasing to nearly one-half million within the next three quarters of the century, when the Black population grew to 1-in-5 (21%) among colonists by the Revolutionary War, highest ever,[77] with percentages later diminishing to 13% nationwide by the Civil War a century later.‡ Most importantly, Blacks represented the vast swath of nonwhites, but with nearly 9-in-10 as slaves.

---

‡ This latter percentage has remained relatively stable ever since.

For the Latino, by contrast, even with the addition of Puerto Rico a century later, they were still few in number relative to Blacks. For example, the estimated population for Blacks ranged from 8 to 10 million in 1900,[78] as compared to barely two million Latinos that same year, but with about 3-in-5 Latinos living outside the continental U.S., back in the Island of Puerto Rico. As a result, the history of Latino education in the continent remained mostly Mexican American until mid-20th century and quite small. Starting the 20th century, the totality of racial groups represented 15% of the U.S. population—13% Black, 2% Latino, and less than 1% for all other nonwhites.[79] Given these demographics, it is reasonable to see how dominant views regarding people of color was that of a black-white dichotomy, especially given the fact that the vast majority of Latinos were much out of view, split between the Southwest and Puerto Rico. As a result, their needs were also more likely to be ignored altogether.

Regardless of numbers at the start of the century, people of color wrestled with the lack of access in contradistinction to the many White European immigrants arriving in droves as new citizens but without the stigma of race and color. For this latter group, melding and fitting into the dominant culture within two to three generations was reasonable.[80] Consequently, racial distinctions were to dominate the first half of the twentieth century as *Plessy* came to further control and overtake years of civic government and the public schools in its racialized treatment and policies toward students of color that did not affect the White European immigrant.

Catholic schools were a godsend for Mexican Americans in the U.S., not unlike the redemption Blacks received in their assistance from the Rosenwald schools. Catholicism for the Latino had been very much a part of the education and culture of the Mexican much before the Mexican-American War. As it was, Catholic schooling continued in Mexico even after schooling fell into disarray as a result of Mexico's independence from Spain in 1821. As such, it also continued when Mexican Americans found themselves neglected in the American milieu after the treaty.

The role of the Catholic Church became even more salient for the Latino child after the treaty, ironically during the height of the "free and public" common schools movement. This turned out to be astounding in the midst of the growth among the public schools. In reality, it was the Catholic school that came to represent a major refuge and life support against the American onslaught, *not* the common schools.

In point of fact, given the wariness of the Mexican family about the new social order in America and the questionable status Americans were imposing on the education of Latinos, it was the Catholic Church that helped fill some of the gap. While this was also the case among some Protestant denominations, it was unquestionably the Catholic Church that dominated influence and overall numbers for the Latino, as it was also the Catholic Church that helped develop the Spanish missions and cathedrals that dotted the Southwest and had been accessible along the Western Coast.

It was precisely because of the exclusion and segregation of the Mexican American that the Catholic Church redoubled its efforts to reaffirm authority over schooling as well as provide domestic assistance to families. It is important to note that the orders for the Catholic Church were now from Europe (not Spain at this time), as the U.S. was considered a missionary site up until the 1900s. In fact, many of the clergy did not speak either English or Spanish when they first arrived in the states.

In short order, Catholic schools began to proliferate the Southwest as Jim Crowism began to affect Mexican entry into the schools. In the Territory of New Mexico as many as "twenty schools" were established from 1853 to 1874.[81] Likewise in California, an "undetermined number" of Catholic schools were established for Mexican boys and girls in several cities, including Santa Barbara, Ventura, and Los Angeles. In Texas, "other schools" for Mexican children were established in El Paso, Brownsville, Corpus Christi, and San Antonio.[82]

Catholic schools provided support to the needs of many Mexican American communities to have alternative means of education through the church as well as the utilization of non-formal and informal structures of schooling and education. Families sought refuge in religious schools as a major source of salvation—figuratively and literally. In seeking alternative means to educate, away from traditional public schools, the Latino experience was not altogether different from the Black experience with the AME during this same period. It was the church that had become the safety blanket that protected many Mexican American children from the full effect of caste segregation that Du Bois and others talked about during that period, as it was "difficult to let others see the full psychological meaning of caste segregation," most especially if one had "never experienced" it firsthand.[83] This reality had become a new and difficult experience for the *Mejicano*, and an unintended consequence after the treaty.

Mexicans had been typecast in their community as well as in their schools, with the latter patterned by the former, but each reinforcing the other. The

Catholic Church, having witnessed persecution in American society (especially during immigrant Irish-Catholic battles for inclusion mid-19th century), entered as a willing partner to assist with alternate schooling for Mexican Americans, given that both had endured suffering at the hands of common foes. The unfortunate part was that it was costly, with Catholic schools nowhere sufficient to fill the need. At times, there were exceptions where some Catholic orders provided free charity for schooling. At the same time, however, it must be acknowledged that some White priests treated Mexican parishioners horribly and established their version of "Juan Crow," with mass for Mexicans in the basement. Notwithstanding, it is not surprising that the respect accorded for parochial education by Latinos in many *barrios* continues to hold sway to this day. Unquestionably, the standard for good education for many Latinos continues to be that of private, parochial education.

Education and Imperialism

BY CLOSE OF THE CENTURY, WITH PLESSY MARKING THE OFFICIAL START OF LEGAL SEGREGATION, THE U.S. HAD REACHED A RATHER SAD LANDMARK. BEYOND FORMALIZING AN APARTHEID SYSTEM, THE COUNTRY HAD ALSO ESTABLISHED ITSELF AS AN IMPERIAL POWER. The decided victory over Spain in the Spanish-American War had given the U.S. full license as an imperial nation. Expansionism had reached new heights, going beyond the protection of the hemisphere through the Monroe Doctrine, as it had become a new empire of colonization that included critical portions of the Caribbean and elsewhere.

The takeover of island nations was rather significant two years after *Plessy*, as it began to round out a picture of internal colonization as well as international control and educational subordination. Ironically, it also assured that more Hispanic groups would be added to the U.S. arsenal of Latino nationalities, another unintended consequence. The narrative of internalized *racism* had now combined with external *imperialism* to epitomize the contradictions of a republic that flaunted freedom abroad while usurping the rights of racial groups from within. With official segregation in place, the country had embarked in a new inglorious era, with colonialism added to its arsenal of imperialism. This represented an altogether new phase that bolstered pro-expansionism for the nation on track toward a greater power continuum. This gave it license to also interfere with other Latin American countries in the 20th century like Colombia, Nicaragua, Panamá, among others.

These new conditions became well established in starting a new century, as it conclusively paved the way for policy that would turn out to be highly unjust, becoming the acid test of basic American values and beliefs. It is notable to indicate that after Cuba and the Philippines became independent decades later, Puerto Rico and Guam continued as territorial acquisitions with virtually no representation and voice in Congress to this day except for a Congressional representative for each but with no vote to break a tie. Despite the granting of citizenship, neither island can vote in U.S. presidential elections.

For Puerto Rico, the U.S. takeover of the island meant changing the language of instruction immediately. This was not only demagogic, but absolutely destructive to the culture. Enactment occurred immediately, not incrementally. Takeover also meant changing the name of the Island to "Porto Rico," merely because it was easier for Americans to pronounce, though fully nonsensical in the Spanish language. This took over three decades to reverse.[84]

English language instruction was decided by federal policy in 1899 when Victor S. Clark was appointed President of the Puerto Rico Board of Education by William Torrey Harris, U.S. Commissioner of Education, as cited earlier. With educational instruction across the island becoming fully English, several groups of schoolteachers were soon sent to New York City—primarily Columbia University—to study the English language during the first decade of the century, as hardly any island teacher or administrator knew the language of English.

Given the island's 400-year colonial history under Spain, Spanish had been the mother tongue for nearly half a millennium for government, commerce, and public education. The imposition of English as the official language of instruction created an upheaval, as it forced language dominance to the detriment of subject-matter teaching and sound pedagogy.[85] As this action occurred absent any teacher orientation or textbook to guide teachers, English textbooks became as important to instructors as it was for students. This "Clark Policy," as it came to be known, forcibly imposed English on Puerto Rico and created the highest K–12 dropout rate in island history. Here again, education became the perfect vehicle for Americanization, as it imposed English and American values upon youth instead of needed academic instruction, as little could be learned in island schools after third grade without English knowledge.[86]

This mandate was not only short-sighted, but represented egregious repression and outright colonialism, with education as the most powerful weapon by which to delimit achievement while introducing foreign values all at once. Obviously, the policy was independent of pedagogy and sound teaching.[87] During the next forty-eight years, at least seven different language combinations and grade mixes were tried, none yielding favorable results.[88] As thousands of Puerto Ricans dropped out of school, many of our grandparents went without schooling due to these policies, affecting nearly every islander for several generations.

The story of the Philippine Islands was not unlike that for Puerto Rico, with those islands also receiving domestication, with education disguised as "modernity." In the Philippines, it was the U.S. soldier that presided over the first American classes before U.S. teachers came. This endeared the expression in the Philippines, "Education with a krog" (the U.S. army rifle of the day).[89] Kipling's poem, *The White Man's Burden* (1899), later rewritten to memorialize the Philippines, was penned in response to the influence of the West to colonize people of color around the world. As Robert Coloma (2004) concludes in his review of educational policy in the Philippines, "The U.S. placed their [its] hopes and confidence in education to provide answers to their problems and made social amelioration the schools' primary function."[90] One big difference between the Philippines and parallel language and cultural imposition that occurred for Guam and Puerto Rico is that the Philippines Islands obtained independence in 1946, ridding themselves of a burden that still rages with the other islands. Another major difference was that this occurred only after losing the Philippine-American War (1899–1902) that began almost immediately after the signing of the Treaty with Spain (1898), whereas no wars resulted from other island nations.

In an ironic historical twist, a cadre of teachers was needed to "bring education" to the Philippines at the turn of the century. This was when Carter G. Woodson, later known as the "Father of Black History," went to the Philippines in 1903. He went to help establish a new school system, after the war had been settled. Woodson was one of about 1,000 teachers recruited between 1902 and 1903 to help with the education of local Filipinos. As it turned out, the purpose was to indoctrinate about patriotism through American history and its heroes, and to establish the English language through cultural reorientation. It became obvious that the books and subjects Filipino children were being taught were completely foreign to them, unrelated to their reality, as designed by White Americans in the states.[91]

Interestingly, it was Woodson's past legacy as coalminer now turned schoolteacher that emboldened him to reflect on American schooling as well as his own personal struggles in graduate school decades later when able to provide strong evidence that gave impetus to his seminal book, *The Mis-Education of the Negro* (1933). He had much to reflect, given that he had witnessed both sides of the issue as a multiculturalist. This provided credibility to an unabashed statement in his book about oppression: "When you control a man's thinking you do not have to worry about his actions. You do not have to tell him not to stand here or go yonder." Instead, "He will find his 'proper place' and will stay in it."[92]

Counting the Latino

COUNTING THE LATINO HAS BEEN CONFUSING IN U.S. HISTORY, AS IT HAS BEEN LADEN WITH ERRORS AND CONSIDERABLE MISAPPLICATION. A short history is necessary to realize the extent to which this has not only botched research, but also gotten mixed results in counting school children. For example, it became problematic in accounting for the segregation of children based on race, when Latinos were mixed with all other groups, as documented in the *Cisneros* (1970) court decision which recognized Latinos as its own minority group. The logical conclusion was for Hispanics to be counted as their own category of race. However, the Census has not yet reached this logical conclusion. Unfortunately, the 2020 census will not remedy the confusion, as Latinos represent their own unique category of people, as a *bona fide* demographic group, but being split by the Census with two questions, one related to nationality and the other by race, forcefitting between White and Black.

*L*atinos were not highly visible until the latter part of the 20th century. This was principally due to isolation, as the two largest Latino populations lived away from the mainstream and also greatly separated by water. As these lands were widely distant, unity was difficult. There was virtually no opportunity for any powerbase to be formalized between the two Latino groups. As a result, each remained as a fringe and solitary group, highly ignored as a viable group by mainstream society and separated by geography until around the civil rights era, much after *Brown*.

As was the case, it was also difficult to estimate the number of Hispanics even while the population grew considerably during the century. Other than for Puerto Rico, there was no reliable or systematic process by which to count the number Hispanics with high accuracy until the 1980 census.[93] Today, 'Puerto Rico's totals are still separately counted and entered only by footnote, distinctly separate from U.S. totals.[94] In the mainland, the count for Hispanic groups continues to be flawed by one measure or another.

In 1910, as an example, one of the questions asked was about the principle language spoken at home when the respondent was a child. Only persons responding that Spanish was the "mother tongue" used at home during childhood were counted. In 1930, the first decennial census to include Hispanics only counted "Mexicans" as a race and only for the five southwestern states. Unlike any previous census, the 1930 census presumed Mexicans to be non-Whites unless "definitely White." Counts were determined by census enumerators that had been specifically instructed on how to classify and count the Mexican. As it turned out, over 1.4 million persons were classified by enumerators as "Mexican" and therefore non-White, whereas just over 65,000 (barely 4%) were listed as White.[95] As it was, "Mexicans had become racialized as a non-White group."[96] Only after major uproar from Mexican elites and even the Mexican consuls did the census abandon using a separate race category and has since counted Hispanics as a distinct category of White. However, in seeking a solution, it created two categories of Whites: "Hispanic" and "non-Hispanic."[97] This distinction continues to be in effect.

It was not until 1950 that the Bureau of the Census began collecting data on persons with Spanish surnames. Names were matched against the list of Spanish surnames identified from the five southwestern states in 1930. Turns out, these estimates were highly inaccurate. Ten years later, the Census used three different measures: birth or parentage, mother tongue, and surname. This changed again in 1970 when the Census utilized a self-identification question on "Spanish origin," as it introduced a question regarding "origin or descent," where respondents selected from a list of nations; however, counts were for only a small, five percent census sample, not the universe.[98] Incredibly, it was not until 1980 that a universe count was undertaken for Hispanics. This was when the term "Hispanic" was first used as a census category, but as a distinct classification within "White." Subsequently, the term "Latino" has been added to the nomenclature.

It is important to note that prior to 1980, Hispanic estimates were lost among the counts for "Whites," as there existed two levels of whiteness, one for "Hispanics" and the other for "non-Hispanics," but making it difficult to differentiate between the two populations in the actual counts. Resistance to change the category of White for Mexicans had come from the Spanish elite and from the Mexican government itself. There was great resentment to the term "colored" along with all other terms, as they were also not in favor of the category of Mexican or national identity in the place of "White." Their assumption was that Mexicans had the option of selecting to be White. They had underestimated the role of color and phenotype when it came to race in the U.S., most especially in the Deep South.

This position came back to haunt, as it did not work in a racialized context. This is *not* how White society perceived the Mexican (or any other Hispanic). Neil Foley (2005) well captured the dilemma of the Spanish elite by stating they had basically established "a Faustian pact" with whiteness prior to the sixties, after which a new generation of Mexican Americans and Chicanos rejected the accommodationist strategies and sought their identity through "brownness." Foley argued that assimilation was not about what one leaves behind, but about what one is moving toward; that is, what is acquired in the process of cultural exchange and fusion. In the meantime, as MacDonald (2016) rightfully asserts, this census practice had for decades rendered the Latino statistically invisible. In research it was impossible to accurately document the status of Latinos or to assess their general condition.

While Latino counts are possible today, the counts continue to muddle the two categories of race and ethnicity when it comes to Latinos and often mislead the exact counts between the two. In other instances, there is confusion when double counting, with the White category sometimes containing the count for Hispanics, but then reappearing differently in subsequent data analyses for the same group. The obvious solution is to only have one census question, counting the Hispanic as its own racial category, as a demographic statistic without worrying about racial delineations within an already-mixed racial category. To this day, Census does not count Latinos as a unique category of people, fully unaligned with how other racial groups are counted and inconsistent with how the *Cisneros* decision of 1970 identifies Latinos.

Notes

1. Thomas Carter (1970) chronicles the Mexican American as neglected in the American educational process. Among Puerto Ricans, Clarence Senior (1961) calls them "Strangers then Neighbors" and Oscar Handlin (1959) labels them "The Newcomers," up to then virtually unknown.
2. Mora, 2014.
3. Orfield, et al., 2016.

4. Data recompiled by author, originally taken from latest NCES figures from each reported (2017) district total.
5. Taken from 1970 decennial census.
6. Data taken from CGCS website (November 2017): www.cgcs.org/
7. The Peninsular War (1808–1814) was when Spain was partially occupied by French forces and the country was ruled by Joseph Bonaparte (Joseph I).
8. O'Sullivan, 1845.
9. Taken from Department of State Website, https://2001-2009.state.gov/r/pa/ho/time/gp/17661.htm
10. Ibid.
11. The Chinese Exclusion Act of 1882, extended in 1892 by the Geary Act, was partly amended by the Magnuson Act in 1943 and then more fully repealed by the Immigration and Naturalization (INS) Act of 1965 which overruled previous exclusions, including the National Origins Formula.
12. Puerto Ricans in the island and the other colonies went through a different experience, but nonetheless subjugated.
13. MacDonald & Guzmán, 2017.
14. Leonard Pitt, 1966.
15. Blauner, 1972.
16. Donato & Hanson, 2012.
17. Gómez, 2018.
18. Hispanics, primarily Mexican Americans, accounted for 1-in-5 lynchings among over 4,000 lynchings in America.
19. Orozco, 2009. Note that the "dog" was the animal of the dead in ancient Mexico. When ancient inhabitants of Anahuac burned a corpse they killed a red dog and laid it beside the dead body.
20. There were rare exceptions to this generalization such as among upper-class *Hispanos* that held property and political power in the territories of New Mexico and Colorado.
21. Analysis of census data from 1770 to the present shows that African Americans have gone from 21% of the nation's total in 1780 to around 13% today. By contrast, Latinos went from barely 1% in 1850 to nearly 20% today (counting Puerto Rico) and growing quite rapidly.
22. See Morales Carrión (Ed.), 1983, as one of the better known analysts on the political and cultural history of Puerto Rico.
23. The PBS documentary by Rubén Martínez, *When Worlds Collide*, documents part of this story.
24. Tainos were a branch of a larger group of Arawak Indian tribes extending to South America. The Tainos spoke an Arawak-Indian dialect.
25. *La Malinche* initially served as interpreter and intermediary to Cortés.
26. Thornton, 1998. [The first slaves were brought into Hispaniola in 1502, with the first major slave ship from Africa entering the Caribbean in 1517. The first slaves to enter the United States occurred in 1519, two years later when accompanying Ponce de León when exploring Florida.]
27. This resulted in several thousand deaths and injuries as well as considerable economic loss.

28. In addition to Spain, Equatorial Guinea is the only sovereign state in the continent of Africa that is fully Spanish-speaking, though not of Spanish or Latino ancestry. It is a rich country with a population around 1.2 million (2015), but with unevenly distributed wealth.
29. As an example, the deprecatory term "Gachupin" is known in many parts of Latin America, especially Mexico, in reference against the Spaniard.
30. The country in Africa, included elsewhere, is not accounted here. It speaks Spanish but has no Latino origins.
31. San Juan is the oldest city in the United States, initially called Ciudad de Puerto Rico. The city was founded in 1509, just before Ponce de León, one of Columbus' lieutenants, was appointed as the first island governor in 1511.
32. Kanellos, 1997, p. 40.
33. He was also the first bishop appointed to the New World. Though the first church in the New World was established in the Dominican Republic, Puerto Rico hosted the first school with a Catholic bishop.
34. Weber, p. 401.
35. Thomas, 2010.
36. The McGuffey graded primers series (grades 1–6) were sold between 1836 and 1960. Available at: https://en.wikipedia.org/wiki/McGuffey_Readers
37. San Juan is truly the oldest American city, though not part of the U.S. until 1898.
38. Known as California today, Baja and Alta California were separated by the U.S.-Mexico border.
39. MacDonald, 2004, pp. 11–13.
40. Taken from map of California Missions (2014), distributed by East View Press, Minneapolis, MN. www.eastviewpress.com
41. Due to Oñate's despotism and cruelty against the Pueblo Indians, a revolt occurred in 1680 where over 400 colonists were massacred and the Spanish were pushed back. It was not until after the *Reconquista*, as it was called in 1692, that a second wave likely resulted in the early 1700s.
42. Weber, 1992.
43. MacDonald, 2004, p. 14.
44. Thomas, 2010.
45. Interesting is the fact that the territory changed hands between Spain and France several times. Just before the purchase, it belonged to Spain until Napoleon wrestled it away in 1800 only to then sell it in 1803 to the U.S. Under Spanish rule, some 200,000 Mexican settlers had moved into the territory just decades earlier (Hugh Thomas, 2010).
46. Florida did not become a state until 1845.
47. From the Mexican perspective, lost territory from the Mexican-American War in 1848 was the near equivalent of half the entire country of Mexico.
48. The Mexican territory was quite vast. It included the present-day states of California, Arizona, New Mexico, Texas, Nevada, Utah and parts of Wyoming, Colorado, Kansas and Oklahoma. This is equivalent to one-third the continental U.S.
49. By 1879, the federal government had established 145 schools for Native Americans, with 63 of them as boarding schools. By 1891 Native American education was primarily under

federal control, with the exception of missionary schools and others that were privately religious schools.
50. Tyack, p. 23.
51. O'Donnell, p. 137.
52. Ibid.
53. Ibid.
54. Tyack, p. 66.
55. Ibid.
56. Tyack, p. 72.
57. Taken from interview with Luis Cruz, former principal, 2016.
58. Ibid.
59. Taken from interview with Samuel Betances, professor emeritus and national speaker, 2016.
60. Valencia, 2008, p. 9.
61. Foley, 2005.
62. Reynolds, p. 9.
63. California Superintendent of Public Instruction, archives, 1869.
64. San Miguel & Valencia, 1998.
65. Rangel & Alcalá, 1972.
66. Montoya, 2001, p. 20.
67. Carter, p. 10.
68. Ibid.
69. Donato & Hanson, 2012.
70. Ibid.
71. Howard, 2015.
72. Woodson, 1988.
73. Spring, 1997, p. 1.
74. Ibid., p. 1.
75. While nearly all land allocated during the war was later restored to pre-war owners, some Black land ownership did increase through these programs in states like Mississippi during the 19th century.
76. During this period there were always the exceptions at some public university in the territories of New Mexico or Arizona and at the normal training schools in Texas or California, for example, but these were often the exceptions and primarily for the upper class.
77. Verified by U.S. census archival data; also taken from Sol Cohen, *Education in the U.S.*, 1974, p. xxcii (book 1).
78. Census counts report close to 8 million Blacks in 1900, though Du Bois talks about 9 million Blacks in one article, but then references 10 million Blacks in *The Souls of Black Folk* (1903).
79. Based on census data and including Puerto Rico in the count. The total nonwhite population in 1900 would have otherwise been closer to 14%.
80. Handlin, 1982; Molina, 2014.
81. San Miguel & Valencia, 1998, pp. 353 and 355.
82. Ibid., p. 355.

83. Myrdal in foreword to *Dark Ghetto* (1965) by Kenneth Clark, p. ix.
84. The name of the Island was changed to "Porto Rico" at the Treaty of Paris in 1898. It was later changed back to "Puerto Rico" by a joint resolution of Congress in 1931.
85. Kal Wagenheim, p. 167.
86. MacDonald, 2004, p. 93.
87. Negrón De Montilla, 1975.
88. Rodríguez-Arroyo, 2013, p 5.
89. Coloma, p. 27.
90. *Ibid.*, p. 57.
91. Coloma, 2004.
92. Carter G. Woodson quote, https://www.goodreads.com/quotes/156111-when-you-control-a-man-s-thinking-you-do-not-have
93. Puerto Rico was first enumerated by the Census Bureau in 1899, then became part of the U.S. census counts since 1910 for each decennial, but with counts kept separate from the rest of the country.
94. Latest population estimates from 2018 indicate a population of 3.2 million.
95. Woofter, 1933.
96. Foley, 2005, pp. 59–60.
97. *Ibid.*
98. Taken from report by the U.S. Commission on Civil Rights, *Counting the forgotten*, 1974.

· 5 ·

A TRIPARTITE SYSTEM

> At first people refuse to believe that a strange new thing can be done.
> Then they begin to hope it can be done. Then they see it can be done.
> Then it is done and all the world wonders why it was not done centuries ago.
> — Edward Everett Hale

DURING THE *PLESSY* ERA OF SEGREGATION, EDUCATION HAD BECOME FULLY LINKED TO THE COUNTRY'S MOST CRITICAL SOCIAL PROBLEMS, NAMELY RACE AND OPPRESSION. While a large majority of White students were in early elementary school by 1900, Blacks had been pushed out of most schools, with barely one-third receiving an elementary education by 1900.[1] For Hispanics, data were equally grim, with barely one-fourth entering grammar school at the time, and with only handfuls continuing onto public high school.[2] Graver still was the fact that nearly half the schools that served Hispanics were backed by church or charitable funds, as a result of local districts unwilling to allow them entry into the "American" educational mainstream.

Polarization During *Plessy*

BY THE START OF THE 20TH CENTURY, IDEOLOGY HAD STRONGLY OVERTAKEN THE CURRICULUM, AS RACE AND EDUCATION HAD COMBINED. FOR LATINOS, JIM CROW HAD ALSO MIXED WITH NEW BRANDS OF AMERICAN EXPANSIONISM, JINGOISM, AND

IMPERIALISM. Power and control had reached new heights from which progressives and educators could hardly escape.³ While one set of issues pertained to Blacks and another to Latinos, both groups struggled deeply with lack of educational progress, as these were tied to race. Education no longer dodged issues around race, as open season to hunt was now granted through *Plessy* and education had become another tool for subjugation.

While claiming to operate at arm's length, educational policymakers let Jim Crowism imbue school policies throughout the public schools. Issues around the "negro problem" and the racial tone of Manifest Destiny and imperialism had permeated so much daily talk among the populace that it led Du Bois to query in 1903 how it felt to be "a problem" inside the "soul." There is no question about the similarity in the predicament of the African American and the Latino when compared to the Brown man in the Philippines or *trigueño or Negro* (colored) in Puerto Rico or stateside. All were products of oppression and massive miseducation. For the colonies as well as for persons of color back home, all wrestled with the "problem" posed by Du Bois on the racialization of differences *within* and *outside* America's national borders. Color had become the issue of the day. It had transformed into the dominant feature of policy and culture throughout the first half of the 20th century.

In part, this is what then President Teddy Roosevelt referenced as his wish at the turn of the 19th century: to eradicate the concept of the hyphenated-American, where all would become one American.⁴ This may be feasible for the European immigrant, but neither Latinos nor Blacks were ever a hyphenated group, as they were never truly in the "melting pot."⁵ The stigma of color could never mix with White, most especially when mixture through marriage was outlawed, as even a drop of Black blood was miscegenation and illegal with Whites. Legally considered White, Mexican intermarriage with Whites was permitted, albeit with disdain and also less common with the population of White women increasing in the West. With *Plessy* continuing its stranglehold with Jim Crow laws, minority groups could not be free, as there was little distinction between Black, Brown or Indian blood.

Given the large growth of immigrants at the turn of the century, the dominant belief had been that any youngster could rise above the most humble origins and make good on the nation's promise of opportunity for all. While some educators may have wanted the Horatio Alger story turn toward educational success for everyone, the premise was possible if the student was White.

Disappointingly during this tumult, neither key educational leaders of the period nor public officials would support innovative alternatives, as *Plessy* directives were quite formidable and non-reversible. Even reformers were afraid to breach the subject of inequality or racism. These attitudes fostered silent dissent, when not fully consenting. In the meantime, racial minorities were left out. As a result, educational progress came to a near halt. What was accomplished was due to the sheer doggedness of a small but growing middle class of Black and Latino leaders, barely if at all. During this era, Latinos lacked advocates with sufficient social capital, political will, or economic means. The most viable option was the avenue through the courts. It was but a small band of Mexican American activists, many of whom had served in World War I that demanded their rights as citizens. They founded the League of United Latin American Citizens (LULAC) which opened its doors in 1929.[6]

With immigration in full swing, equality of opportunity for Latinos meant that only a small number of students would qualify for "academic" education, as "the great majority would get vocational or industrial training."[7] To have done otherwise would have been considered "unfair" and "antidemocratic" for students of color, despite citizenship. This proved hard to accept, as districts were continually gerrymandered not to provide educational services for the non-acceptable, albeit a qualified Latino and minority student. There arose little distinction between *de facto* and *de jure* exclusion, or between one racial group and another.

For the Mexican American it was a time when Jim Crow laws were integrated into the Mexican community.[8] Traditional dual systems of separate had transformed into *tripartite* systems by the early 1900s, as Latino children were forced into Mexican schools. Prior to *Plessy* it had been the "practice." Post-*Plessy*, tripartite education had become universally common during the first third of the century, albeit variable by state and within states. In some sectors of California, for example, Mexicans were placed in Black schools. Yet legally, only Texas had full *de jure* segregation of Blacks in their constitution.

Conditions in Texas were the poorest among the Southwestern states, stemming from its racist orientation as a former slave state to all people of color. Barely half the Mexican American, school-aged children were attending school in Texas in the early 1900s. According to the data by Robert Margo (1990), Hispanic statistics were even grimmer than for African Americans.[9] In reality, compulsory attendance laws were a "dead letter" for racial groups. As agricultural needs trumped the rights of children, school officials looked the other way, rarely enforcing child labor laws when powerful farmers needed their labor. The pipelines to higher levels of schooling were largely blocked. As MacDonald (2016) shows, White public high schools refused to enroll more than a handful of Mexicans, if at all during that era. Ironically, because of their racial category as White, the federal government did not provide the equivalent of a Historically-Black school for Mexican Americans. Catholic Colleges filled this gap for the few that could muster the financial resources. Once again, Latinos got hit from both sides, too colored to be White, and too White to be counted as Black, thus receiving the benefits of neither.

The low level of secondary school enrollment is revealed in California, where more than 3,000 children of Mexican descent were enrolled in Imperial County elementary schools in 1926—over one-third of the entire K–12 total—but with only 51 students (4% of the total enrollment) in high school.[10] Similarly in Ontario County, California, with 10% of the total K–12 enrollment being Mexican American, only two students of Mexican descent out of a class of 293 graduated from high school in 1930.[11]

California's poor showing for high school enrollment and graduation among Mexican American youth was echoed in the adjoining states of the Southwest. Careful review of state-by-state data revealed that little had changed by the decades of the 1930s and 1940s, as comparable rates continued almost unabated from the turn of the century,[12] even after New Mexico and Arizona became states in 1912. It was the role of Catholic schools that permitted a slim margin of students in high school to attain leadership status that later became critical.

Pedagogically, evidence was overwhelming that segregation did not work well enough to assure comparable facilities or services in racial schools. Despite evidence to the contrary, anti-pedagogical practices continued undeterred and for the most part unchallenged for the Mexican American. It was expected that schools were to operate separate systems for the acculturation of the Mexican American, yet research from that period indicates that Spanish-speaking children in "mixed" classrooms progressed in English language acquisition much more rapidly than those in segregated classes. These studies did not matter, as segregation continued unfazed.[13] In 1946, the first Regional Conference for the Education of the Spanish-speaking People in the Southwest proclaimed that Mexican children learned English best when in constant contact with English-speaking peers. If acculturation was the answer, the process took longer under segregation, but such knowledge had little effect in changing practices for the next twenty years.[14] It was not what research indicated, but what policy dictated, as the latter superseded facts.

Maybe this was the point, since "The bulk of professional opinion during this period was stuck on the side of segregation."[15] These issues had little to do with reason and everything to do with race. Carey McWilliams (1968) documented that as late as 1947 "Segregation was the rule whenever Mexicans resided in sizeable colonies," lasting from "cradle to grave." [16] As expertly testified as attorney and later as State Commissioner of Immigration and Housing for the State of California, and then as researcher and author, this was a practice that was truly "hard to change."

Added to the isolation of Mexican American students from available high schools that would accept them, grade retention was common. By the time many Mexican Americans had reached eighth grade, many had already celebrated sixteen years of age.[17] Unquestionably, grade retention was independent from academic progress.

As a result, few Mexican Americans were well prepared for work above working class wages, even after going through the schooling process, except for the lucky few and some of the best and brightest, for little learning was taking place in the Mexican school. In his seminal book on Mexican American education Thomas Carter (1970) pointed out, "School programs for Mexican American children by the 1930s emphasized vocational and manual arts training. The learning of English and cleanliness, and the adoption of such American 'core values' as thrift and punctuality were the themes of the day" affirming standard practices.[18] None of this related to academic learning or the basic 3Rs.

Reform by its many names, including the Progressive Movement, was more about strengthening the workforce and, at times, expanding curricular offerings and approaches, than about outreach and basic education for students of color. It was also about maintaining people in their place. Most reform efforts, and there were many, kept most of the strong and vibrant Latino workers in manual labor.[19] The assumption here was that these youngsters lacked the aptitude to do well in school. As victims, they were to blame.

While these views were as regressive and anti-democratic as they were racist and exclusive, progressive workers kept at bay. In retrospect, it is ironic as it is disheartening to know that even the progressive movement during this period was progressive almost exclusively along class, gender, and racial lines. After WWII, when the nation went back to work, so-called progressives continued to lose their opportunity to maximize well-educated people or for growing any of the professions from the ranks of the poor or the disenfranchised. This was shameful as it was exasperating, with all but a handful of progressives suffering from an elusive backbone in the struggle.

Schooling in America remained flawed, despite being touted as the solution to the nation's race problem, as proclaimed by policymakers at the time. It was a stance most ardently voiced by White supremacists and flamboyant politicians. The reality was that in American schools it was virtually impossible for the narrative of racialization not to penetrate the classroom, tarnishing the learning process. Among racial groups, education had undoubtedly transformed into domination through domestication, as a total barrier for minority achievement.[20] In the new century, saturated with segregation and animosity, Brown and nonwhite had become another form of Black, as all minorities fell into the same exclusionary, non-melting pot. For Latinos, despite parochial education, educational progress had otherwise been stunted.

As America never settled the race issue before going abroad to conquer other races and nations, its policies fell into a state of continual conflict and contradiction. By bringing other races into America—a seemingly ironic twist—the country had compounded its dilemma of race. One wonders why this was the case, except to ensure a subservient class. Yet, for any society, keeping increasingly large numbers of people ill-educated runs counter to the logic of good health for any republic.

With contrary constructs intersecting at every turn, favorable conditions were botched the first half of the 1900s in education. *The Washington Post* summed up part of this racial divide and confusion by quoting a policymaker about the Filipinos in 1902 as, "Little, savage negritos, living away up in the mountain forests. They have black skins and their hair is kinky as that of an African."[21] This depiction seemed to dominate the American mind under *Plessy*. Latinos, like Filipinos, were viewed similarly. They were just another version of Black. *Bottom line:* The template for racial inferiority had become virtually indistinguishable between black and brown and red and yellow, as colors also became racially designated. As most were brought into the Union by force, race remained unresolved and color lines continued to be problematic.

Educational Contradictions

DURING THIS PERIOD, THE PURPOSES OF EDUCATION LAID BARE. LINKED WITH RACE, EDUCATION HAD BECOME MERELY UTILITARIAN. That is why prominent politicians and business leaders made such a big issue regarding the differences between the educational approaches of two prominent Black men: W.E.B. Du Bois and Booker T. Washington. Why was this important? And why did they promote a debate between these two statesmen? While differences between these intellectuals stemmed from the 1895 Atlanta Compromise debates,* the issue was about the purposes of education and who should be educated. This created heated controversies during the first half of the next century. Du Bois favored high academic achievement and the education of at least a talented tenth of the Black community, whereas Washington focused more strongly on getting Blacks employed by gaining basic skills to further their entry into the trade industries for upward mobility and higher wages. Washington was highly utilitarian and practical in his approach which focused on the immediate needs of workers, while Du Bois focused on the long-term benefits of education and what it meant socially.

Upon further examination, the controversy seemed clearer and at a more sinister level for Whites than at first evident. White elites downplayed the salient points where both scholars agreed, that of upholding *self-determination, self-reliance* and *liberty*. Instead, they preferred that two prominent Black men quibble about the "type" of education that would best benefit the Black youngster, rather than the "right" to an education "regardless" of type. For the White businessman, opportunity was not the issue, so it was downplayed. The glaring point was that despite differences between the two men and their followers that led some to uphold the Niagara Movement of 1905 that railed against accommodation and conciliation by Blacks,[22] their bond of commonality from 1895 was firmly and roundly dismissed by the White elite, as White bias was about creating divisions, not about forging bonds. Further on point, White bias was more about assuring that Black minorities would keep in their place, subservient not illustrious. The issue centered on keeping Blacks away from ever competing in the upper rungs of society, as they were never to be elevated to positions where they could gain the capacity to question, for God forbid they would overturn the rigidly established boundaries of a White-dominant society.

It is powerful to retrospectively note that Du Bois and Washington were quite ahead of their time and that their controversy was not just a "Black" controversy after all, as it was more deeply philosophical and also quite pragmatic. Embedded in their stance was that which became a controversy that

---

* The compromise was that Blacks would work and submit to White political rule, with less emphasis on integration and social justice, while Southern Whites would guarantee that Blacks would receive basic education and due process of law. Northerners would work at funding Black charities. This was subsequently subverted by *Plessy*.

later spread across the entire spectrum of the educational establishment. Pure and simple, the debate was about "utilitarian" education as different from "knowledge" education. This juxtaposed education that was to maintain the status quo and oppression as different from liberation and leadership, as Du Bois and his followers advocated. As such, both men were much ahead of their time. It was about whether new workers should be prepared for a trade rather than equipping them with strong intellectual faculties and high virtues to engage with the ruling class, and sufficiently equipped to make decisions in board rooms and assert leadership in policy formation.

Not so ironically, related debates continue with similar resonance today, including discussions concerning the role of education for the preparation of minority students before they enter the workforce versus a more practical and vocational education for children of color. As Whites favored utilitarian, technical, and manual skills, they supported Booker T. Washington and promoted his brand of education.

Not long afterwards, leaders like historian Carter G. Woodson and the poet Langston Hughes addressed issues of diversity and the common themes among black and brown, but from the viewpoint of forming common bonds. These issues were also of little interest to dominant White majorities. Both Woodson and Hughes were multilingual with extensive overseas experience with disenfranchised racial groups, the former with Filipinos and the latter with Mexicans.[23] They were not highly successful in gaining needed support in bringing diverse racial communities together, but not for lack of effort. It is likely the educational community would be leaps ahead of today's status quo on these issue should they have been successful in engaging the country on diversity issues half a century ago. The White establishment and its educators were too narrowly focused around issues of domination and control that they could not think ahead about more encompassing issues and posterity.

Unabated Segregation

WITH *PLESSY* IN FULL BLOOM, THE COUNTRY NOW HAD LEGAL PERMISSION TO CONTINUE HIGHLY SEGREGATED AND FULLY DIVIDED. SIDELINE ISSUES WERE DISMISSED. The purpose was to prepare a brute workforce, a cotton gin of the human kind as one reporter coined it. As per the times, no agency or department from municipal, state, or federal government dared assist the Mexican American community in their struggles as they were unimportant distractions, neither for Blacks nor for other racial groups until partial relief from social efforts like President Franklin D. Roosevelt's New Deal programs. This was expanded somewhat later such as the Works Progress Administration (WPA) that was a works program for the unemployed.

Latinos were stripped from full participation in schooling as they had been barred from certain labor positions. In effect, they were to join Blacks as another arm for the dominant society to also plunder. As a result, Latinos leaders received no help from local government and were forced to seek assistance through alternate means, including international channels. They sought action through complicated diplomatic means via consulate offices to fight for their rights by way of the State Department, akin to foreign nationals when seeking criminal justice.[24] The reliance on consuls provided minimal relief for educational access in a rather limited and localized manner, and only for particular cases, not at-large.[25] For these cases, it only allowed certain Mexican children to attend segregated White institutions, most especially high schools, with the rest remaining in highly-isolated Mexican schools. Unsurprisingly, diplomacy only redressed the needs of a very limited number, and all too often the more well-to-do.

Over time, demographics proved important. Mexican nationals crossed the border and increased dramatically during the first third of the 20th century. This was partly due to the fact that borders were quite porous at the time, as workers went where there was need, with each border community benefitting their respective country. With the Mexican Revolution in 1910, many nationals fled to the U.S. the following two decades.

The Mexican flow increased even more during the second decade *after* the 1910 revolution, when economic conditions fully worsened in Mexico. The need for agricultural workers rewarded immigrant labor by offering better wages on the U.S. side of the border for painstaking jobs American workers were unwilling to take. Mexicans, prompted by both sides, took full advantage and fluctuated as needed. A difficult, but still reinforcing factor about immigration emerged from the industrial sector, where the hardest and most dangerous jobs were taken by Mexican Americans and Blacks.[26]

Yet, with the Great Depression came the Mexican Repatriation of many Mexicans from 1929 through 1939, where about half a million Mexican nationals as well as American citizens were sent back to Mexico.[27] Hatred against Mexicans had intensified as it spread further during this period onward, with many anti-Mexican movements developing across the Southwest, most especially among border towns.[28]

Initially, the rapid development of the cotton industry, for example, had attracted Mexicans to Texas, with the Latino hub feeding the industrial Midwest through the harvest of agricultural products and the meat industry. As Vargas (1993) details, Mexicans were also replacing Black workers in the Southwest because Blacks were no longer satisfied with agrarian labor. Their inclination was to leave the fields altogether in the Great Migration north. Mexicans then took the jobs many Blacks began deserting. Over time, however, "repressive working conditions and low wages eventually motivated tens of thousands to seek alternative work in the Midwest."[29]

Later, the "Bracero Program" was introduced as a war-related program to address the labor shortage caused by World War II. The Mexican Farm Labor Agreement was established with the Mexican government in 1942. The Act made official what was already occurring, except that it was then "legally" possible for more single male Mexican workers to come, as the program inadvertently bypassed strict INS restrictions. This was ironic, and in contrast to earlier deportation, as it brought more Mexican workers than ever into the U.S. continent. Interestingly, Puerto Rican workers were not invited because they were too costly. As U.S. citizens now, Puerto Rican workers could demand higher wages.

Traditional thinking was that the Mexican (or any other Latino) came to the U.S. mainly to take advantage of American wages and that this has been a one-way process. To the contrary, American firms incentivized workers to work with government consent and thus cross the border. Between the "savagery of Mexico" and "tyranny of the North," some chose *El Norte* as the lesser evil, enduring dangerous voyages to the North and tackling a risky future.[30] These were the options Mexican workers had to balance daily to make ends meet.

With *Plessy in vogue, caste rules were expected to be known by everyone, as they had presumably become obvious and clear to the Mexican American.* The rule of law had expanded as common knowledge on how communities were to behave and accordingly respond. Nomenclature was that schools with "Spanish or Mexican" children, for example, were called "Mexican," whereas White children were simply known as "American." As schools were identified by type of student, labels denoting race sufficed to denote the rank and importance for any school under review.[31]

Mexican schools were highly monolithic, as they were also significantly different from segregated Black schools. Added to the horrors of segregation, Mexican schools had definitive *disadvantages* to the segregated Black schools. For example, nearly all teachers were African American in Black-segregated schools, with many instructors holding distinguished credentials because employment for credentialed Blacks was scarce, with school-teaching as an alternative that was prestigious and difficult to attain. As a result, Black teachers had high credentials, as they were also strongly committed to teach Black children. These teachers came to be known as the "warrior teachers," knowing full well how powerfully strong their impact would be on younger generations.

By contrast at the Mexican school, hardly any teacher was Mexican American. Nearly all teachers were White, and often poorly credentialed and seldom fond of Latinos. They also represented the lower rung of the teaching ladder, last resort for employment and poorly motivated to teach. In addition, facilities and resources at the school were deplorable, as there was no pressure to ensure "legally" separate but equal facilities under the law for the Mexican school. These schools operated under the radar. This was in stark contrast to Black-segregated schools that faced episodic inspections to comply with the so-called "equality" mandate of *Plessy*, even if irregular and seldom rigorous.

For the most part, Mexican schools were dilapidated, one-room schoolhouses, outside the scrutiny; hence, absent from regulators. This meant that the same education for a segregated Black child would seldom be the same education for a segregated Latino child. Beyond the number of years completed against age for the Mexican American student and the appalling conditions of school buildings, the quality of instruction for Latino youngsters was considerably lower.

In reference to Mexican schools, it is ironic to quote President Lyndon Johnson, as former schoolteacher and principal at a Mexican School in Cotulla, Texas in 1928 as an exception to the rule. Yet, it was years later that he reflected on the deplorable conditions at his school in a public statement in 1966:

> I have come back to Cotulla this afternoon, not just because this school is part of my past, but because this school is a part of America's future … I was working my way through the San Marcos Teachers College … In those days [1928] … We had no lunch facilities. We had no school buses. We had very little money for educating people of this community. We did not have money to buy our playground equipment, our volleyballs, [and] our softball bats … I took my first month's salary and invested in those things for my children. About the only thing we had an ample supply of was determination … I worked as principal … I worked as a playground supervisor. I coached the boys' baseball team. I was a debate coach … In my spare time, sometimes I acted as assistant janitor.[32]

As referenced, while no laws allowed for or required separate schools for Mexicans based on race, the vast majority of districts segregated Mexicans into separate and highly under-resourced schools and classrooms as a matter of course.[33] The practice of segregating Mexican American pupils was conducted outside legal structures. These measures ensured segregation was about changing district boundaries and maintaining "best" schools far away from *colonias*. Insistence was that Mexicans attend local, Mexican-dominant schools for the purposes of language instruction. It was these conditions that gave further rise to the Mexican school and segregated facilities.

De facto segregation overtook when *de jure* was not legally permissible. Various practices fed the conditions for *de facto* segregation, as White supremacy felt it necessary. Here the term *de facto* may be misleading, as documentation from the period clearly indicates that non-legal means were utilized to segregate schools through extralegal processes. While common in practice, this was seldom reported and less often documented. Machinations of this type were all too common, where even outlandish means of isolation were sanctioned to keep Mexican children away from Whites so as to ensure social distance.[34] Otherwise, Anglo parents would object and force alternative means for their children not to attend classes with "dirty" and "diseased" Mexicans.[35]

Through "multiple ruses and ploys," justification to separate Mexican American students from Anglo children was based on deeply-ingrained beliefs that Hispanic children belonged to a "different class," rationalized by a racial ideology of superiority.[36] As basic levels of education were viewed to be necessary for the workforce, higher access was restricted so that there was no need for higher skills at the secondary or collegiate level for the Mexican American child. The practice ensured non-competition with a sector of society ultimately reserved for the Anglo. The educational system not only bifurcated how different children accessed education, but also focused on outcomes that would ensure non-egalitarian results. These actions were not by fiat, but ill-intended by willful design.

Second-Class Schooling

GOING BACK TO *PLESSY*, AS DOCUMENTED, BASIC SCHOOLING WAS HIGHLY LIMITED FOR THE MEXICAN STUDENT DURING THIS PERIOD. EDUCATIONAL ACCESS HAD OCCURRED IN THE "CONTEXT OF INCREASING SOCIETAL DISCRIMINATION SO AS TO ENSURE THE GENERAL SUBSERVIENCE OF MEXICAN AMERICANS."[37] This meant schools had continued as segregated and fully unequal. In actuality, it was as if the Southwest was shielded and unaffected from what happened elsewhere. By the 1930s, "the educational template for Mexican American students was one of forced, widespread segregation, and inferior schooling."[38]

Three major groups of Mexican American students were denied full access to public education during the first half of the twentieth century. These were (1) high school students, (2) postsecondary students, and (3) migrant children.[39] Access to schooling, even at the lower grades, was also highly limited, with waiting lists.

More specifically, the enrollment of Mexican-origin, school-age children between the ages of 5 and 17 ranged from a low of 17% in Texas to about 50% in the Territory of New Mexico in 1900. Three decades later in 1930, the picture had changed moderately, but not significantly. The state with the lowest percentage was Texas, with 50%; and the highest was New Mexico, with about 74%.[40] These enrollment statistics began to slowly improve two decades later, but primarily after *Brown*, from a national average of 53% in 1942 to 79% by 1960.[41] Relative to other groups across the country, these were still the most deplorable statistics to start the sixties.

As earlier mentioned, all states had compulsory school attendance after Mississippi became the last state to enact compulsory attendance laws in 1918. While restrictions in many of the schools segregated the Mexican child away from mainstream students, enforced attendance aided Latino adolescents because it blocked authorities from otherwise keeping them from education. Regulations were more strictly enforced in the Midwest, where Latinos were now migrating after the First World War.

Though the plain states were with many fewer Mexican families at the turn of the century, migratory patterns to the Midwest began occurring soon after the war. Some initially came with the migrant agricultural stream and then stayed in the Midwest. Others came as first-generation workers directly from Mexico to work on the railroads in Kansas, Illinois and Indiana. This was also the case for others coming to work in various industries such as steel and meatpacking. By midcentury, especially after the Second World War, additional others had come as second- and third-generation Mexican families from the Southwest.

In navigating much of the data on Mexican American students during the *Plessy* period it is important to note that not all Mexican Americans did poorly in school. In period research, Manuel (1930) notes that in the late

1920s, approximately 10 percent of the Mexican American, school-aged population in Texas was completing high school.[42] Though his figures represent the most favorable estimates in the literature and only for certain districts, they indicated favorably changing trends. Research from Grebler, Moore & Guzmán (1970), however, indicate more accurately that even as late as 1950 barely 10% of Mexican men had completed high school, with California ranking highest in completion rates and Texas ranking lowest in the Southwest. Catholic and private schools performed at slightly higher academic levels than the public schools, but with many fewer students, as most parents could not afford private schools. Also, most of these schools were at the primary level.[43]

In higher education, several studies indicate that the number of Mexican American students attending college even by mid-20th century was extremely small, much under one percent.[44] Disappointingly, by the early sixties, advancement into higher education was still severely limited, with the low number of Mexican Americans that had graduated from high school as the major factor blocking college entrance. Though eighth grade was the highest level reached by most, many were unable to reach upper elementary grades during the first four decades of the twentieth century.

Historian Victoria M. MacDonald (2016) describes how these discriminatory actions created a "fractured pipeline" of postsecondary access for Latinos. As she well documents, an impactful negative consequence of this truncated education resulted in few Mexican American veterans eligible to take advantage of the college portion of the GI Bill. As it turned out, early Latino college students were pioneers during the period 1848 to 1960, when students from middle- and working-class families had just started entering college.[45] In contrast, the Black experience saw a less fractured pipeline, albeit fully segregated, but with the option of attending segregated high schools and then continuing onto HBCUs.

For Mexican Americans, the period 1920 to 1960 was an era of intense segregation and discrimination throughout the Southwest, accompanied by much violence. Texas, as previously mentioned, officially established its first Mexican school in 1902, but by 1930 "90% of South Texas schools were segregated." By the 1940s, "separate schools for Mexican Americans existed in at least 122 school districts in 59 represented counties" across the State.[46]

Grace Stanley (1920), an educator writing about her experiences in California wrote about the issues facing public schools and local community attitudes toward the Mexican American. Among her observations, she pointedly depicted the following:

> One of the first demands made from a community in which there is a large Mexican population is for a separate school. The reasons advanced for this demand are generally from a selfish viewpoint of the English-speaking public and are based largely on the theory that the Mexican is a menace to the health and morals of the community.[47]

In California, in a study of 31 school districts, as conducted by Ward Leis (1931), more than 80% of these districts were highly segregated, with many of the remaining 20% maintaining segregated practices through special Mexican classrooms and Americanization programs.[48] Leis also documented that school officials routinely segregated Mexican American students for the first several grades, and further added that while official segregation ended after third grade, "excessive dropping out by these children was a large factor in [later] discontinuing segregation,"[49] with other instances of a truncated system.

As was the case quite often, community elders or mothers representing the PTA would approach the school district with a petition to create a "Mexican school" so as to separate children of other races from their White children, claiming it was instructionally-driven. More than likely, the Mexican school also provided services to youngsters from other racial groups. But this approach merely acquiesced to the White public and kept these children far away from the mainstream.

By the mid-1930s, based on these and related data, both Texas and California were operating more segregated schools for Mexican Americans than for Blacks. This was partly because of the larger numbers of Mexican Americans, but also because segregation was just as rampant for either group. A decade later (1945), the most segregated group in the entire State of California continued to be the Mexican American student.[50] The case for other states like Arizona, Nevada and New Mexico, were not altogether different as Donato (1997), Valencia (2005), and others have documented.

This was undoubtedly the context for California during the period when the *Méndez* (1947) case was tried in Orange County, a small farming community in the southern part of California and settled in the Circuit Court of California, as earlier cited. The decision challenged Mexican "remedial" schools, becoming "the most significant case involving Mexican Americans and desegregation."[51] It hailed California as the first state to desegregate its schools after *Plessy*, as it also opened the gates for *Brown* a decade later.

The question as to why this was occurring at this time is important to understand. It is crucial to recall that *all* public facilities were closed to racial minorities. This included parks and recreational areas as well as other public facilities such as swimming pools, restaurants, theatres, even restrooms and drinking fountains. The indelible outcome was that all racial minorities in the U.S. at one time or another experienced exclusion from formal schooling.[52] It must be noted, however, this was applied rather differentially from state to state and from one locality to another. While the pattern was similar, it was apportioned unevenly, quite often colored by the history and context of the community, with the Deep South and the Southwest serving as the epitome of extreme subjugation.

These trends led to great fear, even paranoia, and justifiably so. This kept Mexican Americans huddled together, in racial isolation for self-protection. Many towns were comprised of two distinct worlds, though side by side, one for Anglos and the other for Mexican Americans. Assignment for the latter was primarily based on name and complexion, living defensively in *colonias*. It should be noted that such restrictive covenants and other extra-legal means had kept Mexicans in the most segregated and worse sectors of their community decades earlier, but the new fear of deportation merely re-strengthened isolation once again as it also led to a northern migration.

Evidence that Mexican American students were experiencing massive school inequalities surged to the extent that organizations were formed to defend its rights such as LULAC, as previously mentioned. As the quality of schools had remained uneven and inferior during this period, documentation by LULAC showed considerably greater disparity among schools attended by Mexican students as compared to Anglo students in the center of Texas.[53] Deplorable conditions had propelled the organization to advocate and accept major court battles. Gathered data from court cases included teacher-student ratios, facilities costs, teacher pay, and other funding allocations such as disproportionate school resources.

A large national study sponsored by the Office of Education known as the Reynolds study (1933) concluded that Mexican American students were attending highly inferior schools and posted the following results: (1) most Mexican American children attended highly segregated schools; (2) very few Mexican American pupils were reaching the upper elementary grades;

(3) teaching materials were inadequate in both amount available and appropriateness for Mexican American children; (4) teachers reported being ill-equipped to teach the Mexican American student, particularly Spanish speakers; (5) the percent of Mexican American teachers was extremely small; (6) many Mexican American students were still not attending school as compared to other students; and (7) there was an exceedingly high percentage of Mexican American students below grade level, with a high percent being retained for multiple years.

In an extensive analysis of census data, Chapa (1988) found that in 1940 there was a schooling gap of nearly 3.0 years between the number of years in school completion between Mexican Americans in California (ages 25–64) and Whites. Forty years later (1979), however, the same analysis yielded a difference of 2.4 years. As her research noted, such differences admittedly yielded little statistical change within the span of four decades.

Much of the documentation by Latino educators like George I. Sánchez during the mid-1950s also corroborates these data, as he also indicated how similar patterns repeated from one district to another and across state lines. In a major survey of school districts that Sánchez & Strickland (1948) conducted, findings across multiple districts concluded that Mexican schools were "inferior in every respect," ranging from facilities to teachers, curricula, allocation, and the like.[54]

It is interesting to also note that by the mid-1950s, with segregation still in the balance for Latinos, there was an attempt by LULAC to have preschool places where children were taught basic vocabulary words in English so as to have the advantage of English instruction before entering school. These were called "Little schools of the 400," beginning in the summer of 1957 in Texas and later spreading out. As the program was inconsistently funded, it gave way over time after Head Start became a national federal program the following decade.

In reviewing these and related data, there is a strong and positive correlation between increases in Mexican American population numbers and school segregation. As the Mexican population rose, especially after 1910, school segregation trends also increased. In actual practice, it meant that at the start of the century access to schools had been severely limited, as there were many out-of-school Mexican youth; but as more Mexican Americans attended school, the new crop of students attended even *more* highly-segregated schools, with likely dismal facilities and few resources. At the same time, high school attendance rates continued at considerably lower rates than for other racial groups. Despite winning various lawsuits between the 1930s and 1950s, conditions remained virtually unchanged in the Southwest, and just slightly better for those in the Midwest.

By mid-20th century, with high schools as the gateway to college, there was still a limited number of Latinos receiving high school diplomas. Blockage had been so effective that even by 1950 the national percentage of high school attendance for Latinos in the Southwest was barely 1 in 10 compared to 1 in 5 for Whites.[55] Comparable data for the decade of 1960 was not much different, with corresponding percentages of 25% for Whites and 14% for Latinos.[56] Relative to Blacks, data was still slightly lower for Latinos for both male and female enrollees and graduates, alike.[57]

Latino discrimination in the schools appeared in several ways. One was exclusion, especially from high school, where less than 10% attended up until the mid-1950s. The other was the Mexican school, where segregation was fully evident, consigned to a tripartite system. Another level of discrimination was that which existed *within* schools, namely the segregation of students by classroom. A still further level of discrimination was through specialized curricula, whether for English language instruction, special education, vocational education, or any other. By whatever method or justification available, the inevitable outcome was limited education and exclusion from the mainstream. Up until the major reforms of the sixties, obtained through legislation (e.g., ESEA) and the 1964 Civil Right Act, most public schools had paid scant attention to what was happening to racial students, Hispanics most definitely among them.

Identity and Race

IN OVERCOMING SEVERE CONDITIONS OF EXCLUSION, DISCRIMINATION AND INEQUITY, THE COURTS HAD BECOME HAVENS OF LAST RESORT IN EDUCATION, AS THERE WAS NOWHERE ELSE TO TURN. While this is a sad commentary given the *Plessy* decision, it well reflected the desperation that existed among Hispanics. Understandably, with scarce resources and few options, Latinos had little recourse but to seek refuge through the legal system. Obviously, the era of segregation was not solely for the African American or the Latino. There was the total isolation of the Native American in the reservation,[58] as there was also blatant segregation against Asians, initially the Chinese then others

Asian Americans as well as the Filipinos and later Japanese Americans. Similarly for the Mexican American, major cases of litigation were brought in defense of equity, most especially in the schools such as exclusion from White schools and internal segregation within schools themselves, with "Mexican classrooms" and disproportionate representation in special education classes coupled with extensive grade retention, as documented by myriad lawsuits.

During the *Plessy* era, at least nine cases of blatant school discrimination were brought by Mexican Americans prior to *Brown*. Inequality by exclusion and segregation had become major issues during the first half of the 20th century.[59] As it turned out, more headway was accomplished from confrontation in the courtroom and legal battles than through legislation or executive orders.

The Mexican American community fought tooth and nail to change the educational system through the courts as well as in the community, as they refused to become passive victims. With limited social capital or the financial means to overcome race discrimination, it was through the development of political and economic power over time that Mexican Americans were able to access the courts and exert influence to curb outrageous practices besetting Latino children, as they received little assistance from the federal government. Major cases were assisted by civil rights organizations, especially LULAC in the pre-Civil Rights era.[60] This was buttressed further by several cases post-*Brown*.

The legal history of Hispanics has been rich in the documentation of abuse, but poor in resources to exact greater power and influence. As litigated cases were won locally, they were lost in the reality of practice and implementation. Nationally, while landmark decisions heightened progress, remedies suffered considerable setbacks in their enforcement and scope, with little local progress and change in practice. It is less that plaintiffs did not win, but that legal victories did not yield needed changes in practice or in the implementation of tougher policies. During this period, legal precedents (*de jure*) and practice (*de facto*) became strange bedfellows, where practices fell short in follow-up to legal mandates and statutes.

From the start, the controversy regarding race haunted the status of the Latino, encroaching even on citizenship rights, not just education. Debates and court cases over the definition as to whether they were "White" or "not White" consumed the American mentality for the entire second half of the 19th century and nearly three-quarters of the 20th century. This was shameful but true.

Turns out, the issue of identity for Hispanics as a separate and identifiable group was not well settled until much later in 1970 with the *Cisneros v. Corpus Christi ISD* ruling that Latinos were neither White nor Black, but a distinct class of its own. For a long period in the meantime, this fact had crippled Latino advancement every which way. While controversy was to be expected, as Americans were ambivalent about color and race, it did not fit a binary, Black-White dichotomy that had become confusing and divisive for the Latino. It was an absurd construct from the start for Hispanics, but one that crippled progress.

The point here was that classifying Mexican Americans (and other Latinos later) as either Black or White could never yield the right answer, as they were neither. While this was basic, the national mindset resisted the logical third option that they were uniquely different as a demographic group, not an anthropological category for race.[61] Lack of education and orientation from those who presumably should have known better fed the flames of confusion. Some of this, however, was willful as it was manipulative. It was less a lack of knowledge as it was outright prejudice and ill will. As with many social ills, these problems and lack of sound resolution were poured onto the schools unresolved, causing greater confusion and havoc for within-school segregation as well as within the classroom itself.

It is important to look back and underscore that the Treaty of Guadalupe Hidalgo guaranteed the full rights of American citizenship with no assumption about a "not-White" racial category. Nonetheless, the U.S. government had assured Mexicans the full rights of citizenship, not an almost White definition. Whiteness was an implicit assumption. The climate became such that they were socially *redefined* as "Mexicans" in a pejorative manner as not-quite-White, though now as a U.S. citizen. As a result, rights were thwarted as unbecoming a White. More specifically in Texas, the first of the states in the Southwest in 1845, the rights of Mexican Americans had slowly diminished through various subterfuges and machinations, both at the state level and among local jurisdictions. The missing nail in the coffin was to deny Mexican Americans the right to vote altogether because they were not American enough despite the treaty, though the latter never fully occurred.

In reviewing Latino-related court cases since 1848, there have been distinct anomalies and contradictions, but the re. Rodríguez (1897) decision from Texas ranks as an example of a special case without parallel. It well documented the ambivalence toward race as it regarded the Latino in the context of American attitudes toward color. As an unresolved verdict, this was a decision that would haunt the status and legal definition of Hispanics for another seven decades.

Adjudication wrestled with the definition of Latinos as a race or "category" of people. The case fell on a Monday (May 11, 1896), exactly one week prior to *Plessy*, but it took a year to decide. As it turned out, it was one year after the *Plessy* verdict that a key statute affecting Mexican Americans was finally added to the books by the *Rodríguez* decision in 1897, with color and citizenship at its heart. This time, it affected the definition of the Mexican American and eligibility for citizenship, seemingly independent of color.

This case was about a "copper-colored" man, with "straight black hair" and "high cheek bones" from the State of Texas that entered the Federal courthouse in San Antonio to submit an application for citizenship. As alleged by a lower court, "He [Ricardo Rodríguez] is not a White person, nor an African, nor of African descent, and is therefore not capable of becoming an American citizen."[62]

As the case moved up the courts, it was argued that the State Constitution of Texas together with the Fourteenth Amendment of the U.S. Constitution as well as the Treaty of Guadalupe Hidalgo were each in agreement that persons like Rodríguez were eligible for citizenship. After a year in deliberation, Rodríguez was granted citizenship in Federal Court, but not without the proviso that he was a "pure blooded Mexican." The category was later labeled by scholars as the "other White" category, seemingly reserved later for Mexican Americans, based on this particular ruling and for years to come.

Despite the "win" for citizenship, it put Mexican Americans on the defensive regarding racial status. The underlying question was, "Who was of the White race?" Despite the decision of the Court, the Immigration and Naturalization Service (INS) had come up with its own conclusion on the matter based on phenotype *independently*: "Mexicans who were White were given full citizenship, while mestizos, Christianized Indians, and afro-mestizos came under different racial laws."[63] Rather than a solution, the state of ambivalence compounded the acceptance of Mexican Americans, eventually banning them from White schools. This put Mexican Americans in an undefined status that muddied much case law the better part of the 20th century.

As one interpreter described it, color now became an issue of begrudging consent.[64] In arguing to be "White" to be accepted as a citizen, but truly *not* fully White because Rodríguez was a pure-blooded Mexican, resolution hung on the balance. The decision prompted litigation to later become ambivalent for Mexicans to side with Blacks as a distinct and discriminated race for fear of losing their "whiteness" at the other end. As quibbling over color became divisive for Blacks and Browns to work together to jointly defend "persons of color," it was equally perplexing for schools trying to sort among Blacks, Browns, and Whites in conformity with *Plessy*. Regardless of how the argument was made by districts or state law, or how the Black and Brown community dealt with the issue in court, treatment continued disdainfully against the Latino, with the full brunt of hatred and prejudice uppermost.

As but one example of the color and identity problem that later arose for Mexican Americans in 1935, a federal judge had ruled that three Mexicans immigrants were ineligible for citizenship because they were "not White," as required by federal law. The country of Mexico protested and President Roosevelt decided to circumvent the decision by assuring that the federal government would recognize Hispanics as "White." Thereon, the State Department as well as the Census Bureau and the Labor Department codified people of Mexican descent as Whites. However, it had been the 1930 Southwestern Census that had already established a "Mexican" category that was distinctly not White. This decision further encouraged LULAC and others to re-assert "whiteness" in legal cases. These actions led to the long-term handicap of separating Mexican Americans from joining as plaintiffs with Black court cases, including *Brown*. Turns out, it was plain for all to see how muddled the issue had become.

In fact, the issue was even more convoluted. Concomitant with the census categorization, the *Del Río ISD v. Salvatierra* (1930) case had defined Mexican Americans as "other White." This occurred when parents sued the school board for segregation in the border town of Río, Texas. Over a decade later in *Méndez v. Westminster* (1946), the High Court ruled against the segregation of Hispanic children in question by affirming that their segregation was indeed unconstitutional and violated the 14th Amendment. However, it also argued that segregation of these children was not racially biased as they were defined as "other White," hence not interfering with *Plessy*. However, two decades later in *Hernández v. Texas* (1954), just before *Brown*, the High Court had ruled that Mexican Americans were a "distinct" class, separate from Whites.[65] Obviously, these rulings were in contradistinction. As previously stated, it was not until *Cisneros* (1970) that a full and final determination was made that Mexican Americans were an "identifiable ethnic-minority group." It is this latter ruling that would stand for all Latinos thereon.[66] Accordingly, Hispanics were no longer another category of White, except that the Census has yet to catch up with this distinction, as alluded earlier.

This latter decision exemplifies how population shifts enter policy formation principally because population numbers had become too large for school districts to ignore. It had become the huge elephant in the room crying out against racism. This *quantitative* shift had now transformed into a *qualitative* issue. The impression until *Cisneros* (1970) was that *Brown* was not impacting Latinos in schools, as Hispanics had been fractionally represented among student populations involving Blacks and Whites. The *Cisneros* ruling conclusively determined that Latinos were to be counted as a separate group. Thereon, courts have been forced to treat Latino students as a distinctly separate group for the purposes of school desegregation.

Resolved by *Cisneros*, desegregation plans now include Hispanics as another racial category along with Whites and Blacks.[67] Prior strategies had been all over the map, with different legal opinions regarding varying claims about "whiteness." For the Latino, the legal world regarding identity changed in 1970, as the ruling holds firm to this day.

In retrospect, it is somewhat ironic that it was precisely the following decade (1980) when the term "Hispanic" entered the American lexicon, coming into common usage to "count" Hispanics in the full (100%) census in 1980.[68] Until then, the concept of Hispanics as an identifiable group had remained controversial despite the fact that Latinos had been fighting against the category of whiteness since the sixties. Nonetheless, as we learned from the previous chapter, the census continues to use two categories of White: "Whites, not of Hispanic origin" and "Hispanics."

The Color of Reform

SCHOOLING CONDITIONS DID NOT CHANGE MUCH FOR LATINOS EVEN AFTER BROWN, AS IT WAS NOT UNTIL THE LATTER 1960S THAT CONDITIONS BEGAN TO CHANGE, AND THEN VERY SLOWLY. Even in the midst of signing historic education legislation mid-1960s, President Johnson took opportunity to share a nostalgic memory of his days as a teacher and principal at a Mexican school in a rather reflective manner, as he wanted to dramatize how important it was to change the conditions of schooling since his days at a Mexican school. A year later, at another historic signing, he again reviewed this history. This time he shared statistics the country was still facing as it regarded Mexican American children *after* 38 years:

> Three out of every four Mexican-American children now in a Texas school will drop out before they get to the eighth grade... One out of every three Mexican Americans in Texas who are older than 14 have had less than 5 years of school ... [And] What

is the percent of the Mexican Americans [in school] with less than 8 years of school? ... Over half [53%] of all the Mexican-American children [that stay in school] have less than 8 years of school.[69]

Undeniably, these were catastrophic statistics. It was data like these together with figures cited by President Kennedy several years earlier regarding "the Negro," that mounted pressure to improve the American educational system. It was precisely during this mid-decade awakening that the largest revamping of education took place through legislation, but it also took major agitation and push from Black and Latino activists and grassroots groups. Executive action occurred less from benign kindness, then from political expediency. Otherwise, it is quite likely the status quo would not have changed at the time. Apparently, *Brown* was insufficient, as legislation was still needed to enforce policy, as policies needed stronger prongs.

As pressure mounted, especially after the March on Washington during the summer of 1963, it was during the Johnson years that a torrent of reforms through education legislation and executive action were thrust upon public schools and higher education institutions like never before. This time it came from a former schoolteacher turned President. Johnson signed more than 80 education bills. Yet without doubt the Elementary and Secondary Education Act (ESEA) of 1965 came to represent the most significant education legislation of the century. Measures were needed to ensure legal compliance, beyond the mere "spirit" of the law. The decade of bareness since *Brown* had clearly shown that voluntary action by municipal or state government would not occur unless forced by law. For racial minorities, it was an opportunity to ensure equality.

The color line stood strongly against reform. While the Civil Rights era ushered a new period of activism in American education, and symbolized a War on Poverty and a push toward educational parity and equality, a racial war was raging. Despite Johnson's pronouncements and executive action, predominant thinking from the period still held on to misguided hereditary and "limited capacity" theories about the ability of racial groups to succeed in school, a strong racist holdover from the belief regarding minority inferiority. Baby boomers may still recall the harm such thinking caused, as it dominated the thinking of many teachers. The force of law guided by research and social justice combatted racist ideology and fought against the beliefs about the inferiority of students of color. New activism was beginning to affect teacher expectations and increase college options for students that had been previously ignored and marginalized.

Yet, vestiges from the faulty thinking of a former high-level education reformer like Charles Eliot[70] and well-known child and educational psychologist G. Stanley Hall, both former adherents to the eugenics movement, now had their former thinking influence a new generation of White social scientists that became similarly biased during the fifties and sixties. This new group exerted a continuing influence over the educational establishment. Now it was academia that catapulted the dialogue back to the future all over again.

New data was now added to previous mounds of research that had supported deficit conclusions, expanding upon the notion that nonwhites had a plurality of deficits that would be impossible to overcome through education. Though with tenuous evidence, such beliefs that had been validated by former IQ tests were back in vogue. New data had now combined racial inferiority with the eugenics thrust from the 1920s and recast as newly formulated deficit theories nonetheless. This brought thinking like the "culture of poverty" into vogue, placing minority children once again in a limited position to succeed. New studies were updated to support past conclusions. Such new compilations were verified with a strong stamp of approval from eminent educational psychologists, measurement specialists, and research experts.

Whether new adherents to this mode of thinking believed in inferiority or not, consequences from their actions yielded equally devastating results. For doubters among them, it confirmed an old psychological principle that asserts how certain ideologies, including racist perceptions, continue long after the evidence that gave rise to them are proven false. To the detriment of students at that time, evidence emanating from "science" overwhelmingly supported the theories about inferiority, with insufficient scholars contradicting. While seemingly astonishing, this just occurred barely a lifespan ago, with academia—the last bastion of evidence-based research—further justifying the status quo.

Let's take stock and quickly review. Charles Eliot who had rightfully opposed the banning of Blacks into Harvard at the turn of the century, as earlier mentioned, had still proclaimed that the mixture of racial groups was a grave danger to society with inflammatory statements like "Each nation should keep its stock pure" and "There should be no blending of races."[71] Worse, he had become an outspoken supporter of forced sterilization of persons declared to be "feebleminded," "physically disabled," "criminalistic," or "otherwise flawed."

Indiana in 1907, after enacting the nation's first eugenics sterilization law, was later lauded by him when he said four years later that it was the law that "blazed the trail which all states must follow, if they would protect themselves from moral degeneracy."[72] While eugenics suffered a slow death by the 1930s, especially after the rise of Nazism, his influence and that of his followers fueled subsequent theories that continued to fault the minority victim, while exonerating dominant White society.

Flawed research continued to influence educational thinking in the same manner, albeit with new theories and in new ways by followers of eugenics like psychologist E. L. Thorndike and leaders in scientific racism like Henry H. Goddard, Robert Yerkes, and Lewis Terman. Even some of the progressives in education did not strongly challenge the system, as different from John Dewey's positions. Prominent educators and social scientists tinkered around the edges of "White" education, never taking issue with the fundamental failings of dual and tripartite systems. Their beliefs truly left minority students out of the picture of redemption through education.

Within barely a decade, a new and improved theory, this time espousing a "culture of poverty" arose and became significant in the research literature. This first emanated from an ethnographic orientation based on the Latino family with research led by scholars like Oscar Lewis from the University of Illinois, who had studied under anthropologists like Ruth Benedict and Margaret Mead. Lewis' principal research on Mexican families (1961; 1969) and with Puerto Rican families in *La Vida* (1966) led the pack, as he was highly influential. From late-1950s to mid-1960s he came to be known as the "father" of the culture of poverty thesis. His research gave credence to conditions of poverty that acted like a vicious cycle, as a vortex from which many prominent social scientists were unable to escape. Poverty became the new culprit for family disintegration, violence, pathology, and economic failure, as it was also the explanation given for why Latino and Black children most especially could not perform well in school. This exonerated the system and placed responsibility squarely on children and family.

Following Lewis' lead, research studies like the Coleman Report, *Equal Educational Opportunity* (1966), provided stronger quantitative and statistical credibility to this theory. This time around, arguments had come from a sociologist who had been greatly influenced by Lewis. For education, Coleman's research represented the largest body of data in the history of education. It was voluminous, highly "empirical," well "documented," and "statistically significant." Conclusions favored an educational crisis that primarily rested on the lap of poverty and family disintegration, basically taking educational deficits back to the home life of the student, as the new culprit for failure, with schools a poor substitute to make up the difference.

In short time, prominent thinking was further collaborated by additional research, including rather costly studies like those from brilliant academicians like Christopher Jencks, et al., from Harvard, *Inequality* (1972), and prior to him the likes of Daniel Patrick Moynihan in what came to be known as the report on *The Negro Family* (1965) that had highly praised Oscar Lewis for his pioneering work. Moynihan's statements on the Black family in particular had created a firestorm among Black researchers, with pointed statements that were blameworthy such as "The social pathology affecting the Negro community can be traced to the weakness of family structure" and "Most Negro youth are in danger of being caught up in the 'tangle of pathology' that affects their world."[73] His bottom line was that Blacks and Latinos were caught between "poverty" and "culture," hard to be rescued from heritable and/or cultural antecedents, but victims nonetheless.

Collateral damage has been the belief that schools can only do so much. Predominant policies, structures, and many educational practices seemed to cling for the educational enterprise to escape from working harder, as problems stemming from family factors such as culture and poverty can hardly be overcome by the school. Such thinking was not much different from colonialists who disparaged poor Whites centuries earlier. I am reminded of an educator's comment about this type of thinking when she said: "We all too often use people and their cultures as an excuse for low expectations."[74]

The stain of blaming the victim, without examining in greater detail how teaching can impact the lives of students, continues to influence educational thinking. By default, it supports lax expectations for Black and Latino children. While President Johnson's reforms had brought considerable improvements to the larger context of education that included favorable improvements in resource allocation, they were still insufficient to override a wave of deterministic beliefs about the limitation of educational practice. Seemingly, cultural deficits and beliefs about impoverishment led to patronizing approaches about the education of minority children. During the decade of the sixties, little was expected due to deprivation and deficiency. Prominent thinking belittled the potential for an entire generation of students and worked at cross-purposes to what Johnson was championing through legislation. It was a strange mix because one of Johnson's strongest advisers and proponents for educational achievement and the problem of culture and poverty was Moynihan himself, as adviser to the War on Poverty.

As it turned out, the Moynihan Report followed by the Coleman Report and then Jencks' Report on inequality led many educators to believe schools were strongly limited in their influence to turn students around to beat the odds. The result was a *fait accompli*, with the fault falling on the backs of students as victims, as William Ryan (1976) later pointed out. Many schools had absolved themselves from that responsibility. In the 1980s, teachers like Jaime Escalante, from the movie *Stand and Deliver*, well demonstrated that impoverishment was not the full story. He and scores of outstanding teachers like Uri Triesman from Berkeley at that time were making a decided difference among low-income, minority students. They did not use the excuse that children could not be taught, but that teaching could make the difference. They argued that if only teachers could learn how and schools could provide the right supports, low-poverty students could well achieve.

To have greater impact, schools need to drastically change their policies and teachers learn to better connect with their students. The major challenge is having the right teachers on the school bus of achievement. A plus factor for today is that there are excellent examples of outstanding teachers that have shown how positive results are attainable, as there are also outstanding districts that have conclusively demonstrated how groups of schools can succeed against the odds utilizing local per-pupil allocation, albeit with unequal resources.

Past chapters have provided a brief review of the Latino story from several vantage points. For one, it has shown how the Spanish and English systems of education differed significantly in both their approach as well as fundamental beliefs about the development of an educated class of people, albeit both dogmatic and highly authoritarian in approach. Past chapters also captured how Latino groups were oppressed and colonized within the context of White Supremacy, disallowing them to prosper and excel in school. While schools, by themselves, are certainly not the full answer to current conditions, they can play considerably stronger roles in creating more favorable conditions and opportunities for student success. By extension, the culprit is not so much the students, despite their background, but the system through faulty policies, practices, and wrongful assumptions about racial groups and the low income.

Our historical review concludes that although much has changed, basic beliefs and attitudes about people of color have not changed in major ways, as these continue to create significant barriers and crippling attitudes about the achievement of minority students, with Latinos receiving the brunt of the avalanche as the largest racial group. We also learned that while some problems have been resolved, major issues linger as their remnants have not vanished.

The next chapter focuses on several significant trends in greater detail, while also highlighting key issues that dominate the educational landscape.

Notes

1. Woodson, 2005. Also, Doxey Wilkerson (1936) documented that by the end of the 1930s, 19% of Black students between 14 and 17 years of age were enrolled in high school.
2. Ravitch, 2000, p. 38.
3. Cremin (1961) indicates this in his review of progressive education, though not as strongly as others have since.
4. Taken from Theodore Roosevelt's speech, "American for Americans," 1916.
5. This is in reference to Israel Zangwill's play by that title in 1908 that Roosevelt highly praised.
6. LULAC was formed in 1929, exactly two decades after the NAACP in 1909.
7. Ravitch, 2000, p. 57.
8. Olivas, 2008.
9. Margo, 1990, p.10, indicating that Black enrollment was just over 60% for both males and females.
10. Wollenberg, p. 322.
11. *Ibid*.
12. McWilliams, 1947.
13. Burma, 1954.
14. McWilliams, 1947.
15. Wollenberg, p. 360.
16. McWilliams, 1968, p. 24.
17. Valencia, 2011; Chapa, 1988.
18. Carter, 1970, pp. 10–11.
19. There were a host of educational movements active during this period. They included the vocational education movement, social efficiency movement, mental measurement movement, child-centered movement, activity movement, curriculum revision movement, mental hygiene movement, and the social reconstruction movement, among others.
20. Excellent Black universities like Howard, Moorehouse, and Spellman among other Black universities being the exception.
21. *The Washington Post*, November 30, 1902.
22. The Niagara Movement was founded in 1905 by key Black leaders. As a civil rights organization, it was in opposition to racial segregation and disenfranchisement. It opposed the policies of accommodation and conciliation by Black leaders such as Booker T. Washington.
23. Young Langston Hughes would stay for short periods of time with his father in Mexico, as he also dealt with his dad's estate later, after which he periodically visited Mexico. Fluent

in Spanish, he was later hailed as an important poet in Spanish that preceded his later notoriety in the U.S. during the 1930s as part of the Harlem Renaissance.
24. MacDonald, 2004.
25. MacDonald & Guzmán, 2017.
26. Vargas, 1993.
27. Known as the Mexican Repatriation, this was a mass deportation of Mexicans from the U.S. between 1929 and 1939. Estimates range from 400,000 to 600,000, though likely closer to one-half million were deported. It is estimated that nearly 60% of those deported were birthright citizens of the U.S.
28. Hoffman, 1974.
29. *Ibid.*, p. 15.
30. McWilliams, 1968.
31. MacDonald & Cook, 2017.
32. Quote taken from the American Presidency Project, "Remarks at the Welhausen Elementary School, Cotulla, TX," http://www.presidency.ucsb.edu/ws/?pid=28003
33. Vigil, p. xxi.
34. Donato, 1997.
35. Martínez, 2007.
36. Donato, 1997.
37. Valencia, 2005, p. 395.
38. *Ibid.*, p. 395.
39. California, Nevada and Colorado had compulsory laws in the late 1800s, and Texas enacted such a law in 1915. New Mexico and Arizona became states in 1912, when compulsory attendance laws were also enacted.
40. MacDonald, 2006.
41. Carter & Segura, 1979.
42. Manuel, 1930.
43. Little, 1944.
44. Weinberg, 1977.
45. *Ibid.*
46. Montejano, 1987, p. 160.
47. Grace Stanley quoted in Wollenberg, 1976, p. 111.
48. Bowman, p. 9.
49. Leis, 1931, p. 66.
50. Wollenberg, p. 358.
51. Valencia, 2008.
52. Chesler et al., 2005.
53. San Miguel & Valencia, p. 371.
54. *Ibid.*
55. Recall that data for Latinos was difficult to extrapolate, as information on Hispanics was restricted to only the five Southwestern states, where the majority still lived. Data are taken from the 1950 and 1960 Special Reports, U.S. Census of Population, *Persons of Spanish Surname*.

56. Data are taken from average numbers (males and females), as extrapolated by statistical means from national census for White students comparable to data for Mexican American students from the Southwest, years 1950 and 1960, as compiled by MacDonald & Cook from their recent analysis, 2016.
57. Derived from the MacDonald and Cook (2016) compilation.
58. By 1879, the federal government had established 145 schools for Native Americans, with 63 of these as boarding schools. By 1891, nearly all public education for Native Americans was under federal control, though these conditions have considerably changed today.
59. Valencia, 2008.
60. The Mexican Legal Defense Fund (MALDEF) was founded in 1968 and was patterned after the NAACP. PRLDEF, the Puerto Rican legal equivalent, was founded in New York City in 1972. Both were created with substantial funding from The Ford Foundation.
61. During desegregation in the 1970s there were heated arguments about how Latinos were to be identified between "Blacks" and "Whites." In some instances, Latino children were literally split apart on the basis of color, with lighter-skinned going to White schools and darker-skinned going to Black schools, at times separating siblings that went to different schools.
62. Donato & Hanson, 2012, p. 209.
63. Menchaca, 2001, p. 217.
64. Donato & Hanson, 2012.
65. Ibid.
66. Ibid.
67. Valencia, 2005.
68. U.S. Census, September 1993.
69. From speech delivered November 7, 1966 at the Wellhausen Elementary School in Cotulla, Texas.
70. Adam Cohen, 2016.
71. Ibid., p. 49.
72. Eliot, "The Suppression of Moral Defectives," paper delivered in 1911.
73. Moynihan, p. 19.
74. Taken from interview I conducted with JoAnn Gamma in 2017, co-founder of IDEA Charter Schools.

· 6 ·

CONTEMPORARY ISSUES

Discontent is the first step in the progress of a man or a nation.
Oscar Wilde

A HOST OF ISSUES HAVE BEEN DISCUSSED THROUGHOUT THE PREVIOUS CHAPTERS, BUT SEVERAL IN PARTICULAR NEED TO BE STRONGLY HIGHLIGHTED. While many are ongoing, several important issues have been lingering since the mid-sixties and need to be tackled more strongly and rather directly. Several pertain to court cases, while others are more specific to particular trends among K–12 public schools as well as for higher education. Quite specifically, this chapter aims to review school funding, English language acquisition, higher education, and several other topics that are urgent for Latinos.

School Funding

ONE OF THE MOST LOPSIDED CONDITIONS THAT HAS FACED BLACK AND LATINO STUDENTS THROUGHOUT THE PAST CENTURY HAS BEEN DISPROPORTIONATE FUNDING ALLOCATION, as fiscal allocation highly correlates with student outcomes. Resource-rich districts continually outperform resource-poor districts, regardless of achievement measure.[1] Most ashamedly, our country continues to have wider inequities in school funding and allocation than nearly any other industrialized nation. The processes and formulas being used today are remnants of more than a century ago. It is time such formulaic unevenness is stopped and brought to the reality of today's imbalance among schools.

For school funding, multiple decisions have been adjudicated that indicate the level of inequity in our schools such as SAN ANTONIO ISD V. RODRÍGUEZ (1973), where Latino parents sued the San Antonio school district because affluent districts spent *considerably* more dollars per pupil.[2] This inequity, as parents contended, amounted to discrimination against minority children that were predominant among the poorer residential areas of the state. The case was lost in a 5–4 decision from the High Court. Disturbed by the decision, Thurgood Marshall took an unusual step to read a part of his dissent from the bench:

> In *Brown v. Board of Education*, this Court held that segregation of children in public schools on the basis of race deprived Negro children of equal educational opportunities and therefore denied them the equal protection of the laws.... After twenty years of small, often difficult steps toward that great end [of school integration], the Court today took a giant step backwards.[3]

Later, in *Edgewood ISD v. Kirby et al.* (1989), the *Rodríguez* case was again addressed, as filed by the Mexican American Legal Defense Fund (MALDEF).[4] Here the State Supreme Court found that the public school finance system had violated the Texas state constitution and ruled it unconstitutional by unanimous vote, alleging inequitable funding. Parallel cases also had been litigated for African Americans. While certain decisions yielded favorable rulings, implementation and follow through were difficult to enforce, as decisions relied on the willingness of local and regional authorities to ensure equity. Sadly, implementation has been haphazard and not uniform after the wins. In other instances, local courts have not followed up favorably in rectifying imbalances. As a result, inequitable conditions persist in most neighborhood schools.

According to recent (2015) reports released by civil rights groups, "Funding for public education in most states is inadequate and inequitable."[5] Statistics from national data now indicate that "Children of low-income families are now the majority in U.S. public schools."[6] These conditions have created major obstacles for the nation's growing minority and low-income children as they try to beat the odds while wrestling with unequal and highly disproportionate funding. Despite the many rumblings that education is too costly, states spent less on education in 2012 than they did in 2008, relative to their economic productivity. Wade Henderson, president of the Leadership Conference Education Fund, has vehemently stated that "School funding is one of the sleeper civil rights issues of our time."[7]

Language, Pedagogy and Rights

AS IT REGARDS LANGUAGE EDUCATION, THE ASPIRA CONSENT DECREE OF 1974 IN NEW YORK CITY IS IMPORTANT TO HIGHLIGHT. A consent decree is a settlement of a lawsuit (or criminal case) in which a person (or institute) agrees to take specific action without admitting fault or guilt for the condition that led to the lawsuit. In pursuing viable responses to extremely high dropout rates and the harsh experiences of limited English proficient (LEP) children (denoted today as English language learners),* a group of Puerto Rican organizations that included ASPIRA, the United Bronx Parents, and PRLDEF collaborated to address the failures of the City in response to needed instructional services for these children. The ASPIRA decision was a settlement contained in a court order, as it related to the language rights of children. It established bilingual education as a legally enforceable entitlement for the City's non-English-speaking students.

The consent decree initially resulted from *ASPIRA of New York, Inc. v. Board of Education* (1972). The agreement settled in 1974 decreed by consent that LEP students had the right to receive appropriate language instruction. As it was argued, if the City required all children to attend school, but a child did not know English well enough to be instructed in English, the child had the civil right to be taught in a language that was understood until English competence was achieved. As a negotiated settlement, in lieu of continuance in court, the decree mandated that the City's public schools provide core content instruction in Spanish for LEP students along with dual language education, bilingual education, or some other form of English language instruction, including English as a Second Language (ESL). This was a rare win, and one that should be replicated in many urban centers across the country.

---

* It is important to note that the original term LEP has now become ELL for English language learners. The State of California uses the term EL for the same designation. ELL and EL are used synonymously throughout the book.

In San Francisco, the Chinese community had brought forth a similar complaint in LAU V. NICHOLS (1974). The *Lau* ruling claimed that San Francisco's Unified School District violated the constitutional rights of Chinese children by failing to provide language education services for Chinese-dominant school children, constituting a violation of their rights to an equal educational opportunity, as they could not learn in English. School policy, as alleged, violated the Civil Rights Act of 1964 and therefore demanded it provide students with "appropriate relief." It was this statute that had application for language-minority children, as it was interpreted by the Supreme Court "as also prohibiting language discrimination."[8] For non-English-speaking communities, the *Lau* decision had extended the equal opportunity provisions of *Brown* for English language learners. It also inferred that to do so did not mean re-segregation of students as in former days when justification for language learning meant attending segregated, Mexican schools. Hence, *Lau* remedies were provided in 1975 for the purposes of adequate implementation. Remedies would assist districts so that when schools had 20 or more students of the same language group other than English, they were to have a process that established (1) a means for identifying these students, (2) assessment of the English language proficiency of the students, as well as (3) provisions for appropriate bilingual education instruction.

In response to the needs of the nation's English language learners (ELLs), Congress had previously passed the 1968 Bilingual Education Act (BEA), also known as Title VII of the ESEA, which recognized "the special educational needs of the large numbers of children of limited English-speaking ability in the United States" and provided "financial assistance to local educational agencies to develop and carry out new and imaginative elementary and secondary school programs designed to meet these special needs."[9] Although the legislation recognized that change was necessary to adequately address the needs of language-minority children, it defined the problem as a deficiency in knowledge of the English language rather than as the need to change the educational underachievement of all language-minority children.[10] As there had not been a policy for limited English proficient (LEP) children or ELLs, Title VII represented a victory for the nation's language minorities, quite especially for Latinos, its largest representative.

Bilingualism and dual language instruction thus became more than an issue of voluntary participation in the government-funded Bilingual Education Act, but a shift to a constitutional issue of civil rights. As the Supreme Court had upheld this as a denial of equal education, it ruled in favor of the plaintiffs, it was the *Lau* remedies that provided leverage for the plaintiffs for ASPIRA and later entered into a consent decree with NYC, as the City realized the language rights of learners had been violated.

The ASPIRA Consent Decree mandated that the Board of Education provide English language learners with access to an English-instructional program and that ELL students be identified and classified as such. An important point was that while the transitional bilingual education programs established during this period through Title VII had been the source of considerable debate since its inception, the consent decree represented much more than the provision of linguistically-appropriate services. From a policy perspective, the 1969 Decentralization law and the 1974 ASPIRA Consent Decree helped resolve ambiguity regarding how institutional structures should be organized to address the educational needs of linguistically-disenfranchised communities, including those for which English was a second language. Here the struggles for desegregation and language rights had at times overlapped (and sometimes conflicted), as federal policy and court rulings compelled the school system to desegregate while also needing to provide adequate educational opportunity.

More recently, anti-bilingual and anti-dual language forces have gained momentum and defined their intent to "sunset" the consent decree. Efforts to dismantle these programs represent a return to pre-*Lau* and pre-*Brown* structures that were clearly ineffective in the past, with explicit denial of the rights of non-English speaking students. In reflecting on the aftermath of the consent decree, Angelo Falcón (2001) formerly from PRLDEF called it *De'tras Pa'lante*, as the "backwards-forward" motion of a past-present, with laws emanating from both directions.[11] Advocates from the Latino community as well as from the Chinese community and other language-minority groups are poised to ensure such decrees remain intact and are fully protected, but this condition remains unresolved in many ELL communities.

High School Dropouts

BY THE LAST THIRD OF THE 20TH CENTURY, THE CONDITION OF EDUCATION FOR LATINOS HAD NOT IMPROVED SIGNIFICANTLY. High school graduation was exceedingly low relative to other groups. Completion rates had become a measure of educational achievement. Findings meant that very few Latinos were continuing onto college, with most not entering the workforce well prepared for higher-skilled jobs, a key to social and economic mobility. Latino dropout studies were commissioned from the late 1960s to the end of the 20th century. Toward this end, ASPIRA of America[12] was one of the first Latino organizations that commissioned an analysis of the high school "dropout problem" at that time from among 400,000 Puerto Rican students nationwide in 1968.[13] Results of a commissioned study by Robert J. Margolis for ASPIRA called *The Losers* were astounding, paralleling statistical findings from the Coleman Report that indicated "Puerto Rican children in the United States lagged behind both urban white and urban Negroes in verbal ability, reading comprehension and math."[14] Among sixth graders, for example, Puerto Rican students were already "three years behind the average white child," [15] with less than half the enrollment finishing high school.

Among parallel studies during that period, research by education professor Isidro Lucas (1971) in Chicago documented the trend at three high schools with the highest Puerto Rican enrollment for the City. His findings were even more alarming, uncovering a dropout rate of 71.4% across the three high schools.[16] Obviously, something was not going well with the education of Latinos.

Subsequent investigations of high school dropouts indicated a disturbing pattern nationwide that went beyond Puerto Ricans, equally impacting multi-generations of Latinos from Mexico and other Spanish-speaking countries. Sometime later, as a result of continuing trends, the federal government commissioned senior researcher Walter Secada and colleagues in 1995 to undertake what became known as the Hispanic Dropout Project. Their completed report in 1998, called *No More Excuses*, concluded that dropout rates for Hispanics were 2.5 times the rate for Blacks and 3.5 times the rate for Whites.

Findings also indicated the trend was far more serious because data applied to a rapidly growing number of the nation's students, with rates remaining relatively stagnant but numbers increasing geometrically. "Over the last 25 years," as the report stated, "the overall Hispanic dropout rate started higher and has remained between 30 and 35 percent during that same period."[17] The study confirmed that traditional thinking had plonked the dropout problem onto the student, their parents, or their language, with conclusions about antecedents grossly inaccurate. *No More Excuses* unequivocally concluded that "Such misinformation created inaction ... by turning Hispanic students into victims."[18]

While such findings and recommendations were not new, they reflected what many minority researchers like Ron Edmonds (1979) had been saying all along about school effectiveness, reform, finance, and equity—messages school systems had failed to heed. Different from the Coleman (1966) findings concluding that family background and income were the major determinants of student achievement, the Effective Schools Movement led by Ron Edmonds and later by Larry Lezotte and Wilbur B. Brookover (among others), noted that school characteristics can positively affect student achievement in dramatic ways, as the "correlates of effective schools." Their findings were not altogether different from research among schools in England such as *Fifteen Thousand Hours* (1979) that basically claimed that from the age of 5 until school leaving, schools and teachers can dramatically impact the development of children under their care.

The belief about effective schools led to different perspectives that were held about the extent schools can impact a child's development. It was widely "different from believing education cannot compensate for society."[19] To the contrary, it could considerably. Schooling conditions can influence in major ways. These findings underscored the preface to *No More Excuses* that was addressed to then Secretary of Education, Richard J. Riley, stating: "We mourn the truncated education of our children as we worry about their future ... their unfulfilled dreams ... and we are outraged at the conditions that made possible such a shocking state of affairs."[20] Briefly stated, faltering educational outcomes were not the fault of the children or their families.

As per *No More Excuses*, Hispanics at the turn of this century accounted for more than "90% of all immigrant dropouts." Undoubtedly, the return on investment (ROI) to stay in school was considerable. If all Latinos completed high school, for example, lifetime earnings were estimated to be "nearly equal to the total assets in 1994 of Disney, McDonalds and Microsoft combined."[21]

Findings concluded that "dropping out is not a random act, but the logical outcome of the social forces that limit Hispanics' role in society."[22] In fact, findings were congruent with a statement by a participant at one of the hearings: "Dropping out is sometimes a healthy response to an intolerable situation." According to the research, addressing the condition of Latinos in education will require "A concerted and long-term investment of human and fiscal resources" that will not be solved by "political grandstanding" or "sound bites news reporting."[23] Understandably, it will take a large-scale effort, with much coordination among sectors that normally do not collaborate. Final conclusions from the report indicated students can succeed under the right schooling conditions, as it pointed to effective practices and how positive outcomes could be achieved, echoing Ron Edmonds from two decades earlier.

Back to the Future

A REPORT ON LATINO EDUCATION THAT HAD JUST PRECEDED SECADA'S STUDY BY TWO YEARS HAD UNDERSCORED SIMILAR THEMES, ALBEIT MORE BROADLY. This came from a newly-formed Presidential Advisory Commission on Educational Excellence for Hispanic Americans: *Our Nation on the Fault Line* (1996). The report was the first federal report that focused specifically on Latino educational achievement. It made a bold assertion, namely that "The educational attainment for Hispanic Americans is in a state of crisis." It further concluded that "although achievement gaps for some measures of educational attainment were narrowing, the disparity in overall performance between Hispanic Americans and other Americans *had become intolerable* [emphasis added]"[24] and that "literacy levels for Hispanic American adults" had remained comparatively low to that of other racial groups.[25]

In short, this latter report was another powerful indictment on the lack of Latino educational progress, as it conveyed lack of success after many attempts at reform, including minimal results since the release of A Nation at Risk more than a decade earlier. The bottom line for the decade of the 1990s was that such a state of affairs was an uncomfortable place from which to launch a new century. Obviously, the education of Latinos had not made the forward leap expected from the 1980s—the so-called decade of the Hispanic. Progress in education had also not advanced as expected from earlier years as a result of ESEA and the War on Poverty. Ironically, it has been incidental and untimely that the phrase "Decade of the Hispanic" was first used inadvertently in an article released by *U.S. News & World Report* in 1978 that captured the headlines. It had morphed from a phrase used by activist María Elena Toraño when she said: "The blacks had the decade of the '60s and women had the '70s. The '80s will be the decade for Hispanics."[26] As it had turned out, the decade of the Hispanic had truly been a misnomer.

In contradistinction, the 1980s witnessed the Latino not being included in the educational accomplishments of reform and advancement, as acknowledged by the two reports just reviewed and other limitations on Latino progress during the decade of the 1990s. In point of fact, the last decade of the century witnessed a considerable backlash from Whites to dismantle helpful programs for Latinos rather than improving overall conditions. As evident, systems were working at cross-purposes to major educational achievement. Few were focusing on the big picture and its inherent contradictions.

This trend was especially marked by the State of California where the largest Latino population resided. In California, the 1990s witnessed a trilogy of hard-hitting, anti-Latino ballot propositions that came down hard within a four-year period that decade, greatly blocking educational progress at every possible juncture. It is important to understand this backlash and how it held up the progress of Latinos in school once again.

Among the first of the California ballot initiatives was Proposition 187 in 1994. It aimed to restrict non-citizens from attending public schools. As this went against the *Plyler v. Doe* (1982) Supreme Court decision, it was ruled unconstitutional. In 1999 a court-approved mediation ended the political debate. The agreement confirmed that no child in the State of California can be deprived from receiving education or stripped of health care due to their place of birth. It also made clear that the state could not violate immigration laws by reporting the immigration status of individuals, including children. This condition had created a hostile environment for children in school that was accompanied by great fear. Supporters of the Proposition had maintained that the State could not afford to provide social services for so many people that had entered the country illegally or overstayed their visas.

The second Proposition (#209) in 1996, also known as the California Civil Rights Initiative, aimed to amend the State Constitution to prohibit state government from considering race, sex, or ethnicity in the areas of public employment, public contracting, and public education. It was the first electoral test of affirmative action policies in the country, putting a stop to affirmative action in public higher education. This was nationally disputed and then put under review.

Here it must be noted that affirmative action had been initiated during President Johnson's administration to improve opportunities for African Americans when civil rights legislation was dismantling the legal basis for discrimination. The landmark Civil Rights Act of 1964 and an Executive Order in 1965 began to institute affirmative action policies. This had been monitored by the Equal Employment Opportunity Commission (EEOC) that was established in 1965 to investigate claims of discrimination. Affirmative action was later broadened to include women, Native Americans, Hispanics, and other racial minorities as it more broadly also extended to colleges and universities as well as state and federal agencies, but not put to a vote until the California ballot.

On November 1997, the year after the ballot initiative, the Supreme Court effectively upheld the constitutionality of Proposal 209 by refusing to hear a challenge to its enforcement. It also upheld a lower-court ruling that struck down as unconstitutional the University of Texas' affirmative action program in *Hopwood v. University of Texas Law School* (1996), stating that there was no compelling state interest to warrant using race as a factor in admission decisions. That same year, a ballot proposition similar to California's Proposition 209 was passed by voters from the State of Washington.

In 2003, the Supreme Court reaffirmed the constitutionality of affirmative action in *Grutter v. Bollinger* (2003), although ruling that race could not be the predominant factor in such a decision. As a result, it struck down the university's undergraduate admission policy that awarded points to students on the basis of race in *Gratz v. Bollinger* (2003). Ten years later in *Fisher v. University of Texas at Austin* (2013) the Supreme Court vacated and remanded an appeals court decision that had rejected a challenge to an affirmative action program modeled on the one approved in *Gratz*. Here it required the most demanding form of judicial review. Once the appeals court upheld the program a second time, the Supreme Court affirmed the decision in 2016 in determining that strict scrutiny had been satisfied in *Fisher v. University of Texas* (2016), known as *Fisher II*. Affirmative action has been upheld since then for higher education under the rightful application of the law.

It is important to underscore that the decade of backlash for California ended in 1998, when Proposition 227—the third in California's trilogy—aimed to dismantle bilingual education. This vote eliminated instruction in the native language and replaced it with "structured immersion" in English for "one" year in a sink-or-swim scenario for ELs. This latter Proposition wielded profoundly negative consequences for ELs, now well documented. While the initiative was later rescinded, it remained on the books for two decades, impacting at least one generation of K–12 students for the largest state in the Union.

Along similar lines in arguing for dual language education, prominent researchers like Dr. Eugene García, former dean of the School of Education at University of California-Berkeley and later at Arizona State University, had weighed-in against such practices in his testimony before Congressional hearings. This was when he stated, "children placed in English-only programs do not do well academically," when compared to those enrolled in bilingual programs three to four years later, as English-only leads to major "academic drawbacks" over time.[27] Other researchers also viewed these conditions as "not only oppressive, but also regressive," as they most regrettably had "endangered much of what had been gained through earlier decades of struggle for educational equity."[28]

With the passage of three major Propositions in California completing the final decade of the 20th century together with the *Hopwood* decision against affirmative action, movement was rather indicative of the state-of-the-art just two decades ago against the Hispanic. While decisions have since been remedied and others remanded, it has merely brought Latino progress back to where it had started soon after civil rights, with limited gain after decades of struggle. In looking back, one educator framed it thusly: "The future of educational progress and equality for Latinos has remained at a virtual standstill the last three decades of the century. We have truly gone back to where we started."[29]

California, a state that had pioneered very advanced dual language programs, although debilitated while anti-bilingual education laws were in place, reversed these laws quite recently via a series of court cases and through subsequent voting legislation. The concern remains, however, that pendulum swings continue to debilitate and undermine steady progress forward. If students are to take a step backward to whatever positive steps are taken forward, it means that another hundred years will only bring education back to its current stance. These wins are not progress, merely stasis. These should not be the lessons from the past half century, since Civil Rights. Are we to repeat these again in fast forward? If so, our country will have lost ground with which it will not easily catch up. At this rate, the rest of the world will leave our nation and its children in the dustbin of history.

In now taking stock of current conditions for Latinos in the 21st century as the Hispanic population continues to grow, the educational scene must significantly improve its status. For Hispanics, education cannot be like the movie "*Back to the Future*," with every two steps forward followed by giant leaps backward. We must ensure permanent silver linings for these clouds.

For Arizona, at the very start of the new century in year 2000, English Language Education for Children in Public Schools (Proposition 203) became a ballot initiative that passed against bilingual education and dual language instruction. This meant that where schools had been previously free to use bilingual or immersion methods for ELLs, it was now illegal. This action had the consequence of dissolving primary support for language-minority children. It was a policy based on public opinion, not informed research. Most baffling, the very laws that had failed a hundred years earlier were now in force once again, resurfacing as *avant-garde* practices but truly creating "*déjà vu* all over again."[30] The lessons of California had not been well learned.

Astonishingly, it was just recently in 2018 that the court came down against the state as it had prohibited Mexican American Studies (MAS) from being taught as well as certain ethnic studies materials from being used for educational purposes in the Tucson schools. In principle, leading lawyer Richard Martínez argued that if the state rejects a program that is more effective in educating children, such action suggests that the state does so "not" because it wants to produce better educated children but because it has "discriminatory intent." Federal Judge A. Wallace Tashima, one of the three judges in the ruling from the 9th Circuit Court in California stated in his decision that "racial animus" was at the core of why the MAS program was being outlawed and, as such, the state had violated statutes that infringed on students' First and Fourteenth Amendment rights. The judge further stated that the barring of the MAS program was "motivated by a desire to advance a political agenda by capitalizing on race-based fears."[31]

While new rulings bring heartening news, they have required litigation at great expense and inordinate amounts of energy from the Latino community and its best advocates. While efforts could have been spent in more productive endeavors, the best and brightest of the Latino community is losing valuable time and effort in doubling back to make reparations. At best, these have been distractions to merely bring the community back to current times.

Meanwhile, some of the sobering questions that must be asked continue. These include: "How many times can indefensible actions be taken without irreparable and long-term harm to students?" "How many times must we learn the same lesson?" "How can we get politics out of the equation of learning?" "Where is the country moving in education?" And "How can Latino educators and practitioners harness its best potential to advance the state of the art instead of defending the rights children were to have had from years earlier?" Here the basic question remains: "How can we make it right for the future?"

A critical concern is how easy it has become for public pressure to reverse sound pedagogical practices because of misguided information or by political interference. Schools must be guided by research, not public opinion or political pressure. This is not the way to run effective school systems. Think of a parallel case if a medical system was based on people's opinions or experiences merely because they were once patients. Educators should not allow this to happen to the profession. Education is a right, not a tool for oppression. Otherwise, what has been learned since *Plessy*?

The nation must also refrain by signaling the challenge of education for this century as a Latino "problem." Latinos did *not* create the problem. Hispanic issues in education must be viewed as an American challenge. Multiple players are involved, as everyone is in the same cauldron. To a great extent, the public may be misinformed but only because its leadership is highly clueless. By whatever yardstick, so-called "problems" cannot be ameliorated if public schools are rigged against certain students. According to Rodríguez and Oseguera (2014), what has been underemphasized is the "institutional culture as a culprit for failure" rather than "more importantly as a facilitator of student success."[32]

Dreadful schooling conditions will remain unresolved until sound policies and implementation oversight checkmate unsound practices. The clash between White Supremacy and the Latino condition has been likened to an irresistible force crashing through an impenetrable wall. This is not about mutual destruction but about mutual gain. It is not about elimination but about co-construction. Latino determination and a strong resolve from everyone else must penetrate the impasse, as the struggle is most formidable.

Higher Education

HIGHER EDUCATION IS ANOTHER CRITICAL FACTOR IN THE EDUCATIONAL PROGRESS OF LATINOS. IT MERITS SPECIAL ATTENTION. While it may seem strange to devote a small section to higher education among key topics in education history, it is quite likely that it will occupy most discussions and analyses during the next two decades. For example, the Lumina Foundation and other higher education foundations are now advocating that learning beyond high school is what will build a strong nation.[33] Higher education represents an exciting and newly-evolving demographic shift in education for the Latino.

Concerns about high school dropouts were addressed from the vantage of the 1990s, but the good news is that graduation rates have since increased. According to the Pew Research Center, the Latino high school dropout rate "has fallen to new lows, extending a decades-long decline" to around "10% in 2016,"[34] when barely five years earlier dropout rates had hovered around 16%.[35] At the same time, the national high school dropout rate also reached a record low of 6% in 2016, with Latinos contributing considerably to the overall drop. Nonetheless, according to NCES (2018), Latino students still represent the highest dropout rates among racial minorities.

With a declining dropout rate, the share of Hispanic high school graduates entering college has increased. According to Pew, 47% of Hispanic high school graduates ages 18 to 24 were enrolled in college in 2016, as compared to 32% in 1999. By comparison, the share of college enrollees among 18- to 24-year-old White, Black and Asian high school graduates increased more modestly.[36] Most ironically, as a result of these increases, the dropout rate for Latinos has graduated to the collegiate level, with higher dropout rates from the first year in college than from high school. This means considerably more Latinos are now attending college, unlike the past. It also means that with increasing trends Latinos will soon represent the single largest block of minority students entering college. This further means that concern will soon be shifting from *college entrance* to *college graduation*, as Latinos lag behind in obtaining four-year college and graduate degrees. As a result, there are many areas in this upward climb that will require careful scrutiny and more direct action, though increases are most positive.

Beyond the data that researchers and certain higher education organizations have documented the past decade about higher education, more "analytical" data on what has been transpiring for the Latino is needed, as current research falls short for this group.[37] Christopher Tudico (2010) informs through his extensive review of the historical literature that there is still a dearth of information available for Latinos in higher education, though with more recent coverage on current trends and issues. MacDonald & García (2003) in the first overview of higher education and its historiography since the 1980s found that not a single article focusing on Latino higher education appeared during the previous twenty years in the *History of Higher Education Journal*.[38] As this was indeed stunning at the time, it is also good that these conditions have begun to change most dramatically, with much more research now in progress.[39]

Prior to 1950, Hispanic numbers at institutions of higher education (IHEs) were so low that few noticed. While accurate census counts on "Hispanics" did not occur until 1980, previous calculations on earlier enrollment were fairly accurate. Data today are more accurate, as they are even more carefully collected and scrutinized. The American Association of Hispanics in Higher Education (AAHHE) and *Excelencia* in Education are two organizations that are now providing ongoing research on higher education for Latinos, as they systematically gather and report on basic research, surveys, and trend data.

Back in 1928 when researchers were counting Hispanic-surnamed students in the Texas university system, only 57 undergraduates at UT-Austin had Hispanic surnames, but this included international students which inflated the data and principally focused on the main university campus, not its branches. For other universities, data showed much lower rates of enrollment, less than half a percent, with UT-Austin as one of the highest achievers.[40] By 1966, enrollment had increased to 2.8% at UT-Austin, again one of the highest in the nation.[41] After two generations of graduates, however, these were still unsatisfactory numbers.

At Arizona State University (ASU) in Tempe, a total of 150 Mexicans graduated between the years 1896 and 1936—a span of 30 years—averaging five students per year for nearly the entire state, with no other university remotely close to these ratios. In California, total numbers from the 1900s showed barely several hundred students graduating statewide, a figure that included all state university systems.[42] Latino enrollment began to slowly pick up for the public colleges of California 1920s onward, but with strong advocacy and some leadership from student-led organizations, not by the school administration or the State Government. Among these groups was the Mexican Youth Conference and afterwards the Mexican American Movement (MAM), both playing important roles in recruiting Latino students mid-1930s through the early 1950s.[43] MAM, for example, is the first known Latino college student organization in the continental U.S. Through their publication, *The Mexican Voice*, as a student newspaper at UCLA, it served as a recruitment vehicle across the state, with student totals increasing midcentury.[44] Over time, the University of California eventually came to enroll the largest number of Latino students in the mainland.[45] Some of these students became future leaders in vanguard movements for civil rights.

In 1948, President Truman's Commission on Higher Education spurred the creation of more two-year institutions which increased accessibility and choice for Mexican Americans. While this was an important step, midway the following decade the Immigration and Naturalization Service (INS) instituted "Operation Wetback" under President Eisenhower which deported over half a million undocumented and "other" Mexicans,[46] creating fear and anxiety among Mexican Americans attending school.[47] The process resulted in large-scale violations of peoples' rights, including forced deportation of U.S. citizens. Unfortunately, the number of students with four or more years of college understandably declined for Mexican Americans that decade, with one percent in 1950 barely increasing to two percent ten years later

(2.9% for males and 1.1% for females).[48] Given current immigrant fears, such dips in enrollment will hopefully not recur again for the rest of this century.

While college enrollment has increased slowly for Latinos and other minorities over the years, several "shifts" have been notable. It was not until post-1980 that the country witnessed the fastest minority growth in higher education. In 1980, for example, about 18% of undergraduates were identified as minority, but by 1995 minority rates had increased substantially to 27%.[49] More specifically for Latinos, the latest data from multiple sources, including the Website "bestcolleges.com," indicate that college enrollment rates for Latinos now seem to be sharply rising for both males and females. Breaking from past trends, this represents an *important first shift*. While yet to be realized in baccalaureate degrees, the percentage of college students that identified as Hispanic rose from 4% to 15% between 1976 and 2012.[50] Most recent (2016) data from the Pew Research Center indicates that 2.3 million Hispanics between the ages of 18 and 24 were enrolled in higher education programs in 2014. According to Pew, this represented a threefold increase since 1993.[51]

The growth of Hispanic-Serving Institutions (HSIs) is another indicator of this increase. These are universities with Latino enrollments exceeding 25% or more at the college campus, as monitored by the Hispanic Association for Colleges and Universities (HACU). There are now (2016) some 492 HSIs, but projected to exceed 600 colleges and universities within the next several years.[52] This represents a considerably fast pace in enrollment. As a result, the Census Bureau now projects that 1-in-4 college students will be Hispanic by 2020.[53]

Excelencia in Education now attests that Latinos are also reaching another milestone, where high school graduates are now enrolling in college at the same rate or higher than even their White counterparts for the first time.[54] This represents a critical *second shift*, as it indicates Latinos will now be on the rise for greater college attendance in upcoming years. This is significant progress when compared to past reports on Latino achievement such as *No More Excuses* (1998) just two decades ago.

Also, recent (2016) survey by the Pew Research Center corroborates that Hispanic parents are now beginning to focus more on higher education, as they are starting to value a college degree more strongly.[55] This latter data imply that new trends in higher education are also now more likely to be sustained by parents. This is a significant *third shift* in higher education for Latinos, again indicating that college enrollment numbers are likely to continue rising steadily.

While Latinos are rapidly gaining in degree attainment, more financial support is needed. There is an irony here, as Sarita Brown from *Excelencia* in Education points out:

> Our numbers graduating from high school are growing greatly and more are entering college, but at precisely the time that state support for higher education is being cut. The very people who were able to earn degrees at institutions supported by public dollars some 30 years ago now argue education is a private benefit.[56]

The new challenge is undoubtedly completion of the B.A. degree, as many Hispanics are *not* completing their studies for a variety of reasons, all too often financial. Pew data (2016) indicate that while 22% of Latino students have outstanding student debts, they represent lowest debt ratios among all groups. This is primarily because Latinos are more highly enrolled at two-year institutions with lowest tuition costs, but it may also indicate Latinos are less inclined to undertake debt loans even when these might be helpful. The concern remains, however, that any discontinuity in studies, even if temporary due to lack of funds, correlates highly with non-completion.

Financial prospects are not strong, as funding for the higher education of Latinos has become a major concern. Scholarship opportunities are floundering. Shockingly, fewer opportunities are available today than during the late-1960s. In fact, it was not until much later that scholarships from the Bill and Melinda Gates Foundation and from community stakeholders like the Hispanic Scholarship Fund (HSF) that newer scholarships have become available.

In addition, large funding sources from foundations like The Ford Foundation during the 1960s and 1970s provided much greater funding opportunities for graduate students and faculty. Private and foundation monies are extremely important and must continue, but they pale in comparison to the past, while tuition and fees skyrocket.

In retrospect, it is also important to note that scholarship opportunities by the Federal Government from the past have now been curtailed. At the same time, student loans like the National Defense Student Loans (NDSL) program that was stimulated by the National Defense Education Act (NDEA) and assistance through programs like Federal Traineeships for educators (such as bilingual traineeship scholarships), do not have similar counterparts today. Overall, the federal response has not been anywhere comparable to the past nor has state funding. Both have tapered considerably. It is also not close to the assistance provided by the government after WWII via the GI Bill (where very few Latinos could take advantage of the college portion of this bill) or as indicated during the 1960s when the Higher Education Act was funded. These were major initiatives that truly propelled the nation toward higher achievement. More federal and state assistance is needed as well as other ways by which private industry can help with sponsorship such as through employee benefits. Opportunity is basic to achievement.

National trends now represent a decidedly major improvement toward higher education attainment among Latinos. This is a significant change and a welcome advancement. However, more funds are needed to sustain these trends to keep students enrolled. The stop-and-go process for going to college then stopping to work and re-enrolling later has not worked beneficially for Latinos. In addition, the option of attending lower-level universities or only two-year colleges due to the higher costs of more prestigious universities is an area of concern as it may be hampering Latino student potential for greater career opportunities and higher education attainment, especially with new minority funding from some IHEs.

New Century Struggles

IN EMBARKING UPON ANOTHER MILLENNIUM IN EDUCATION, MUCH HAS BEEN LEARNED ABOUT WHAT HAS WORKED, WHILE MUCH HAS ALSO BEEN UNCOVERED ABOUT SHORTCOMINGS. As history can partially repeat, there are all too many familiar themes and vestiges from the past that keep reoccurring which must be nipped. For K–16 education to work well, it must be relevant and contextual, with supportive institutional climates that are more caring and inclusive. Lower-income districts must also be more substantially funded and supported.

With history as our guide, we have learned that education cannot occur independently from its social context, as norms from society inevitably influence and penetrate the schools, both good and bad. To assume that education is apolitical is naïve, but to assume it is in a downward spiral may also be unfair. Notwithstanding these assertions, however, improvement in education has been relatively stagnant, as it continues to remain highly mediocre, barely average for the modal student. While outcomes cannot be always blamed for the symptoms they reveal, problems also cannot be solved when the government does not assist in the process, nor can it be fixed when improperly diagnosed or when problems are disregarded. Educational difficulties will not resolve by themselves. Educators must hold their own to protect a most noble profession, as education is about the future of the country, a most sacred and honored responsibility. Let's not lose sight that the resolute bottom line is that public schools are not performing well, most especially for minority students, and performing wretchedly for the Latino student in particular.

One major concern from this last conclusion is that the pattern of education is more than benign neglect, as some may view it. It is actually worse, as some aspects border on abject abuse. A major but consistent pattern is that prejudice and inequity have continued long-term, as they are palpitating well today. While forms and conditions have changed to accommodate another camouflage of progress in education, the reality of miseducation has continued. This continuity is as significant a challenge as it is an intolerable state.

For education, the remnants of earlier decades illustrate how good practices and sound theory have been "hijacked" by so-called reforms when it comes to certain children. Others may argue contrarily, as they see that sound reforms have been hijacked by circumstances and events beyond their control. Granted the contrast, the bottom-line yields the same results, with miseducation winning. That has made all the difference. This now brings us to current conditions.

While accountability needs to be protected, inequity looms as a bigger concern, as the latter will always trump the former. Public schools need to be protected from distorted forms of accountability through faulty measures and obtrusive practices, but they are more strongly ailing from scant resources. This is wrong for the country, often resulting from gamesmanship. Autopsies of NCLB reveal that accountability made little impact in addressing performance while schools were devoid of basic resources and needed support. Much more of the latter was needed. While this may seem self-evident in hindsight, much of the country continues to march to a former drumbeat offering little change.

By whatever achievement measure or metrics utilized, Latinos are faring poorly because they continue to lack critical resources and the opportunity to achieve. In absolute candor Latinos lack more than homespun boots to be able to pull themselves by their bootstraps, as public schools have left the Hispanic community barefoot—*descalsos*. Latino students are not being adequately prepared for high achievement. To applaud recent success as a result of schools doing well is to deny students the credit deserved for succeeding despite the odds, fully hiding the culprit. In actuality, Latinos can perform considerably better, provided an opportunity.

Educators cannot afford to be simplistic or solipsistic in thinking. Schools that serve the highest percentage of Hispanic K–12 students continue to lack the most basic resources and continue to lose their best teachers and administrators. These schools also report the highest teacher turnover rates (over 50%) and highest teacher absenteeism.[57] These and related factors combine to contribute low achievement. As this is nowhere as complicated as health reform, the question remains why it cannot be fixed and why it continues unabated. Any lay person would have expected such issues to have dissolved by now.

Critical shortcomings have been at the forefront of concern since ESEA. Why is practice so behind the research? And why are so many funds being spent on testing what we already know from everyday classroom experience, but not on fixing the schools? Then there are the funds on educational research that are not being well spent. We are not researching the right issues. Conservatively, over half a trillion dollars[58] have been spent on educational research since the mid-1960s for too many districts not to know what is going by now. This is wasteful. While universities and private R&D corporations have greatly benefitted from this largesse, students continue struggling with performance and schools continue with inability to meet fiscal needs.

As we have seen through a brief historical review, it is not the absence of knowledge that hinders progress as much as the will to do what is needed to improve schooling in America. Ignorance is no longer an excuse. We are past that stage. The difficulty is not the "what," but the "how" and certainly the "will." I am in full agreement with what Ron Edmonds once expounded nearly half a century ago:

> We can whenever and wherever we choose, successfully teach all children where schooling is of interest to us. We already know more than we need in order to do this. Whether we do it must finally depend on how we feel about the fact that we haven't so far.[59]

Here I am also reminded of what Malcolm X once proclaimed: "We can't lead where we won't go."[60] Pioneering researchers like Isaac L. Kandel (1934), from Columbia University back in the 1930s also clarified educational priorities for the country quite succinctly, especially after extensively studying educational systems worldwide. Among his many insights, one in particular tugs at the heart of today's educational priorities: "If ever American schools became as rigorous and well planned as their athletic programs ... they would be reinvigorated."[61] He well captured both a lesson and an admonition for his day, but we can transplant it for today as these parallels have not changed.

If the nation can perform well in sports and in the Olympics, why not equally well in education? Is education not more pertinent? Ironically, and quite favorably, sports are more balanced in racial numbers and placement and management than education in America. The bottom line in sports is winning. With parallel logic, the bottom line for education is achievement. In sports, it takes diversity to make a great team. For education, the analogy equally underscores the point.

The new American Latino has virtually become the New Black, but data reflects poorly for both groups equally. More ashamedly, it reflects on the systems of education that have been created. If education cannot do best for its neediest schools, the educational system will flounder. As recipients of a faltering educational system, Latinos cannot be blamed for systemic inequities. Education is America's challenge, with Latinos in the numerical forefront. Hispanic communities cannot combat the social poverty of its schools independently of the governments and bureaucracies that manage the schools. This would be unfathomable. Only systems and their select chosen have the power to resolve those imbalances, with educators willing to make it happen and the Latino community capable in rolling up its sleeves to help the process, as thousands of neighbors will also extend wide support.

Reflecting on the state of the color line a century ago, Du Bois was prescient in reminiscing: "The black man's burden is the white man's burden."[62] By parallel logic, the Latino problem is America's problem, and the Latino challenge is America's challenge. While Latinos now carry the numbers to make the case urgent, they alone cannot make the system change. Resolutions from multiple sides can never succeed when only one side is working unilaterally. Success will only occur when all flanks work collaboratively.

The struggle has been long as it has been arduous, with disastrous effects mounting cumulatively. Latino education has been stabbed, with deep scares in recovery. Educational systems are quite aware of where the community has been, as it must also realize how much farther it needs to go. Without question, the matter requires a collective effort, where every citizen plays a role and where every leader must engage. But moral courage is needed to drive the bus, and educators have historically not been the most courageous crusaders.

We need greater courage in leadership and a stronger will to endure the hard work required for success.

In reviewing the history of Latinos in education, recent conditions cannot be well assessed independently of the past; and a dreadful past cannot be the yardstick for the future. So why do we say things are fine? Why is there complacency? The long view of miseducation indicates particular patterns have persisted for decades, but never well confronted and overcome. As we have seen, timidity has reigned. As such, the miseducation of Latinos is not a product of the moment, but a long-standing continuity of travail. Issues have risen to the surface in the past, but unheeded because communities have not had the capacity to battle, and school leadership has lacked the *cojones* to fight. Today should be different. The future is here ever present. A large population cannot tolerate inferior education for long without it also affecting the very fabric of society. We are truly at a most vulnerable and tattered stage.

In surveying history, every nation that has made a major leap forward did so when it placed education as the driver of excellence for its people.[63] If and when Latinos receive their due in instruction, it is the entire country that will become the stronger. Moving onto the ends of equity, balance, and opportunity, the educational process does not merely represent future success for the Latino community and its achievements. Instead, it represents enduring viability for the nation. Education is paramount to a highly-achieving, fully-inclusive and extremely productive nation, where everyone participates in an equitable manner toward excellence, common success, and high productivity.

In reviewing lessons from history, a model in combatting difficult odds comes from Anna Julia Cooper (1892), a Black schoolteacher who wrote from her "heart" and pleaded with a strong "voice." Born into slavery by a White father and a Black servant mother, when she screamed about inequality it was a lesson for all. Here she well cautioned: "It is not the white man versus black, the brown, and the red—it is not even the cause of women vs. man. Nay, 'tis woman's strongest vindication for speaking that the world needs to hear her voice."[64] She then proclaimed: "It would be subversive of every human interest that the cry of one-half the human family be stifled."[65]

In similar manner, the cause for education today remains greatly impoverished if one-half the K–16 body consisting of Latinos, Blacks, and other minorities is not fully enlisted in the finest of schools and enrolled in the best of universities they can attain (rather than afford), alongside the best and the brightest. It is high time we all screamed like Anna Julia that talent is everywhere, but opportunity remains scarce.

It would be hard not to overstate the enormity of the Latino contribution to the wider national community, as the U.S. now houses the most vibrant Latino population ever. The yield from such an awakening can only bring inestimable benefits of unprecedented proportions and at a time of great need as Latino Americans awake. The nation is hurting because our brothers and sisters are hurting. In a very real way, we are each other's better half.

What does all of this mean? I go back to what Anna Julia Cooper echoed a century ago. Our nation "will have to limp along with a wobbling gait and one-sided hesitancy of a man with one eye" if it does not correct its sickness.[66] While hobbling persists in its strive to survive, if not soon corrected, it may not be able to save an ailing body from distress. With limited time available, we can still work to recover, but quickly, within this generation. Coming together to fix the problem is important, but only by working together with the *urgency of time* can success be assured.

Learning from these last chapters reveals that education has gone through a non-heroic strain the past two centuries for the Hispanic. It is a condition from which the country must improve to succeed. The path has not been straight, as it also has been most difficult and far from successful for young, Brown and Black youngsters. As starkly evident, public schools have been grossly inadequate, and all too often dealt an unfair hand. Quite apparently, much needs to be repaired. In assessing the past, Barbara Sizemore rightly sized it years ago: "Although many want to say that the schools did assist the various immigrants, they, in fact, did not. Most immigrants were excluded from effective participation."[67] Challenges were overcome primarily from the grit and hard sweat of the oppressed. Latinos are no exception and must continually work with others to aright these wrongs.

Supremely important to know for many years since *Brown*, the premise was not simply about equal educational opportunity, but about the full value of every citizen and, hence, inestimable value to the country. A pronouncement from Chief Justice Earl Warren at the time sums it well: "Education is perhaps the most important function of state and local governments ... In these days, it is doubtful that any child may reasonably be expected to succeed in life if he is denied the opportunity of an education."[68]

Accordingly, the value of education for any child of color never has been, nor ever will be a minority problem. Education is for everyone, as it is profoundly the most important function that needs protection for America's future. Legally, it is a fundamental right to protect. Legislatively, it is an obligation to ensure. For the school, it is a responsibility that must be met. And for our communities, it is a requisite that everyone be served.

Notes

1. See *Abbeville v. State of South Carolina* (1998).
2. Upon retrial in the reestablished case [*Kirby* (1989)] it was determined that property wealth during that period was grossly disparate. For example, according to Farr & Trachtenberg (1998), "Edgewood I.S.D. drew taxes from $38,854 in property wealth per student; at the same time, Alamo Heights I.S.D. enjoyed $570,109 in property wealth per student" (p. 615). This is a ratio of 15:1.
3. Williams, p. 357.
4. This was originally filed in 1968 and eventually lost in High Court, as *Rodríguez et al. v. San Antonio Independent School District et al.* (1973). It was later reestablished as the *Edgewood* case for the State of Texas.
5. Baker et al., 2015, Rutgers University, Education Law Center (4th report card).
6. Emma Brown, 2015.
7. Ibid.
8. Del Valle, 2003, p. 235.
9. Stewner-Manzanares, 1988.
10. Ibid.
11. Falcón, 2001.
12. Now renamed the ASPIRA Association.
13. While the Puerto Rican enrollment was nearly one-fifth of all students in New York City public schools, only one-eighth were enrolled in the academic high schools.
14. Margolis, p. 2.
15. Ibid., p. 3.
16. Lucas, p. 10. According to Lucas (1971), Margolis had estimated a 60% Puerto Rican dropout rate nationwide.
17. Secada et al., 1998, p. 5.
18. Ibid., p. 1.
19. Rutter et al., 1979, p. 2.
20. Secada et al., 1998.
21. Ibid.
22. Ibid., p. 7.
23. Ibid., p. 2.
24. President's Advisory Commission, *Our Nation on the Fault Line*, 1996, p. 17.
25. Ibid., p. 17.
26. Rivera-Servera, 2012.
27. Eugene García, public testimony before the U.S. House of Representatives, 1998.
28. San Miguel & Valencia, p. 390.
29. Statement taken from interview with a prominent Latino scholar.

30. Palmer & García, 2000.
31. Astor, 2017, http://california-mexicocenter.org/tucsons-mexican-studies-program-was-a-victim-of-racial-animus-judge-says/
32. Rodríguez & Oseguera, 2014, p. 4.
33. See Lumina Foundation's recent report, *A Stronger Nation*, 2019.
34. Gramlich, 2017.
35. Ibid.
36. Ibid.
37. Even an in-depth review of analytical articles or reports in early 2018 yielded miniscule information across key higher education journals as well as searches of extant databases, including ERIC and Google.
38. MacDonald & García, 2003.
39. See publications, for example, from the American Association of Hispanic Higher Education (AAHHE) and the work by *Excelencia* in Education.
40. It must be noted that these data exclude universities from Puerto Rico.
41. MacDonald, 2016.
42. Tudico, 2010.
43. MacDonald, reference article, https://home1.nps.gov/heritageinitiatives/latino/latinothemestudy/education.htm
44. Ibid.
45. The single exception is the University of Puerto Rico, founded in 1903.
46. Data for this operation vary from one-half million to one million.
47. www.history.com/new/operation-wetback-eisenhower-1954-deportation
48. MacDonald, 2016, p. 16.
49. MacDonald & García, 2003.
50. NCES, *The Condition of Latinos in Education*, 2016.
51. Krogstad, 2016.
52. Latest (2018) data from *Excelencia* in Education.
53. Census projections for 2020 population, 2016.
54. Fry & Taylor, 2013.
55. Stepler, 2016. This Pew survey found that 86% of Hispanic parents of children 18 and under said it is "extremely important" or "very important" for their children to earn college degrees. By comparison, 79% of Black parents and 67% of White parents said likewise.
56. Taken from interview with Sarita Brown, 2017.
57. U.S. Department of Education, *The State of Racial Diversity*, 2016.
58. This is a conservative figure calculated merely from average yearly allocations to research organizations from the Department of Education such as the IES and NCES R&D allocation for educational research by university labs and centers since the late 1960s, when the National Institute of Education (now IES) was established. While funds are lower than in the past and while there are fewer labs and centers, there are still ten rather large and comprehensive Regional Educational Laboratories not to mention other university and non-university related R&D centers conducting research.

59. Education quotes, https://www.greatschoolspartnership.org/wp-content/uploads/2017/04/equity-quotes-2.pdf
60. *Ibid.*
61. Kandel, pp. 71–72.
62. Du Bois in Locke, 1925, p. 386.
63. Most recently, Sweden and Poland rank among them.
64. Cooper, 1892, p. 121.
65. *Ibid.*
66. *Ibid.*, p. 122.
67. Sizemore, p. 45.
68. Taken from the majority opinion written by Chief Justice Earl Warren in the *Brown 1* decision, 1954.

EPILOGUE

Learning from History

A different world cannot be built by indifferent people.
Horace Mann

MANY LESSONS COME TO MIND IN CONDENSING THE RECENT REVIEW OF AMERICAN EDUCATION AND LATINOS. As we take stock, let's pause for a moment to reflect why this is so extremely important. Looking back, I recall once listening to an obituary delivered by President Kennedy about an iconic American folk artist and how it was possible for her to achieve such success in this country, the land of the free. It was an inspiring story and one that excited many in our neighborhood, including several artists among us.

As revealed, it was from deep in the farmlands of northern New York State bordering Vermont that profound words were uttered by a legendary and centenarian artist known as Grandma Moses. Born at the time of the Civil War, she eventually became an icon. So important was her desire to paint that she began in earnest at the ripe age of 73. She later claimed she did not have needed time to fully paint until age 78. Her vision of the world is what many of us aspire, as she was the gospel of tranquility, happiness, and much wisdom. In this spirit she once proudly proclaimed with great satisfaction, "Life is what we make of it, always has been, always will be." True enough, as the phrase has resonated in my mind's eye ever since. But is this possible for all

Americans, even persons of color in this new century? Of course it is, we are likely to say without hesitation, as there are now many examples. But truly, is it as easy as it was for Grandma Moses? You would hope so.

Yet for my family, this powerful phrase was always qualified by circumstance, as my very own grandmother once shared. My dear "*abuelita*" held the belief that all would be well if we each just did our part, but that life [*las cosas de la vida*] still would be harder because of whom we were. Over time, circumstances proved "*la vida*" would not be so straight-forward after all for some of us. This I learned watching my family's story unfold from grammar school onward, most especially when I watched my dear uncle Wilson literally fight in the streets for our turf and for "*la dignidad de la familia*" [the dignity of our family] in a sliver of a neighborhood that was then turning Puerto Rican. I was too young to fight, nor did I know how, so I relied on him. Turns out, I painfully learned together with cousins that moving to "America" dealt different odds for people of color, not unlike Anita from *West Side Story*. Looking back, you would think the story no longer relevant to the America of today.

Coming to America, as we would say it from Puerto Rico at that time, meant much to my family, as it was a place to start over again. It was our time for opportunity, a time to shine. That was all "*mi papi*" ever wanted for us before he himself had to fight for his own civil rights. Ironically, the U.S. was a country that was supposed to increase our odds to make it. Yet, I heard that children like me were to undergo nasty events and confront many barriers. I did not want to believe it. Hope was eternal in thinking that the rough and tumble of school years would be over by graduation and all would then be well. All that my parents ever wanted was a fair chance for us to prove our talents. In thinking back, that is why they came, as that is what we later desired for our own children. Our hopes were anchored on a government that would be upheld by an impartial justice system, a third branch of the government that would uphold our rights and keep us safe. To the extent it might not, we as a people would rise up and claim that justice would prevail, much like in the heyday of the Declaration of Independence and much like what happened during civil rights. Despite the blemished history of Latinos and other racial groups, our hopes continued to have us believe the nation would live up to its creed. Hopeful thoughts seemed inbred.

Given the importance education plays, we felt schooling would restrain our lives for a while but eventually set us free. To get an education was the way to make it in America and survive tough *barrios*. End of game. Education was fundamental to the goals of equal educational opportunity, hence my rationale for studying, then later sharing the history of a Latino in education. It was to understand what happened. It was to ask how events occurred. And where am I and my family in the trajectory? Well, that is the thinking that was in all of us. In that process, important learning took place. Throughout my years of education, certain conditions were unsettling to learn. Over a period of time, it became equally important to share. As an educator, I believe the country can still make things happen, as I believe in "the way its spozed to be,"[1] but I have also learned it is easier said than done and I must be part of it. The statement by Granma Moses, "Life is what you make it," I still cherish, but it turned a bit differently for my people, though still sharing her conclusion. Given different trajectories, I hope by God she is correct and our kids make it.

One of the major lessons since then is in thinking about the future of this country and how vulnerable it can become. This may come as a surprise to many of my colleagues. The plain fact is that the future of America is fully connected to the future of the Latino population, but coming at a time when Latinos are being highly disrespected. The latter assertion is fully reinforced by lack of services and poor schooling for our folk coupled with the current climate and rhetoric of our times and the implications of shifting demographics that are now incontrovertible. The population pyramid of the country is already highly Latinized. This makes it imperative to learn more about the Latino population and its importance, but also about the role education must play within this reality. It is also a time to think of about social justice and greater opportunity.

With Latinos as the demographic driver for the nation, attention has to be paid to the general welfare and overall wellbeing of this population, including its prosperity, overall development, and educational progress. This is where social science becomes critically important, as it opens the doors to understanding social groups and its bonds, with history laying the antecedents and context by which social science can help interpret and analyze events. This was the case with the Clarks, Mann, Dewey, Allport, Myrdal, and many other scholars, as it also came with an equally strong voice from Latinos like George Sánchez middle last century, as by our own brand of scholars and researchers today, as per this review.

In seeing how education holds the keys to the wellbeing and success of any population, it is now evidently clear we must pay fuller attention to the educational needs of the Hispanic. For any group, disenfranchised or not, education is not only essential, but serves as the engine that drives its accomplishments.

For the nation, education is that which eventually fuels the economy and feeds productivity. The Latino population must be adequately nourished if it is to contribute to the national economy. Given its numbers, it must. As such, its economic needs and educational priorities must be attended. Otherwise, its frailties will spill over and gravely impact the rest of society. As it takes at least a generation to reverse conditions through education, time is of the essence.

As evidenced from prior chapters, the Latino population is facing major inequities that have been grossly neglected and too easily dismissed, with undereducation ranking high among them. It is with sincere hope and high expectancy that this country will become well aware and highly poised to ameliorate such disparities in rapid time. Otherwise, it will find itself in future shock, battling a "perfect storm" of a major magnitude which by then will be impossible to undo. These are critical realities of incalculable proportions facing the nation.

For the Latino community, the lack of national attention to priorities has been stirring for decades. This has been pushed aside by polemics. To continue in this manner would be at the very peril of the country's future. There is no firmer reason or stronger rationale than to scream loudly and clearly that the country is facing a clear and present danger if it does not act at once. It is a supreme imperative that the Latino population not to be ignored any longer.

It is also important to be cognizant of the broader context of other racial minorities that together with Latinos will represent more than half the U.S. population midcentury. This is not a statement of inference, but already reflected among children less than five years of age across the country, as demographics reveals itself among its youngest cohorts. As a result, impending population changes will require that considerable attention be paid to the welfare of racial minorities, as together with immigrant workers they compose the critical majority and future workforce for the nation. It is also important to be aware that this will occur within the next generation. As we have learned, this is not a minority or Latino problem. It is truly a full-fledged American challenge.

For any nation, the measure of wellness about its future rests on the welfare of its most vulnerable groups, most especially when they represent the largest ratios. It would be highly absurd, irresponsible, and reprehensible to ignore the needs of such populations. The fact that they happen to be populations of "color" more fully dramatizes the challenge, as groups with the greatest needs have also been the most greatly ignored.

EPILOGUE

Earlier chapters reviewed hundreds of events, with many more untouched and others yet to be unearthed. While both the story of the Latino and that for America is vast, their many cycles of development rapidly expanded and greatly intersected in truly staggering ways during the past, yet no issue is more important than their intersection at this particular juncture in American history, as the collective future of all people, literally everyone is at stake. Hence, nothing should stand in the way of a national effort to assure a more prosperous and productive engagement.

As a copartner in America's future, it is important to meaningfully comprehend the Latino community and recognize its assets as well as its educational needs. Other exigencies pale by comparison. To this end, this book has attempted to put into perspective the educational story of the Latino through multiple learnings along the way. Before problems can be resolved, antecedents must be known so that their context is more meaningfully and clearly understood. Here it stands to reason that embedded in any response to a crisis must be a full comprehension of the problem. To get there, it was important to know what had transpired and why it was significant. Let's quickly recap.

We learned from earlier chapters that Latino education in the Americas began in San Juan nearly half a millennium ago when the first school was established (1512) by the first Bishop to the New World. Since then, Latino schooling has been part of U.S. history in one way or another. This legacy has forged many paths over long periods in both the U.S. and its outlier territories. Such routes have interconnected with this country's history to this very day, with recent closures of failing schools a vivid example of how Hispanic children are currently being impacted in real time.

Latinos, as a New World product, have traversed encounters of varying types along a circuitous historical route, yielding epic tales with treks that seem interminable and challenges that hunger for resolution. Over time, Latino Americans that are part of the U.S. fabric have encountered a valiant and arduous journey that has shaped their resilience, but with battle scares still healing. Countless encounters have occurred in multiple ways at multiple times and for multiple years.

As we learned, Hispanics first entered the continent as explorers, then conquerors, later as settlers, interpreters, even as combatants and collaborators in various American battles and wars, with much occurring even before the 20th century. Other roles have played out since. These now range from *bona fide* citizens, to patriots, to captives by the U.S. military as well as refugees, while also disdained as illegals and denoted as an Hispanic invasion.

As citizens to this country, Latinos were once highly discriminated before *Plessy* and then legally degraded during *Plessy*. After *Brown*, they were still treated as forgotten citizens. Lost in the shuffle, they were barely acknowledged as a legitimate group, even after civil rights. More recently, they have been shamed for the stigma of color and perceived as biased citizens, with some demeaned as federal judges and others undergoing the indignity of severe family separation in seeking constitutional asylum at the border. Somehow, the brown stains of prejudice have endured longer than the inhumanity of *Plessy*. This is but a long list made short.

While it has been a never-ending saga, it should not continue as destiny. At some point it must halt. This is not to begrudge or cry over spilled blood, as some narratives have already depicted. It is to more appropriately affirm that in the compilation of facts these add to cumulative effects that portray rather serious but troubling patterns over time that must be properly acknowledged if current conditions are to be redressed, reframed and restored.

The review of education likewise reveals that the public schools of the nineteenth and early twentieth centuries did not help many Latino children. Here we learned that the process of miseducation became real, with other Hispanic children denied basic rights and blocked from entering school. However, we must now assure this is not a repeating pattern.

In reviewing the dark ages of public schooling immediately after the Treaty of Guadalupe Hidalgo, it became obvious to Latino settlers that American education was firmly entrenched on exclusionary practices. Over time, the few that entered schools were placed in dead-end, segregated, one-room shacks that operated as schools, then capped at eighth grade. Inside the classroom, it became less about education and more about socialization and indoctrination, seldom the 3Rs. For Hispanics entering the workforce, they did so because of the overabundant availability of unskilled jobs that did not require education, as field workers, farm hands, and factory gofers. Ironically, it was precisely because of non-schooling many more easily found employment, as the "educated" class was repeatedly rejected.

Conditions grew worse under *Plessy*. By the turn of the century, most Latino students were not so much failing in "Mexican schools" as their education was truncated, with many not having opportunity to attend. Under

Plessy, we learned that the educational system was not one system with major racial disparities, but three distinct systems, each classified by race.

Post-*Brown* and after civil rights, more options became available but primarily during the last third of the century. For example, English language acquisition was granted to ELLs through the Bilingual Education Act (1968), enhanced later by the *Lau* remedies (1974). By the time Latinos became an identifiable group—late in the process—it was for the purposes of desegregating schools (1970) then for census counts (1980), but less to offer special programs.

While the number of high school dropouts declined after the 1990s, achievement gaps persisted with disproportionate school resources creating failing schools along other setbacks like one-sided court orders and ballot propositions sponsored by billionaire funders willfully undoing limited progress achieved, leaping back to previous years. These actions were flamed by racism and aided by social ignorance in proffering insidious propositions in states like California and Arizona, just barely overturned the past two decades after much agony and newer confrontations. Some prohibited language instruction for ELLs, while others barred Mexican American studies, among derisive initiatives. Point being, Latinos continue to face rather difficult conditions that limit their educational progress, with rulings yet to be challenged and legislation still to be enacted. While it has been exasperating, much unfinished business remains.

For this century, contemplating the impact of trends, the Latino now stands at the epicenter. Among key trends are the rapidly changing numerical counts and the changing cultural composition with the "Browning of America." Such Latinization is not trivial, as it is now clear that doing well for the Latino also means doing well for the country. Bottom line conclusion is that the country can no longer afford to cut the nose that will spite its face.

Among lessons learned are remnants from past educational floundering that continues to hound the establishment, as it continues to delimit the educational progress of Latino students. As vestiges from the past, these remain as "challenges" lodged in history, yet to be resolved. By whatever means possible, these warts must be excised. Unaddressed, they will thwart progress. In planning proactively, these conditions are the challenge to the educational achievement for Latinos today.

Among the challenges, the following *ten* (10) rank high in importance. They fall into logical categories or a basket-full of concerns that are extremely important in addressing the education of today's Latinos. While each is specific to the Latino population, not all are exclusively Hispanic as several equally relate to language groups like dual language instruction, with others also vital to all persons of color as well as to low-income populations, as poverty increases in relation to the wealth gap. Collectively, they represent pressing issues, each contributing to favorable outcomes when properly addressed. Let's quickly review these challenges before summarizing their implications.

Challenge #1—Race and Education: The first major issue is that of race and the problem of color in America. Confirmed by many scholars, this continues to weigh heavily on society, affecting every person of color. A vivid example is affirmative action of two types, exceptionalism for Whites and color-race discrimination for nonwhites. Du Bois (1903) had long ago identified the problem of color as the major issue of the 20th century. More recently, Colonel West (1993), declared it as a continuing concern for the 21st century. These affect racial profiling in law enforcement as they equally affect academic profiling of students of color in schools.[2] They also reveal themselves in teacher expectations[3] as well as in "stereotype threat" that plays out in testing and other academic endeavors.[4] These likewise impinge on school leaders as they also affect the everyday decisions of boards. The aftermath of Obama's presidency dismissed the concept of a post-racial society, as too many exceptions became evident. Unquestionably, race continues as a major problem in America which is perpetually seeping into the classroom. In tracking how the concept of race morphed over time, we have learned how its cumulative effects dramatically impact the daily lives of people of color in unexpected ways at different points in time, and certainly in schooling.

Challenge #2—Equity v. Equality: The terms are not synonymous. Equality of education has not always been about equity, and equity is seldom about mere equality. Treating everyone the same is inequitable when differentiation is homogenized. The issue of inequity is of particular concern in the allocation of resources and in school financing as well as differentiation in the classroom and special programs. Wealth gaps have greatly widened the past thirty years, with the U.S. now representing highest poverty levels among OECD industrialized nations with one exception, but also affecting the lives of 1-in-3 children at some point in their lives.[5] With the passage of NCLB, later ESSA and other federal action, the concept of equity has been recast most blandly, under a different rubric through faltering regulations.

Challenge #3—The Achievement Gap: This issue has plagued educators since EEO and the civil rights era. Tens of billions of research dollars have been spent on the topic since, with limited success. In actuality this is about an "opportunity gap," as Sonia Nieto rightfully asserted during our interview.[6] Leila Janah stated the problem clearly when asserting that "Talent is equally distributed, but opportunity is not."[7] This so-called gap has been stagnant for four decades, yet 90/90/90 schools have beaten the odds, among predominantly minority and low-income districts.[8] Outstanding teachers have also overcome the gap.[9] If some minority students can achieve at these schools, then all minority children should likewise achieve in their schools. Achievement gaps are more about negligence and priority than about capacity.

Challenge #4—Parent Engagement: Schools have been highly negligent and rather lax about parent engagement. Parents want to participate, as they want to be involved. Latinos parents want the best for their child, but are uncomfortable with many White middle-class teachers. They also rarely feel welcomed, with too many schools lacking needed language services and culturally-competent staff. Most school staff commutes from distant regions and do not feel at ease with members of the school community. Yet community schools have little difficulty here, as they apparently connect easily with parents. With parents representing the most important person in a child's life and the greatest influence, dollar for dollar they are the best return on investment (ROI) that schools can acquire for raising achievement levels and increasing school safety, but only when schools work with parents as co-equals. Without doubt, the most involved parents have the highly-achieving youngsters.[10] Though every school budget exceeds several million dollars yearly, funds for parent engagement are often relegated to the bottom of the priority list, even when mandated. As Anne Henderson, et al., (2007) tell it, we must move "Beyond the bake sale." The rest may be charades.

Challenge #5—Cultural Compatibility: There is considerable cultural incompatibility and disconnection in the public schools. A critical asset for teachers is relationship-building, often superseding content. Cultural bridges are greatly lacking among many teachers, as they wrestle with meaningful connections with students. At the same time, Latino students want role models, while lacking teachers that understand their culture and relate to their needs. Tapping student affinity and motivation toward higher school performance is favorably enhanced when culture is well understood in the context of instruction and learning.

Challenge #6—Dual language Competence: Nearly 1-in-10 students are ELLs, with rates increasing since 2000. With the majority of ELLs being Hispanic, as nearly 3-in-4 students speak Spanish at home, there is a greater scarcity of English language teachers than for nearly any other subject. Astonishingly, the scarcity is greater today than in the year 2000. This is puzzling, given the lapse in time to recruit and train more. This should not be an excuse for a country that represents the second largest population of Spanish speakers globally. Among the most spoken languages worldwide, Mandarin, English, and Spanish rank with the top four. Here the U.S. has numerical advantages for each of the three, but with great laxity in taking advantage. To this day, there is great resistance for services to English learners. This is worse than even one century ago during the 1890s, when German and other language schools were in vogue.[11] At that time, those schools were perceived as pedagogically sound, providing a most logical, effective and rapid method for the teaching of basic skills to non-English speakers.[12] Concurrently, dual language schools for ELLs are the most effective nationwide, but few in number, while ESL is more often utilized and the least effective method at nearly the same cost.[13] Current practices are fully unbalanced and contrary to what the research literature advises. Common sense together with sound research is not common practice.

Challenge #7—Socio-emotional Learning (SEL): SEL is an important dimension that complements culture and leads to strong personal balance and stability. These are especially necessary for withstanding the complex environments of today's learner. It is important for students to learn how they can maximize interpersonal assets for greater resilience during formative development. For teachers, often working in highly-fragmented and at times polarized settings, the provision of a caring and nurturing environment is essential.[14] The phrase that "kids don't care how much you know until they know how much you care" rings eerily true for many of today's schools. Evidence is clear that emotional intelligence (known as EQ) is equally if not more important than IQ itself for individual resilience and psychic survival as well as for basic sustenance later in life.[15] SEL brings a moral compass into the equation of wellness that is often neglected. Understandably, emotional balance and stability greatly enhance achievement though seldom brought into the classroom as an important factor, even more seldom embedded within the context of culture.

Challenge #8—Education Pipeline: Data from the Department of Education on the educator workforce (2016) indicates that the current workforce does not well reflect the student population. Differences have been widening relative to student populations. Imbalance runs disproportional to what the future requires. The pipeline to replenish is most leaky and often clogged. Teacher recruitment is not attracting a multicultural teaching force, nor is it attracting a highly culturally-competent staff. This is partially due to the low status of educators, with increasing teacher dissatisfaction added to poor working conditions. Dissatisfaction dissuades others from entering. Ranking significantly high is teacher pay that no longer attracts a high-caliber workforce. Among the professions, teachers require a master's degree and continuing education combined with additional work taken home daily. Given their credentials, they are the most underpaid profession. As teacher quality correlates highly with achievement, a highly-competent workforce is required. Among nations high in achievement, teacher quality is highly valued and compensated. For them, nation-building is anchored on education. Here the ROI is exponential, with children as major beneficiaries.

Challenge #9—Higher Education: There is lower Latino representation at IHEs for both administrators and instructional staff as compared to even K–12 public schools.[16] At the other end, good news is that there has been a favorable increase among Latino students entering colleges and universities the past five years. Not as favorable is that most are enrolled in 2-year colleges, with low transfer rates. Among 4-year universities, they cluster in fewer schools compared to other racial minorities. Financial assistance continues to be problematic. Appallingly, fewer dollars exist for grants and scholarships than during the 1960s and 1970s. In retrospect, it is interesting to note that the U.S. economy boomed when the GI Bill incentivized WWII veterans to complete their college years, with another economic spark occurring when national student loans and scholarships peaked after Sputnik. It is time to again re-pump this fire hydrant to beef up college enrollment as it also will bolster the national economy. As Latinos will likely become the largest college-goers the next two decades, it would be wondrous to increase the numbers and facilitate higher graduation rates for new entrants.

Challenge #10—Educational Leadership: Schools should be viewed as gas stations for national prosperity. As such, they must be guided by thoughtful, inclusive, and competent leaders. These educators are the single most powerful and significant player for the effectiveness of a school and its performance. Yet, there are all too few Latino and minority leaders. This is not to say minorities are the answer—as this is less about counting heads and more about making heads count—but there must be greater representation. There are plenty of competent candidates that are being deselected, as minority talent abounds. Quality leadership also suffers from similar drawbacks as the teacher pipeline, the primary feeder to administration. Furthermore, educators are not strongly defending their convictions, especially in the political arena. More gumption is needed in school leadership, as too many ruffians are running roughshod over the schools. Leaders must swat politicians, as politicization has wreaked havoc. Stronger controls and greater aptness in leadership is needed for the flux of politics not to upend the soundness of education. Much has been learned from bygone years, as reviewed. As an inclusive process, leadership is not about one person, but about a collaborative effort and a leadership team. The better the client is understood in the quest for excellence and diversity, the better leadership can adequately respond.

In closure it is important to indicate that there are always lessons from a volume such as this that cannot be fully captured in any review or summary. It is important to say that another learning in our survey of history is that outstanding reformers like Horace Mann in the 19th century and John Dewey in the 20th century were able to transcend the petty politics of their day and focus on the future and wellbeing of society, not constrained by immediate exigencies at hand or flavor of the month in the politics of reform or inaction.

Still another lesson is the need for significant and lasting changes in education. Special government efforts were each sponsored with considerable funding support in the past, going beyond the lip service of good will. Many were also backed by legislation and decision-making from at least two of the three branches of government. In looking back, it would be difficult to single out any major turning point in education where such factors were not operable and at play.

After reviewing several hundred years of education that strongly impacted negatively on racial groups, we cannot expect this will improve without counteraction. To the contrary, educational pace seems to be moving in opposite directions, with potentially disastrous momentum left unfettered. We need to be weary and watchful to ensure tipping points do not capitulate against the public schools and its minority students as was the educational demise under *Plessy*. Similar conditions can recur if certain trends continue to run amuck and unrestrained.

What is truly uniquely different between today and yesterday is the high number of Latinos and other students of color. This fact alone can make all the difference, as demography packs a powerful punch. Here we must caution with what happened in apartheid South Africa not long ago. For the U.S., it was easier to historically miseducate and abandon ten percent of the population of color a century ago, yet more difficult to now ignore a majority-minority school system, but plausible if trends continue unabated. The ten looming challenges forecasted in this epilogue are more thoroughly covered in my upcoming book, *Critical Issues of Latinos and Education in 21st Century America: Where Are We?*

In closing, it is important to note that we are at a turning point in history that cannot continue wholly unchecked and unresolved. Hope is that if a large number of children continue to be underserved, their parents will not allow the worsening of conditions and rise up. Yet, there is no guarantee. Hopefully, government will learn beforehand. As such, it is my sincere hope the country will navigate its way out of today's educational quagmire as the nation will otherwise face incredible difficulties within the lifetime of many readers like you. Lets work collaboratively to avert a perfect storm now looming by the next generation.

Notes

1. Taken from the title of James Herndon's book, 1965.
2. Ochoa, 2013.
3. Rosenthal and Jacobson, 1992.
4. Steele & Aronson, 1995.
5. Stiglitz, 2013.
6. Taken from interview with Sonia Nieto, 2017.
7. Leila Janah quote: https://quotefancy.com/quote/1778710/Leila-Janah-Talent-is-equally-distributed-but-opportunity-is-not
8. Several appear in previous chapters.
9. Jaime Escalante appeared earlier as one of many.
10. Noboa, 2017.
11. Kloss, 1998.
12. Ovando, 2003.
13. Thomas & Collier, 2017.
14. Noddings, 2006.
15. Goleman, 1995.
16. U.S. Department of Education, *The State of Racial Diversity in the Education Workforce*, 2016.

BIBLIOGRAPHY

Albert Shanker Institute (2015). *The State of Teacher Diversity in American Education*. Washington, DC: Author, September 16, 2015 Report. Retrieved November 11, 2015. Available at: https://docs.google.com/viewerng/viewer?url=http://www.shankerinstitute.org/sites/shanker/files/The%2520State%2520of%2520Teacher%2520Diversity%2520in%2520American%2520Education.pdf

Allport, G. W. (1954). *The Nature of Prejudice*. Cambridge, MA: Addison-Wesley Publishing Company.

Anderson, J. D. (1988). *The Education of Blacks in the South, 1860–1935*. Chapel Hill: University of North Carolina Press.

Astor, M. (2017). Tucson's Mexican studies program was a victim of 'racial animus' judge says. *New York Times* (August 23, 2017). http://california-mexicocenter.org/tucsons-mexican-studies-program-was-a-victim-of-racial-animus-judge-says/

Baker, B.; D. Farrie; M. Johnson; T. Luhm; & D. G. Sciarra (4th Ed.)(Spring 2015). *Is School Funding Fair? A national report card*. Education Law Center, Newark, NJ: Rutgers Graduate School of Education.

Balingit, M. (December 4, 2017). U.S. high school graduation rates rise to new high. Retrieved May 30, 2018. Available at: https://www.washingtonpost.com/news/education/wp/2017/12/04/u-s-high-school-graduation-rates-rise-to-new-high/?utm_term=.da1e25846fe1

Baron, E. (May 8, 2018). H-1B: Foreign citizens make up nearly three-fourths of Silicon Valley tech workforce, report says. *Mercury News*. Retrieved June 6, 2018. Available at: https://

www.mercurynews.com/2018/01/17/h-1b-foreign-citizens-make-up-nearly-three-quarters-of-silicon-valley-tech-workforce-report-says/

Barrón, L. (August 7, 2013). *Census: Non-English speakers in U.S. nearly triple in 30 years.* Retrieved July 16, 2016. Available at: http://www.newsmax.com/US/english-language-speakers-report/2013/08/07/id/519251/

Bennis, W. G. (1994). *On Becoming a Leader.* New York City: Addison-Wesley Publishing Company.

Berlin, I. (2015). *The Long Emancipation: The demise of slavery in the United States.* Cambridge, MA: Harvard University Press.

Berman, M. G.; J. Jonides; & D. E. Nee (2006). *Social Cognitive and Affective Neuroscience, 1*(2), 158–161 (September 1, 2006).

Bialik, K. (June 12, 2017). *Key Facts about Race and Marriage, 50 years after Loving V. Virginia.* By Pew Research Center. Retrieved May 28, 2018. Available at: http://www.pewresearch.org/fact-tank/2017/06/12/key-facts-about-race-and-marriage-50-years-after-loving-v-virginia/

Bidgood, J. (April 9, 2015). Black Immigrants have quadrupled since 1980, study says. *New York Times.* Retrieved April 18, 2010. Available at: https://www.nytimes.com/2015/04/10/us/black-immigrants-have-quadrupled-since-1980-study-says.html

Billingsley, A. (1992). *Climbing Jacob's Ladder: The enduring legacy of African-American families.* New York City: Touchstone.

Blanton, C. K. (2014). *George I. Sánchez: The long fight for Mexican American integration.* New Haven, CT: Yale University Press.

Blauner, R. (1972). *Racial Oppression in America.* New York City: Harper & Row.

Bloom, B. S. (1983). *All Our Children Learning: A primer for parents, teachers, and other educators.* New York City: McGraw-Hill.

Bobbitt, F. (1924). *How to Make a Curriculum.* Boston: Houghton Mifflin Co.

Bond, H. M. (1939). *Negro Education in Alabama: A Study on cotton and steel.* Tuscaloosa, AL: University of Alabama Press.

——— (1934). *The Education of the Negro in the American Social Order.* New York City: Prentice-Hall, Inc.

Bowman, K. L. (2001). The New Face of School Desegregation. *Duke Law Journal, 50,* 1751–1808.

Boydston, J. A. (Ed.)(1972). *Guide to the Works of John Dewey.* Carbondale, IL: Southern Illinois University Press.

Brown, A. (2014a). *U.S. Hispanics and Asian Populations Growing, but for Different Reasons.* Washington, DC: Pew Research Center (June 26, 2014).

——— (2014b). *The U.S. Hispanic population has increased sixfold since 1970.* Washington, DC: Pew Research Center (February 26, 2014).

Brown, E. (June 8, 2015). Inequitable school funding called 'one of the sleeper civil rights issues of our time'. Retrieved December 14, 2018. Available at: https://www.washingtonpost.com/news/local/wp/2015/06/08/inequitable-school-funding-called-one-of-the-sleeper-civil-rights-issues-of-our-time/?noredirect=on&utm_term=.8d18829ff904

——— (May 16, 2016). New data shows U.S. schools are resegregating. *The Washington Post*, A1-A2.

Burma, J. H. (1954). *Spanish-Speaking Groups in the United States*. Durham, NC: Duke University Press.

Caliver, A. (1950). Certain Significant Developments in the Education of Negroes during the Past Generation. *The Journal of Negro History*, 35 (2), 111–134.

——— (1940). *Negro High-School Graduates and Nongraduates: Relation of their occupational status to certain school experiences*. Washington, DC: U.S. Office of Education, GPO.

Cameron, C. E.; E. A. Cottone; W. M. Murray; D. W. Grissmer (2016). How are motor skills linked to children's school performance and academic achievement? *Child Development Perspectives*, 10(2), 93–98.

Carter, T. P. (1970). *Mexican Americans in Schools: A history of educational neglect*. New York City: College Entrance Examination Board.

Carter, T. P. & R. D. Segura (1979). *Mexican Americans in School: A decade of change*. Princeton, NJ: College Entrance Examination Board.

Center for American Progress (April 20, 2017). The Facts on Immigration Today: 2017 Edition. Retrieved June 3, 2018. Available at: https://www.americanprogress.org/issues/immigration/reports/2017/04/20/430736/facts-immigration-today-2017-edition/

Chapa, J. (1988). The Question of Mexican American Assimilation: Socioeconomic parity or underclass formation? *Public Affairs Comment*, 35, 1–14.

Chappell, B. (June 22, 2017). *Census finds a more diverse America, as whites lag growth*. Retrieved May 22, 2018. Available at: https://www.npr.org/sections/thetwo-way/2017/06/22/533926978/census-finds-a-more-diverse-america-as-whites-lag-growth

Chesler, M. A; A. E. Lewis; & J. E. Crowfoot (2005). *Challenging Racism in Higher Education: Promoting justice*. Lanham, MD: Rowman & Littlefield Publishers, Inc.

Clark, K. B. (1965). *Dark Ghetto: Dilemmas of Social Power*. New York City: Harper & Row, Publishers.

Clark, K. B. and M. P. Clark (1950). Emotional Factors in Racial Identification and Preference in Negro Children. *Journal of Negro Education*, 19, 341–350.

Cohen, A. (March-April 2016). Harvard's Eugenics Era. *Harvard Magazine*, 118(4), 48–52.

Cohen, S. (Ed.)(1974). *Education in the United States: A documentary history*. New York City: Random House.

Coleman, J. S.; E. Q. Campbell; C. J. Hobson; J. McPartland; A. M. Mood; F. D. Weinfeld; & R. L. York (1966). *Equality of Educational Opportunity*. Washington, DC: Government Printing Office.

College and University Professional Association for Human Resources (CUPA-HR), 2018 annual survey results, at https://www.cupahr.org/surveys/results/administrators-in-higher-education/

Coloma, R. S. (2004). *Empire and Education: Filipino schooling under United States rule, 1900–1910*. Ph.D. dissertation, Ohio State University.

Comer, J. P. and N. M. Haynes (1992). *Summary of School Development Program Effects*. New Haven, CT: Yale Child Study Center.

Connor, P. and G. López (May 18, 2016). 5 Facts about the U.S. Rank in Worldwide Migration. Washington, DC: Pew Research Center.

Cooper, A. J. (1892). *A Voice from the South*. Xenia, OH: The Aldine Printing House.

Cox, W. M. and R. Alm (2015). What D'ya Know? Lifetime learning in pursuit of the American dream. In *Federal Reserve Bank of Dallas, 2004 Annual Report* (pp. 5–23).

Cremin, L. A. (1961). *The Transformation of the School: Progressivism in American education, 1876–1957*. New York City: Vintage Books.

Cubberley, E. P. (1919). *Public Education in the United States*. Boston, MA: Houghton Mifflin Company.

Danzinger, S. and P. Gottschalk (Eds.) (1993). *Uneven Tides: Rising inequality in America*. New York City: Russell Sage Foundation.

Darder, A. and R. D. Torres. (Eds.) (2014) (2nd Ed.). *Latinos and Education: A critical reader*. New York City: Routledge.

Darling-Hammond, L. (2010). *The Flat World and Education: How America's commitment to equity will determine our future*. New York City: Teacher's College Press.

De Tocqueville, A. ([1835] 2000). *Democracy in America*. Chicago: University of Chicago.

Del Valle, S. (2003). *Language Rights and the Law in the United States: Finding our voices*. Clevedon, UK: Multilingual Matters Ltd.

Delpit, L. D. (1995). *Other People's Children: Cultural conflict in the classroom*. New York City: New Press.

Devos, T. and M. R. Banaji (2005). America = White? *Journal of Personality and Social Psychology*, 88: 447–466.

Díaz, Nelson A. (2018). *Not from Here, Not from There/No Soy de Aquí ni de Allá: The Autobiography of Nelson Díaz*. Philadelphia, PA: Temple University Press.

Dickson, V. E. (1923). *Mental Tests and the Classroom Teacher*. New York City: World Book Company.

Donato, R. (1997). *The other Struggle for Equal Schools: Mexican-Americans during the civil rights era*. Albany, NY: State University of New York Press.

Donato, R. and J. S. Hanson (2012). Legally White, Socially Mexican: The politics of *de jure* and *de facto* school segregation in the American Southwest. *Harvard Education Review*, 82(2), 202–225.

——— (April 11, 2017). "In these towns, Mexicans are classified as Negroes": The politics of unofficial segregation in the Kansas Public Schools, 1915–1935. *American Educational Research Journal*, 54(1), 53S-74S.

Du Bois, W. E.B. (1968[1903]). *The Autobiography of W. E. B. Du Bois*. New York City: International Publishers Co., Inc.

——— (1935). Does the Negro Need Separate Schools? *Journal of Negro Education*, 4(July), 328–335.

Duckworth, A. L. (2016). *Grit: The Power of Passion and Perseverance*. New York City: Scribner.

DuFour, R. (May 2004). What is a Professional Learning Community? *Educational Leadership*, 61(8), 6–11.

Durant, W. and A. Durant (1968). *The Lessons of History*. New York City: Simon & Schuster.

Dweck, C. S. (2006). *Mindset: The new psychology of success*. New York City: Random House Publishing Group.

Edmonds, R. R. (1979). Effective Schools for the Urban Poor. *Educational Leadership, 37*(1), 15–18, 20–24 (October).

Edwards, N. (1939). *Equal Educational Opportunity for Youth*. Washington, DC: American Council on Education.

Eliot, C. W. (1911). *The Suppression of Moral Defectives*. Paper presented at the 38thh National Conference of Charities & Corrections, June 7–14, 1911, Boston, MA.

Farr, J. S. and M. Trachtenberg (1998). The Edgewood Drama: An epic quest for education equity. *Yale Law & Public Review, 17*(2), article 2, 607–727.

Fernández-Armesto, F. (2014). *Our America: A Hispanic history of the United States*. New York City: W.W. Norton & Company.

Flores, A. (September 18, 2017). *How the U.S. Hispanic population is changing*. Pew Research Center. Retrieved May 28, 2018. Available at: http://www.pewresearch.org/fact-tank/2017/09/18/how-the-u-s-hispanic-population-is-changing/

Foley, N. (2005). Becoming Hispanic: Mexicans in the making of America. In P. S. Rothenberg, *Privilege: Essential readings on the other side of racism* (pp. 55–65). New York City: Worth Publishers.

Franco, J. (April 20, 2015). 50 Years of Moore's Law: Fun facts, a timeline infographic and Gordon's own thoughts 5 decades later. Retrieved June 16, 2018. Available at: https://www.techspot.com/news/60418-50-years-moore-law-fun-facts-timeline-infographic.html

Franklin, J. H. (1947) (1st Ed.). *From Slavery to Freedom: A history of African Americans*. New York City: Alfred A. Knopf.

Frazier, E. F. (1939). *The Negro Family in the United States*. Chicago: University of Chicago Press.

Freire, P. (1970). *Pedagogy of the Oppressed*. New York City: Seabury Press.

Friedman, T. L. (2005). *The World Is Flat: A brief history of the twenty-first century*. New York City: Picador.

Fry, R. and P. Taylor (2013). *Hispanic High School Graduates Pass Whites in Rate of College Enrollment: High school drop-outs at record low*. Washington, DC: Pew Rxh Center.

Fullan, M. (2014). *The Principal: Three keys to maximizing impact*. San Francisco, CA: Jossey-Bass.

Giridharadas, A. (2018). *Winners Take All: The elite charade of changing the world*. New York City: Alfred A. Knopf.

Gladwell, M. (2002). *The Tipping Point: How little things can make a big difference*. New York City: Little, Brown and Company.

——— (2009). *What the Dog Saw*. New York City: Little, Brown and Company.

Glazer, N. and D. P. Moynihan (1st Ed.) (1963). *Beyond the Melting Pot: The Negroes, Puerto Ricans, Jew, Italians and Irish of New York City*. Cambridge, MA: MIT Press.

Goldin, C. and L. F. Katz (2008). *The Race between Education and Technology*. Cambridge, MA: Harvard University Press.

Goldstein, D. (2014). *The Teacher Wars: A history of America's most embattled profession*. New York City: Penguin Random House, LLC.

Goleman, D. (1995). *Emotional Intelligence: Why it can matter more than IQ*. New York City: Bantam Books.

Gómez, L. E. (2nd Ed.) (2018). *Manifest Destinies: The making of the Mexican American race*. New York City: New York University.

Gongloff, M. (November 8, 2017). 45 million Americans still stuck below poverty line: Census. Retrieved June 1, 2018. Available at: https://www.huffingtonpost.com/2014/09/16/poverty-household-income_n_5828974.html

González, G. G. (1990). *Chicano Education in the Era of Segregation*. Philadelphia: Balch Institute Press.

Gordon, M. M. (1964). *Assimilation in American Life: The role of race, religion, and national origins*. New York City: Oxford University Press.

Gramlich, J. (September 20, 2017). *Hispanic Dropout Rate Hits New Low, College Enrollment at New High*. Washington, DC: Pew Research Center.

Grebler, L.; J. W. Moore; & R. C. Guzmán (1970). *The Mexican-American People: The nation's second largest minority*. New York City: Free Press.

Greer, C. (1972). *The Great School Legend: A revisionist interpretation of American public education*. New York City: Basic Books, Inc., Publishers.

Hacker, A. (1992). *Two Nations: Black and White, Separate, Hostile, Unequal*. New York City: Scribner.

Handlin, O. (1982). Education and the European Immigrants, 1820–1920. In B.J. Weiss (Ed.), *American Education and the European Immigrant: 1840–1940* (pp. 3–16). Chicago: University of Illinois Press.

——— (1959). *The Newcomers: Negroes and Puerto Ricans in a changing metropolis*. New York City: Anchor Books.

——— (1951). *The Uprooted: The epic story of the great migrations that made the American people*. Boston: Little, Brown & Company.

Hanushek, E. A. (2016). What Matters for Student Achievement: Updating Coleman on the Influence of Families and Schools. *Education Next*, 16(2), 18–26 (Spring 2016).

Hayes, C. (2017). *A Colony in a Nation*. New York City: W.W. Norton & Company, Inc.

Heckman, J. J. (2013). *Giving Kids a Fair Chance*. Cambridge, MA: MIT Press.

Heckman, J. J. and A. B. Krueger (2003). *Inequality in America: What role for human capital policies?* Cambridge, MA: MIT Press.

Henderson, A. T.; K. L. Mapp; V. R. Johnson; & D. Davies (2007). *Beyond the Bake Sale: The essential guide to family-school partnerships*. New York City: The New Press.

Hendrie, C. (1999). In Black and White. *Educational Week*, March 24, 1999.

Herbold, H. (Winter 1994). It was never a level playing field: Blacks and the G.I. Bill. *Journal of Blacks in Higher Education*, 6, 104–108.

Herndon, J. (1965). The Way It Spozed to Be. New York City: Simon & Schuster, Inc.

Hoffman, A. (1974). *Unwanted Mexican Americans in the Great Depression: Repatriation pressures, 1929–1939*. Tucson: University of Arizona Press.

Honig, B. (1985). *Last Chance for Our Children: How you can help save our schools*. Menlo Park, CA: Addison-Wesley Publishing Company, Inc.

Howard, C. A. C. (spring 2015). *"I've always been for education": Mexicana/o Participation in Formal, Non-formal, and Informal Education in the Midwest, 1910–1955.* Ph.D. dissertation, University of Iowa.

Hugo López, M. (August 20, 2012). *Hispanic Student Enrollments Reach New Highs in 2011.* Washington, DC: Report by the Pew Research Center.

Human Rights Advocate (May 5, 2017). 2017 World Best Education Systems—first quarter report. Retrieved May 30, 2018. Available at: https://worldtop20.org/2017-world-best-education-systems-1st-quarter-report

Heyns, B. (1978). *Summer learning and the effects of schooling.* New York City: Academia Press.

Ignatiev, N. (1995). *How the Irish became White.* New York City: Routledge.

Jackson, A. and A. Kiersz (December 6, 2016). The latest ranking of top countries in math, reading, and science is out—and the US didn't crack the top 10. Retrieved May 30, 2018. Available at: http://www.businessinsider.com/pisa-worldwide-ranking-of-math-science-reading-skills-2016-12

Jencks, C., et al. (1972). *Inequality: A reassessment of the effect of family and schooling in America.* New York City: Basic Books, Inc.

Jensen, A. R. (1979). How much can we boost IQ and scholastic achievement? *Harvard Educational Review,* 39(1), 1–123 (winter).

Kandel, I. L. (1934). *The Dilemmas of Democracy.* Cambridge, MA: Harvard University Press.

Kanellos, N. (1997). *Hispanic Firsts: 500 years of extraordinary achievement.* Detroit: Visible Ink Press.

Katz, M. B. (2001)(2nd Ed.). *The Irony of Early School Reform: Educational innovation in mid-nineteenth century Massachusetts.* New York City: Teachers College Press.

Kim, L. M; M. Tienda; & A. Zajacova (June 22, 2001). *Trends in Educational Achievement of Minority Students Since Brown v. Board of Education.* Princeton, NJ: Princeton University, Office of Population Research.

Kloss, H. (1998). *The American Bilingual Tradition: Language in education.* Rowley, Mexican American: Newbury House.

Kotter, J. P. and H. Rathgeber (2016). *That's Not How We Do It Here!* New York City: Penguin Random House LLC.

Kousser, J. M. (1986). Dead End: The development of nineteenth century litigation on racial discrimination in schools. Oxford, England: Oxford University Press.

Krogstad, J. M. (July 28, 2016). *5 Facts about Latinos and Education.* Washington, DC: Pew Research Center.

Kurlansky, M. (2005). *1968: The Year that Rocked the World.* New York City: Random House, Inc.

Landgrave, M. and A. Nowrasteh (2017). Criminal Immigrants: The numbers, demographics, and countries of origin. Washington, DC: Cato Institute.

Lee, T. (May 7, 2014). Education racial gap wide as ever according to NAEP. Retrieved May 30, 2018. Available at: http://www.msnbc.com/msnbc/student-proficiency-stagnant-race-gap-wide

Leis, W. A. (1931). *The Status of Education for Mexican Children in Four Border States.* Unpublished master's thesis, University of Southern California, Los Angeles, CA.

Lewis, O. (1966). *La Vida: A Puerto Rican family in the culture of poverty—San Juan and New York*. New York City: Random House.

———— (1961). *Children of Sánchez: Autobiography of a Mexican family*. New York City: Vantage Books.

Little, W. (1944). *Spanish-Speaking Children in Texas*. Austin: University of Texas Press.

Livingston, G. (June 6, 2017). *The Rise of Multiethnic and Multiracial Babies in the U.S. By Pew Research Center*. Retrieved May 28, 2018. Available at: http://www.pewresearch.org/fact-tank/2017/06/06/the-rise-of-multiracial-and-multiethnic-babies-in-the-u-s/

Locke, A. L. (1925b)(Ed.). *The New Negro: An interpretation*. New York City: Albert and Charles Boni, Inc.

Lockridge, K. A. (1974). *Literacy in Colonial New England*. New York City: W.W. Norton & Company, Inc.

Long, J. (1990). *Duel of Eagles: The Mexican and U.S. fight for the Alamo: The Mexican and the U.S. fight for the Alamo*. New York City: William Morrow and Company, Inc.

Lucas, I. (1971). *Puerto Rican Dropouts in Chicago: Numbers and motivations*. Final Report, U. S. Office of Education, Bureau of Research. Chicago: DHEW, 1971 (March).

Lumina Foundation (2019). *A Stronger Nation: Learning beyond high school builds American talent*. Retrieved April 11, 2019. Available at: http://strongernation.luminafoundation.org/report/2019/#nation

MacDonald, V. M. (2016). *The Fractured Pipeline: Mexican American access to high schooling, 1920–1954*. [Unpublished manuscript]

———— (Ed.) (2004). *Latino Education in the United States: A narrated history, 1513–2000*. New York City: Palgrave/Macmillan.

MacDonald, V. M. and A. Cook (2017). Before Chicana Civil Rights: Three generations of Mexican American women in higher education in the Southwest, 1920–1965. In M. A. Nash (Ed.), *Women's Higher Education in the United States: New historical perspectives* (pp. 233–254). New York: Palgrave Macmillan.

MacDonald, V. M. and T. García (2003). Latino Higher Education: Historical pathways to Access. In J. Castellanos and L. Jones (Eds.), *The Majority in the Minority: Retaining Latina/o faculty, administrators, and students in the 21st century* (pp. 15–43). Sterling, VA: Stylus Press.

MacDonald, V. M. and G. Guzmán (2017). Revolution and World War I Civil Rights: Transnational relations and Mexican Consul records in Mexican American Educational History, 1910–1929. *Education's Histories*, 4 (December 28, 2017). https://scholarworks.umt.edu/eduhist/vol4/iss1/5

MacDonald, V. M. and J. Rivera (2015). History's Prism in Education: A spectrum of legacies across centuries of Mexican American agency; experience and activism 1600s-2000s. In R. E. Zambrana and S. Hurtado (Eds.), *The Magic Key: The educational journey of Mexican Americans from K–12 to college and beyond* (pp. 25–52), Austin, TX: University of Texas Press.

Malcolm X (1965). *The Autobiography of Malcolm X*. New York City: Grove Press.

Malik, S. (May 21, 2015). *Asian Immigrants to the United States Today*. Washington, DC: Center for American Progress.

Manuel, H. T. (1930). *The Education of Mexican and Spanish-Speaking Children in Texas.* Austin, TX: Fund for Research in the Social Sciences, University of Texas.

Margo, R. A. (1990). *Race and Schooling in the South, 1880–1950: An economic history.* Chicago: University Chicago Press, National Bureau of Economic Research.

Margolis, R. J. (1968). *The Losers: A report on Puerto Ricans and the public schools.* New York City: Aspira of America, Inc.

Martínez, S. L. M. (2007). *The Education of Mexican Descent in the Southwest, 1940–1980: An exploratory analysis of enrollment and achievement in the high school movement.* Ph.D. dissertation, University of Kansas.

Marzano, R. J. (2003). *What Works in Schools: Translating research into action.* Alexandria, Virginia: Association for Supervision and Curriculum Development.

Maxwell, L. A. (2014). U. S. School Enrollment Hits Majority-Minority Milestone. *Education Today,* August 18, 2014.

May, V. M. (2015). *Anna Julia Copper (1858–1964): Black Feminist Scholar, Educator, and Activist.* Retrieved September 2, 2017. Available at: file:///C:/Users/Abdin/Downloads/NC.Women.AJC.2014.PDF

McAlister, L. N. (3rd Ed.) (1989). *Spain and Portugal in the New World, 1492–1700.* Minneapolis, MN: University of Minnesota Press.

McCarthy, N. (February 12, 2018). The world's most spoken languages. https://www.statista.com/chart/12868/the-worlds-most-spoken-languages/

McBride, J. (1996). *The Color of Water: A black man's tribute to his white mother.* New York City: Riverhead Books.

McGaha, R... (1990). *The Journal of S. Elizabeth Dusenbury, 1852–1857, Portrait of a Teacher's Development.* Ph.D. dissertation, Iowa State University.

McNight, J. (1995). *The Careless Society: Community and its Counterfeits.* New York City: Basic Books.

McWilliams, C. (1968). *North from Mexico: the Spanish-Speaking people of the United States.* New York City: Greenwood Press.

——— (1947). Spectrum of Segregation. *Survey Graphic* 36(1), 22–25, 106–107 (January).

Meacham, J. (2018). *Soul of a Nation: The battle for our better angels.* New York City: Random House.

Meléndez, E. and C. Vargas-Ramos (2017)(Eds.). *State of Puerto Ricans 2017.* New York City: Centro Press, Center for Puerto Rican Studies.

Menchaca, M. (2001). *Recovering History, Constructing Race: The Indian, black and white roots of Mexican Americans.* Austin: University of Texas Press.

Mitchell, C. (January 25, 2018). The National Shortage of ELL Teachers has Caught the Eye of Congress. Education Week. http://blogs.edweek.org/edweek/learning-the-language/2018/01/solve_ell_teacher_shortage.html

Molina, N. (2014). *How Race is Made in America: Immigration, citizenship, and the historical power of racial scripts.* Berkeley and Los Angeles: University of California Press.

Mondale, S. and S. B. Patton (Eds.)(2001). *School: The story of American public education.* Boston: Beacon Press.

Montejano, D. (1987). *Anglos and Mexicans in the Making of Texas, 1836–1986*. Austin, TX: University of Texas Press.

Montoya, M. E. (2001). A Brief History of Chicana/o School Segregation: One rationale for affirmative action. *Berkeley Law Raza Journal, 12*(2): 159–172.

Mora, G. C. (2014). *Making Hispanics: How activists, bureaucrats & media constructed a new America*. Chicago, IL: University of Chicago Press.

Morales Carrión, A. (Ed.) (1983). *Puerto Rico: A political and cultural history*. New York City: W. W. Norton & Company, Inc.

Morgan, J. E. (1938). *Horace Mann at Antioch*. Washington, DC: NEA.

Moynihan, D. P. (1965). *The Negro Family: The case for national action*. Washington, DC: U.S. Government Printing Office.

Muhammad, A. (2015). *Overcoming the Achievement Gap: Liberating mindsets to effect change*. Bloomington, IN: Solution Tree Press.

Mullis, Ina S.; M. O. Martin; A. M. Kenney; & P. Foy (2007). *PIRLS 2006 International Study*. Boston, MA: Boston College.

Murray, D. (1899). *The History of Education in New Jersey*. Washington, DC: Government Printing Office.

Myrdal, G. (1944). *An American Dilemma: The Negro problem & modern democracy*. New York City: Harper & Row, Publishers.

Nagdy, M. and M. Roser (2016). *Primary Education*. Retrieved November 1, 2016; Available at https://ourworldindata.org/primary-education-and-schools/

Nation's Report Card (2015). 2015 Mathematics & Reading Assessments. Retrieved May 30, 2018. Available at: https://www.nationsreportcard.gov/reading_math_2015/#reading?grade=4

Negrón de Montilla, A. (1975). *Americanization in Puerto Rico and the Public School System 1900–1930*. Río Piedras, PR: Universidad de Puerto Rico.

Noboa-Ríos, A. (2017). *FLI Impact Study Report 2017*. Washington, DC: ICI, Inc. (Evaluation Report submitted to San Bernardino County Unified School District.)

Noddings, N. (2006). Educating Whole People: A response to Jonathan Cohen. *Harvard Education Review, 76*(2), 238–242.

Noguera, P. A. and J. Y. Wing (Eds.) (2006). *Unfinished Business: Closing the racial achievement gap in our schools*. San Francisco: Jossey-Bass

Novak, M. (2nd Ed.) (1996). *Unmeltable Ethnics: Politics and culture in American life*. New Brunswick, NJ: Transaction Publishers.

Ochoa, G. L. (2013). *Academic Profiling: Latinos, Asian Americans, and the achievement gap*. Minneapolis: University of Minnesota Press.

O'Donnell, E. T. (2011). *Turning Points in American History: Course guidebook*. Chantilly, VA: The Teaching Company.

O'Donnell, M. (April 2018). Commander v. Chief. *The Atlantic*. Retrieved: June 21, 2018. Available at: https://www.theatlantic.com/magazine/archive/2018/04/commander-v-chief/554045/

OECD (2017). *Education at a Glance 2017: OECD Indicators*. OECD Publications. Retrieved May 30, 2018. Available at: http://www.oecd.org/edu/education-at-a-glance-19991487.htm

——— (2018). *PISA 2015: Results in Focus*. Retrieved May 30, 2018. Available at: https://www.oecd.org/pisa/pisa-2015-results-in-focus.pdf

Olivas, M. A. (Fall 2008). The "Trial of the Century" that Never Was: Staff Sgt. Macario García, the Congressional Medal of Honor, and the Oasis Café. *Indiana Law Journal*, 83(4), 1391–1402.

Orfield, G. (1999). Politics Matters: Educational policy and Chicano students. In J. F. Moreno (Ed.), *The Elusive Quest for Equality: 150 years of Chicano/Chicana education*. Cambridge, MA: Harvard Education Review.

Orfield, G.; E. Jongyeon; E. Frankenburg; & G. Siegel-Hawley (May 16, 2016). *Brown at 62: School Segregation by Race, Poverty and State*. Los Angeles: The Civil Rights Project/Proyecto Derechos Civiles.

Orozco, C. E. (2009). *No Mexicans, Women, or Dogs Allowed: The rise of the Mexican American civil rights movement*. Austin: University of Texas Press.

O'Sullivan, J. L. (1845). Annexation. *United States Magazine and Democratic Review*, 17(1), 5–11.

Ovando, C. J. (2003). Bilingual Education in the United States: Historical development and current issues. *Bilingual Research Journal*, 27(1), 1–24 (Spring).

Palmer, D. K. and E. E. García (2000). Voices from the Field: Bilingual educators speak candidly about Proposal 227. *Bilingual Research Journal*, 24(1), 1–10.

Pantoja, A.; B. Blourock; & J. Bowman (1972). *Badges & Indicia of Slavery: Cultural pluralism redefined*. Lincoln, NE: Nebraska Curriculum Development Center.

Peabody, E. P. (1882). The origin and growth of the kindergarten. *Education*, 2, 507–527.

Perry, T.; C. Steele; & A. Hilliard III (2003). *Young, Gifted, and Black: Promoting high achievement among African American students*. Boston, MA: Beacon Press.

Pitt, L. (1966). *Decline of the Californios: A social history of the Spanish-speaking Californios, 1846–1890*. Berkeley and Los Angeles: University of California Press.

Powell, B. (2010). *An Economic Case for Immigration*. Article taken from the Library of Economics and Liberty. Retrieved March 9, 2016. Available at: http://www.econlib.org/library/Columns/y2010/Powellimmigration.html

President's Advisory Commission on Educational Excellence for Hispanic Americans (1996). *Our Nation on the Fault Line: Hispanic American education*. Washington, DC: GPO.

Rangel J. C. and C. M. Alcalá (1972). Project Report: De Jure segregation of Chicanos in Texas schools. *Harvard Civil Rights—Civil Liberties Law Review*, 7 (March 1972), 307–391.

Ravitch, D. (2000). *Left Back: A century of battles over school reform*. New York City: Touchstone.

——— (2010). *The Death and Life of the Great American School System: How testing and choice are undermining education*. New York City: Basic Books.

——— (2013). *Reign of Error: The hoax of the privatization movement and the danger to America's public schools*. New York City: Vintage Books.

Reyes, L. O. (2006). The Aspira Consent Decree: A thirtieth anniversary retrospective of bilingual education in New York City. *Harvard Education Review* 76(3), 369–400.

Reynolds, A. (1933). *The Education of Spanish-Speaking Children in Five Southwestern States* (Bulletin 1933, No. 11). Washington, DC: U.S. Department of the Interior, GPO.

Richman, J. (1905). "The Immigrant Child." *NEA Addresses and Proceedings*, 44th Annual Meeting, Asbury Park, NJ, pp. 113–121.

Rivas, J. (February 17, 2012). Latinos Most Likely Ethnic Group to 'Mary-Out' of Race. In *Colorlines*, published by *Race Forward*. Retrieved July 16, 2016. Available at: http://www.colorlines.com/articles/latinos-most-likely-ethnic-group-marry-out-race

Rivera-Servera, R. (2012). *Performing Queer Latinidad: Dance, sexuality, politics*. Ann Arbor, MI: University of Michigan Press.

Rodríguez, L. F. and L. Oseguera (2014). Our Deliberate Success: Recognizing what works for Latina/o students across the education pipeline. Paper commissioned for the 9th Annual Conference of the AAHHE.

Rodríguez-Arroyo, S. (2013). The Never-Ending Story of Language Policy in Puerto Rico. *Teacher Education Faculty Publications*. Paper 74. Retrieved April 28, 2015. Available at: http://digitalcommons.unomaha.edu/tedfacpub/74

Rosenthal, R. and L. Jacobson (1992) (Expanded Ed.). *Pygmalion in the Classroom*. New York City: Irvington.

Rutter, M.; B. Maughan; P. Mortimore; & J. Ouston (1979). *Fifteen Thousand Hours: Secondary schools and their effects on children*. Cambridge, MA: Harvard University Press.

Ryan, W. (1976) (2nd edition). *Blaming the Victim*. New York City: Vintage Books.

Salisbury, H. E. (1958). *The Shook-Up Generation*. New York City: Harper & Row.

San Miguel, G., Jr. and R. Donato (2010). Latino Education in Twentieth-Century America: A brief history. In E. G. Murillo, Jr. and S. Villenas (Eds.), *Handbook of Latinos and Education: Theory, research, and practice* (pp. 27–62). New York City: Routledge.

San Miguel, G., Jr. and R. R. Valencia (1998). From the Treaty of Guadalupe Hidalgo to Hopwood: The educational plight and struggle of Mexican Americans in the southwest. *Harvard Educational Review*, 68, 353–412 (fall).

Sánchez, G. I. and V. Strickland (1948). Spanish Names Spells Discrimination. *The Nation's School*, 41(1), 22–24 (January).

Schlesinger, A. M. (1941). *Political and Social Growth of the American People, 1865–1940*. New York City: Macmillan.

Secada, W.; R. Chávez-Chávez; E. García; C. Muñoz; J. Oakes; I. Santiago-Santiago; & R. Slavin (1998). *No More Excuses: The final report of the Hispanic Dropout Project*. Washington, DC: U.S. Department of Education.

Seda Bonilla, E. (1971). Ethnic Studies and Cultural Pluralism. *The Rican Journal: A journal of contemporary Puerto Rican thought*, 1(1), 56–65 (fall).

Senior, C. (1961). *The Puerto Ricans: Strangers then neighbors*. Chicago: Quadrangle Books.

Seward, Z. M. (April 3, 2013). The First Mobile Phone Call Made 40 Years Ago Today. Retrieved June 3, 2018. Available at: https://www.theatlantic.com/technology/archive/2013/04/the-first-mobile-phone-call-was-made-40-years-ago-today/274611/

Silicon Valley marks 50 years of Moore's Law (April 17, 2018). Mercurynews.com Retrieved June 3, 2018. Available at: https://www.chicoer.com/2015/04/17/silicon-valley-marks-50-years-of-moores-law-2/

Sizemore, B. (1973). Making the Schools a Vehicle for Cultural Pluralism. In M.D. Stent, W.R. Hazard, & H.N. Rivlin, *Cultural Pluralism in Education* (pp. 43–53). New York City: Appleton-Century-Crofts.

Snyder, T. D. (Ed.) (January 1993). *120 Years of American Education: A statistical portrait.* Washington, DC: National Center for Education Statistics.

Stanley, G. (September 15, 1920). Special Schools for Mexicans. *The Survey, 44,* 714–715.

Statista (2018). Number of internet users worldwide from 2005 to 2017 (in millions). Retrieved August 18, 2018. Available at: https://www.statista.com/statistics/273018/number-of-internet-users-worldwide/

Steele, C. M. and J. Aranson (November 1995). Stereotype threat and the intellectual test performance of African Americans. *Journal of Personality and Social Psychology, 69*(5), 797–811.

Steele, S. (2015). *Shame: How America's past sins have polarized our country.* New York City: Basic Books.

Stepler, R. (2016). *Hispanic, Black Parents see College Degree for Children's Success.* Washington, DC: Pew Research Center.

Stewner-Manzanares, G. (Fall 1988). *The Bilingual Education Act: Twenty years later.* Washington, DC: National Clearinghouse on Bilingual Education, occasional paper, no. 6.

Stiglitz, J. E. (2013). *The Price of Inequality: How today's divided society endangers our future.* New York City: W. W. Norton & Company.

Suarez, R. (2013). *Latino Americans: The 500-year legacy that shaped the nation.* New York City: Penguin Group.

Surgenor, E. W. (2014). *Creating Educational Access, Equity, and Opportunity for All: Real change requires redesigning public education to reflect today's world.* Lanham, MD: Rowman & Littlefield.

Takaki, R. (1993). *A Different Mirror: A history of multicultural America.* Boston, MA: Little, Brown and Company.

Taylor, A. H. (1976). *Travail and Triumph: Black life and culture in the South since the Civil War.* Westport, CT: Greenwood Press.

Thomas, H. (2010). *The Golden Age: The Spanish empire of Charles V.* New York City: Penguin Books.

Thomas, W. P. and V. P. Collier (2017). *Why Dual Language Schooling?* Albuquerque, NM: Fuente Press.

Thornton, J. (1998). *Africa and Africans in the Making of the Atlantic World, 1400–1800 (2nd ed.).* New York City: Cambridge University Press.

Tudico, C. (2010). *The Mexican-American Experience in California Higher Education, 1848–1945.* Ph.D. dissertation, University of Pennsylvania.

Tyack, D. B. (Ed.) (1974). *The One Best System: A history of American urban education.* Cambridge, MA: Harvard University Press.

United Nations, Department of Economic and Social Affairs, Population Division (2017). *International Migration Report 2017: Highlights.* New York City: Author (ST/ESA/SER.A/404).

U.S. Bureau of Education (1916). *Negro Education: A study of the private higher schools for colored people in the United States* ("Prepared in cooperation with the Phelps-Stokes Fund under the direction of Thomas Jesse Jones, specialist in the education of racial groups, Bureau of Education"). Bulletin, no. 38 & 39 (1916). Washington, DC: U.S. Government Printing Office.

——— (1980). Current Population Surveys, 1980, *The Social and Economic Status of the Black Population in the U.S.: A historical view, 1790–1778* (Series P-23, No. 80). Washington, DC: GPO.

——— (1975). *Historical Statistics of the United States, Colonial Times to 1970.* Bicentennial Edition. Part 2, Series Z, pp. 1–19. Washington, DC: GPO.

——— (1998). *Population of the 61 Urban Places: 1820.* Washington, DC: GPO.

——— (1998). *Population of the 100 Largest Urban Places: 1860.* Washington, DC: GPO.

U.S. Commission on Civil Rights (1974). *Counting the Forgotten: The 1970 Census count of persons of Spanish Speaking background in the United States.* GPO: Author (April).

U.S. Department of Education (1983). *A Nation at Risk.* Washington, DC: National Commission on Excellence in Education.

——— (2010). Characteristics of the 100 Largest Public Elementary and Secondary School Districts in the United States, 2008–09. National Center for Education Statistics. Washington, DC: Author.

——— (2017). *Characteristics of Public Elementary and Secondary Schools in the United States: Results from the 2015–16 National Teacher and Principal Survey, First Look.* Washington, DC: Author.

——— (2018). *Digest of Education Statistics: 2018.* Washington, DC: NCES.

——— (2015). *Program for International Student Assessment.* Retrieved May 30, 2018. Available at: https://nces.ed.gov/surveys/pisa/pisa2015/pisa2015highlights_2.asp

——— (2017). *The Condition of Education 2017* (NCES 2017–144), Undergraduate Retention and Graduation Rates.

——— (2018). *The Condition of Education 2018.* Washington, DC: NCES.

——— (2016). *The State of Racial Diversity in the Educator Workforce.* Washington, DC: Author.

——— (2015). *Trends in International Mathematics and Science Study (TIMSS).* Retrieved May 30, 2018. Available at: https://nces.ed.gov/timss/timss2015/

Valencia, R. R. (2008). *Chicano Students and the Courts: The Mexican American legal struggle for educational equality.* New York City: New York University Press.

——— (2005). The Mexican American Struggle for Equal Educational Opportunity in *Méndez v. Westminster*: Helping to pave the way for *Brown v. Board of Education. Teachers College Record, 107*(3): 389–423 (March 2005).

——— (2011). The Plight of Chicano Students: An overview of schooling conditions and outcomes. In R. R. Valencia (Ed.). *Chicano School Failure and Success: Past, present, and future.* New York City: Routledge.

Valenzuela, A. (1999). *Subtractive Schooling: U.S.-Mexico youth and the politics of caring.* Albany, NY: State University of New York Press.

Vargas, Z. (1993). *Proletarians of the North: A history of Mexican industrial workers in Detroit and the Midwest, 1917–1933.* Berkeley, CA: University of California Press.

Vigil, A. (1994). *The Corn Women: Stories and legend of the Hispanic Southwest*. Englewood, CA: Libraries Unlimited, Inc.

Wagenheim, K. (1970). *Puerto Rico: A profile*. New York City: Praeger.

Wang, W. (June 12, 2015). *Interracial Marriage: Who is 'marrying out'?* Washington, DC: Pew Research Center.

Waters, M. and M. G. Pineau (2015). *The Integration of Immigrants into American Society*. Washington, DC: National Academy of Sciences.

Weaver, G. R. (2013). *Intercultural Relations: Communication, identity, and conflict*. Boston, MA: Pearson Learning Solutions.

Weber, D. J. (1992). *The Spanish Frontier in Northern New Spain*. New haven, CT: Yale University Press.

Weinberg, M. (1977). *A Chance to Learn: The history of race and education in the United States*. London: Cambridge University Press.

West, C. (2017[1993]). *Race Matters*. Boston, MA: Beacon Press.

Wilkerson, D. A. (1936). A Determination of the Peculiar Problems of Negroes in Contemporary American Society. *The Journal of Negro Education*, 5(3), 324–350.

Williams, J. (1998). *Thurgood Marshall: American revolutionary*. New York City: Three Rivers Press.

Wilson, R. A. (Ed.)(1997). *Character Above All: Ten presidents from FDR to George Bush*. New York City: Simon & Schuster.

Winfield, A. G. (2007). *Eugenics and Education in America*. New York City: Peter Lang.

Wollenberg, C. (1976). *All Deliberate Speed: Segregation and exclusion in California schools, 1855–1912*. Berkeley, CA: University of California Press.

Woodson, C. G. (2005[1933]). *The Mis-Education of the Negro*. Mineola, NY: Dover Publications, Inc.

Woofter, T. J., Jr. (1933). *Races and Ethnic Groups in American Life*. New York City: McGraw-Hill Book Company, Inc.

World Bank (2016). *Digital Dividends: Strengthening the Analog Foundation of the Digital Revolution*. Washington, DC: Author.

Yablonsky, L. (1962). *The Violent Gang*. New York City: The MacMillan Company.

Yam, K. (June 16, 2017). Number of multiracial, multiethnic babies has tripled in 35 years: Report. Huffington Post. Retrieved January 21, 2018. Available at: https://www.huffpostbrasil.com/entry/pew-research-multiracial-multiethnic-babies_us_594009bfe4b0b13f2c6e2440

Zinn, H. (2003). *A People's History of the United States*. New York City: HarperCollins Publishers.

Zong, J. and J. Batalova (January 6, 2016). *Asian Immigration in the United States*. Washington, DC: Migration Policy Institute, Migration Information Source.

INDEX

A

Academic Profiling, 81
achievement gap, 4–5, 12, 222–223
   decrease in, 1960s–1970s, 100, 104
   early research on, 85–86
Adams, John, 19
Adams, John Quincy, 45
African Americans, 2, 4, 13, 35, 118, 124
   educational exclusion of, 39–40, 83
   emancipation of, 51–52
   Freedman's Bureau and, 53–54, 57
   GI Bill and, 104
   Great Migration of, 54, 87, 118, 166
   growth in public school enrollment of, 61–62
   Historically Black Colleges and Universities (HBCUs) and, 34, 42–43, 57, 59, 83, 105
   Jones Report on, 82–83
   racism against, 73–76
   segregation of, after emancipation, 53–59
   see also tripartite system
African Methodist Episcopal (AME) church, 56, 123
Agar, Herbert Sebastian, 15
Alcott, Luisa May, 45
Alger, Horatio, 36, 158
Allport, Gordon, 74–75
American Association of Hispanics in Higher Education (AAHHE), 202
American Board of Christian Foreign Missions (ABCFM), 41
American Dictionary of the English Language, An, 43
American Dilemma, An, 75
American education, 16–17
   Americanization process in, 140–143
   colonial era, 17–20
   common schools movement in, 15, 21, 35–37
   compulsory education policies in, 22, 93, 159–160

contradictions in, 162–164
curriculum in, 35–37
desegregation of higher education in, 96–97, 105
development of public schooling in, 31–37, 135–138
dual systems of (see dual systems)
early reformers in, 69–76
education as a right and, 20–27
exclusion of racial minorities from (see exclusion, educational)
expansion of higher education and, 25–26
financing of, 37, 99
growth and expansion through the 19th century, 38–46
imperialism and, 147–150, 158
increased White enrollment in, early twentieth century, 58–59
as key to success, 216–217
legacy of the civil rights movement for, 102–105
National Performance Goals for, 107–108
A Nation at Risk report on, 104, 105–107
new century struggles in, 206–212
pipeline, 224–225
presented as solution to race problem, 162
progressivism in, 73–75, 76–77, 161
racism in, 73–76
reform in (see reform, educational)
standardization of schools in, 23
teachers in, 24–25
testing and profiling of students in, 76–81
as White, Christian, and Protestant, 45–46
see also public schooling; tripartite system
American history, Latino void in, 11
American imperialism, 147–150, 158
Americanization process, 140–143
American-Philippine War, 121
American Sociological Association (ASA), 69
American Spelling Book, 35

American Women's Educational Association, 39
America's Challenge: Latinos and Education in 21st Century America-Where Are We?, 227
Amherst College, 43, 49
analysis of variance (ANOVA), 76
Anderson, James, 56
Anthony, Susan B., 39
Antioch College, 43, 49
apartheid, 226
Asian exclusion, 27–29, 63, 174–175
ASPIRA of New York, Inc., v. Board of Education, 191, 193, 194
Association of American Universities, 59
Atlanta Compromise, 163

B

Bacon, Francis, 69
Bailey v. Alabama, 52
Barnard, Henry, 34, 38, 40, 46, 54
Beecher, Catherine, 38–40
Benedict, Ruth, 182
Berlin, Ira, 2
Betances, Samuel, 137
bilingual education, 36, 192–193, 198–199, 220–221
Bilingual Education Act, 220–221
Bill and Melinda Gates Foundation, 205
Billingsley, A., 53
Binet, Alfred, 80, 81
Birth of a Nation, The, 73
Blackboard Jungle, 93
Blaming the Victim, 81
Bobbitt, John Franklin, 72
Bowdoin College, 49
Bowen High School, 101
Bracero Program, 92, 117, 166
Brookover, Wilbur B., 195
Brown v. Board of Education, 30, 61–62, 74–75, 94–95, 219
aftermath of, 95–98

Bureau of Indian Affairs (BIA), 30
Bureau of the Census, 151
Bush, George H., 107, 108

C

California ballot initiatives, 197–199
Caliver, Ambrose, 85
Canterbury Female Boarding School, 40
Capone, Al, 3
Carnegie Foundation, 75
Carter, Thomas, 161
Castro, Sal, 101
Catholic Church
  higher education, 160
  schools run by, 41, 46, 123, 129, 131–132, 133, 145–147
Chapa, J., 173
Charles III, King, 130
Cheney College, 42
Chicago, Latino neighborhoods of, 2–3
Chinese Exclusion Act of 1885, 27–28, 66
Chinese Social and Political Science Association, 73
Chi-squared test, 76
Churchill, Winston, 17
Cisneros v. Corpus Christi ISD, 150, 176, 178–179
Civil Rights Act of 1964, 174, 197, 220
civil rights movement, 180–181
  Elementary and Secondary Education Act (ESEA) and, 98–99
  events of 1968 and, 100–101
  Higher Education Act of 1965 and, 42, 99
  James Meredith and, 43, 96–97
  John Kennedy and, 95–97
  legacy of, 102–105
  Little Rock Nine and, 96
  Lyndon Johnson and, 98–99
  March on Washington, 97–98
  Montgomery bus boycott, 1955, and, 96
  see also post-war America

Civil War, American, 19, 20, 34, 38, 42, 135
  Reconstruction Era after, 51–52, 144
Clark, Kenneth, 74, 81, 142
Clark, Mamie, 74, 81, 142
Clark, Victor S., 69–70, 148
Clinton, Bill, 108
Clyatt v. United States, 51
Coleman Report, 182, 184, 195
College Entrance Examination Board (CEEB), 70
Coloma, Robert, 149
colonial education, 17–20, 129–132
Columbus, Christopher, 126
Commission on Higher Education, 203
Committee of Ten, 23–24, 69
common schools movement, 15, 20, 35–37
compulsory education, 22, 93, 159–160
Cooper, Anna Julia, 55, 72, 74, 143, 144, 210–211
Cooper v. Aaron, 96
counting of Latinos, 150–152
Crandall, Prudence, 38–40
Crisis, The, 72, 81
Cruz, Luis, 137
Cuba, 118, 121
Cubberley, Ellwood P., 71, 81, 84
cultural compatibility, 223
culture of poverty, 182–183
curriculum, early public school, 35–37
Curriculum, The, 72

D

Daley, Richard J., 101
Dartmouth College, 49
Del Río ISD v. Salvatierra, 178
Democracy in America, 40
demographics, changes in American, 144–145
De Tocqueville, Alexis, 40
Dewey, John, 73–74, 182, 226
Dickinson, Emily, 45

Dickson, Virgil, 78
disenfranchisement, segregation as, 83–87
Doane, George W., 35
"doll study," 74
Dominican Republic, 122
Douglass, Frederick, 56, 64
dropouts, 193–195, 201–202, 221
dual language competence, 223–224
dual language programs. *see* bilingual education
dual systems, 62–68, 81–82, 91–92
   calamitous times in, 92–95
   failure of policymakers and educational theorists to address, 73–75
   in post-war America, 93–95
   see also tripartite system
Du Bois, W.E.B., 27, 54–55, 71–72, 74, 134, 144, 146
   on color as major issue of the 20th century, 209, 222
   on the dual system of education, 81–82
   impact of, 162–164
   on racialization of differences within and outside America, 158
Duel of Eagles, 2
"dunce" caps, 44, 60
Dusenbury, Elizabeth, 45

E

Edgewood ISD v. Kirby et al., 190
Edmonds, Ron, 194–195, 208
educational leadership, 225–226
education as a right, 20–27
Education of the Negro in the American Social Order, The, 61
education pipeline, 224–225
Edwards, Newton, 86
egalitarianism, 72
Eisenhower, Dwight, 95, 96, 203
Elementary and Secondary Education Act (ESEA), 98–99, 180, 196, 208

elementary schools, development of American, 22–23, 37
Eliot, Charles W., 70–71, 73, 84, 181
Eliot, T. S., 70
El Salvador, 122
emancipation, 51–52
   segregation after, 53–59
emotional intelligence (EQ), 224
English Language Education for Children in Public Schools law, 199–200
English language learners (ELLs), 12–13, 198, 223–224
English-only policies, 141–142
Equal Educational Opportunity for Youth, 86, 182
Equal Employment Opportunity Commission (EEOC), 197
equity v. equality, 222
Escalante, Jaime, 184
eugenics movement, 72, 73, 181–182
Every Student Succeeds Act (ESSA), 110, 111, 222
Excelencia in Education, 202, 204
exclusion, educational, 26–27
   African Americans, 39–40, 83
   Asian, 27–29, 63, 174–175
   Latino, 30–31, 63, 83, 138–147
   testing and profiling used for, 77–81

F

Falcón, Angelo, 193
Faubus, Orval, 96
Fifteenth Amendment, 53
Fifteen Thousand Hours, 195
financial aid, higher education, 104–105, 205–206
Fisher, Roland, 76
Fisher v. University of Texas at Austin, 198
Foley, Neil, 152
Ford Foundation, 205
Fourteenth Amendment, 28, 30, 53

Franklin, Benjamin, 19
Franklin, John Hope, 74
Frazier, E. Franklin, 74
Freedman's Bureau, 53–55, 57
Freire, Paulo, 65
funding of public schools, 37, 99, 189–191

G

Gadsden Purchase, 132
Galton, Francis, 76
gangs, 93
García, Eugene, 198
García, Lily Eskelsen, 111
García, T., 202
García-Márquez, Gabriel, 128
gender and teaching, 25, 39–40
GI Bill, 104, 170, 206
"Gilded Age," 53, 59
Goals 2000, 108, 109
Goddard, Henry H., 182
Golden Age of capitalism, 53
Goldin, C., 59
Goldstein, Dana, 39
Gong Lum v. Rice, 28
Grandma Moses, 215–216
Grant, Ulysses S., 56
Gratz v. Bollinger, 198
Great Depression, 29, 31, 165
Great Migration, 54, 87, 118, 166
Grutter v. Bollinger, 198
Guadalupe Hidalgo, Treaty of, 66, 121, 125, 132, 141, 176–177, 220
Guam, 122, 149

H

Hacker, Andrew, 82
Haiti, 122
Hale, Edward Everett, 157
Hall, G. Stanley, 181
Handlin, Oscar, 46

Harris, William Torrey, 69–70, 148
Harvard Classics, 70
Harvard University, 17, 71, 181
Hayes, Chris, 134
Hellman, Lillian, 51
Henderson, Anne, 223
Henderson, Wade, 191
Hernández v. Texas, 30, 94–95, 178
higher education
    Catholic, 160
    desegregation of, 96–97, 105
    development of American, 25–26, 34
    financial aid for, 104–105, 205–206
    inclusion of African Americans and Native Americans in, 34, 42–43
    Latinos in, 201–206, 225
Higher Education Act of 1965, 43, 99, 206
high schools
    development of American, 22–24
    dropouts from, 193–195, 201–202, 221
    Latino graduation rates from, 170
Hispanic Dropout Project, 194
Hispanic Scholarship Fund (HSF), 205
Hispanic-Serving Institutions (HSIs), 204
Historically Black Colleges and Universities (HBCUs), 34, 42–43, 57, 59, 83, 105
Historical Methods, 82
History of Higher Education Journal, 202
Honduras, 122
Honig, Bill, 104
Hopwood v. University of Texas Law School, 198, 199
How the Irish Became White, 46
Hughes, Langston, 164
Humboldt's Gift, 3

I

identity and race of Latinos, 122–123, 174–179
Immigration and Naturalization Act of 1965, 29
Immigration and Naturalization Service (INS), 177, 203

imperialism and education, 147–150, 158
industrialization, American, 52–53
Inequality, 183
IQ scores, 77, 78–81, 104, 181, 224

J

Jackson, Andrew, 20
Janah, Leila, 222
Jefferson, Thomas, 11, 18–19, 72
Jencks, Christopher, 183
Jesuits, 130–131
Jim Crow, 53, 54, 60, 85, 142, 158
   Latinos and, 122–123, 140
Johnson, Andrew, 51
Johnson, Lyndon B., 75, 98–99, 102, 103, 167, 183, 197
Johnson-Reed law of 1924, 29
Jones, Thomas Jesse, 82–83
Jones Report, 82–83
Journal of Negro History, The, 72

K

Kandel, Isaac L., 208
Katz, L. F., 59
Kennedy, John F., 75, 95–97, 215
Kennedy, Robert, 98, 100
kindergarten, 36
King, Martin Luther, Jr., 97–98, 100
Kipling, Rudyard, 149
KKK, 53, 73
knowledge education, 164
"Know-Nothing Party," 133
Kousser, J. Morgan, 82

L

language, pedagogy, and rights, 191–193
Latinization of public schools, 2, 4, 11–12, 118–119, 221
Latinizmo, 128–129

Latino education, 1–2, 11, 111–112, 117–120
   Americanization process in, 140–143
   bilingual education in, 36, 192–193, 198–199, 220–221
   Catholic Church and, 41, 46, 123, 129, 131–132, 133, 145–147
   challenges in today's, 137–138, 221–226
   court decisions affecting, 176–178
   high growth and poor academic progress in, 5
   imperialism and, 147–150
   importance of addressing educational needs of, 219–220
   reforms and, 179–184, 196–197
   as second-class, 168–174
   segregation in, 60–61, 118–119
   in Spanish schools, 129–132
   see also tripartite system
Latinos
   California ballot initiatives affecting, 197–199
   citizenship and acculturation of, 123–125
   counting of, 150–152
   development of education in the U.S. and, 135–138
   dropout rates among, 201–202
   educational exclusion of, 30–31, 83, 138–147
   English-language learner (ELL), 12–13, 223–224
   ethnic, cultural, and racial diversity of, 127, 128–129
   in higher education, 201–206, 225
   Hispanic-Serving Institutions (HSIs) for, 204
   historical challenges faced by, 210–211
   labeling of, 128–129
   lack of national attention on needs of, 218
   mestizo, 126, 127
   1960s protests by, 101–102
   post-war life for, 92–95
   racial identity of, 122–123, 174–179
   segregation of, 161

Spanish colonialism and, 120–122, 126–129
twentieth century immigration of, 117–118
in the U.S., 132–135
see also Mexican Americans
Lau v. Nichols, 192–193, 220–221
La Vida, 182
leadership, educational, 225–226
Leadership Conference Education Fund, 191
League of United Latin American Citizens (LULAC), 30, 60, 172, 173, 175, 178
Leguizamo, John, 1
Leis, Ward, 171
Lewis, Oscar, 182, 183
Lezotte, Larry, 195
liberty, 163
limited English proficient (LEP) children, 191, 192
Lincoln, Abraham, 51, 98
Little, Malcolm, 86
Little Rock Nine, 96
Lockwood, Belva, 40
Long, Jeff, 2
Louisiana Purchase, 19, 132
Lucas, Isidro, 194
Lumina Foundation, 201

M

MacDonald, Victoria M., 130, 152, 160, 170, 202
Mailer, Norman, 100
Malcolm X, 86, 208
Manifest Destiny, 32, 120–121, 122, 132, 135, 158
Mann, Horace, 33–35, 38, 40–46, 54, 69, 70, 74, 215, 226
Manso, Alonso, 129
Manuel, H. T., 169–170
March on Washington, 97–98
Margo, Robert, 159
Marshall, Thurgood, 74

May, Vivian, 55
McGuffey Readers, 35–36, 130
McKinkley, William, 122
McWilliams, Carey, 161
Mead, Margaret, 182
Mejicanos, 133, 134
Méndez v. Westminster, 30–31, 94, 171, 178
Meredith, James, 43, 96–97
mestizos, 126, 127
Mexican American Legal Defense Fund (MAL-DEF), 190
Mexican American Movement (MAM), 203
Mexican Americans, 2, 4, 56, 83, 91
acculturation and citizenship of, 123–124, 134–135, 139
adjustment of, after the Mexican-American War, 143–144
Bracero Program, 92, 117, 166
Catholic Church and education of, 41, 123, 133, 145–147
manual arts programs for, 161
migration north by, 117–118
19th century education of, 57
re. Rodríguez case and, 176–178
second-class schooling for, 168–174
significant court cases affecting, 94–95
treatment of, in public schools, 139–140
walkout of East L.A. public schools, 101
White teachers in schools for, 167
Zoot-Suit, 92
see also Latino education; Latinos
Mexican-American Studies (MAS), 200
Mexican-American War, 20, 65–66, 121, 132
adjustment for Mexican Americans after, 143–144
Mexican Farm Labor, 166
Mexican Revolution, 122, 130, 165
Mexican Voice, The, 203
Mexican Youth Conference, 203
Miami and the Siege of Chicago, 100
Middlebury College, 49
minority population growth, 144–145
Mis-education of the Negro American, 74, 119, 150

Monroe Doctrine, 120
Montgomery bus boycott, 1955, 96
Mora, Cristina, 129
Moreno, Rita, 216
Morrill Act of 1890, 25
Morrill Land-Grant Act of 1862, 25, 34
Morris, Robert, 59
Moynihan, Daniel Patrick, 183–184
mutual-aid societies, 92
Myrdal, Gunnar, 75, 82

N

National Association for the Advancement of Colored People (NAACP), 60, 62, 81
National Center on Education Statistics (NCES), 13, 118
National Defense Education Act (NDEA), 205
National Defense Student Loans (NDSL), 104–105, 205
National Educational Goals, 108
National Education Association (NEA), 23, 34, 39, 69, 111
National Origins Act of 1924, 29
National Performance Goals, 107–108
National Teachers Association, 23
Nation at Risk, A, 104–108, 196
Native Americans, 20, 87, 124, 174
  citizenship of, 122
  displacement of, 20, 135
  education of, 123
  Tribal Colleges and Universities (TCUs), 42–43
Nature of Prejudice, The, 74–75
Negro Education in Alabama, 61, 82
Negro Family, The, 183
New Deal programs, 165
New Negro, The, 72
New York Free School Society, 20–21
Niagara Movement, 163
Nicaragua, 122
Nieto, Sonia, 222

Nixon, Richard, 102
No Child Left Behind (NCLB), 109–111, 222
No More Excuses, 194, 195
Normal Schools, 38, 41–42, 55

O

Obama, Barack, 222
Oberlin College, 42, 43
Ochoa, Gilda, 81
One Best System, The, 8
Orfield, Gary, 118
Orwell, George, 115
Oseguera, L., 201
Our Nation on the Fault Line, 196
Ovando, C. E., 36

P

Panamá, 122
parent engagement, 223
Pearson, Karl, 76
Pearson Learning, 111
Peninsular War, 120
Peonage Act of 1867, 51–52
pipeline, education, 224–225
Plessy v. Ferguson, 28, 30, 54, 59–62, 77, 95, 219
  polarization during, 157–162
Plyler v. Doe, 197
polarization during *Plessy*, 157–162
post-war America, 92–95
  riots of the 1960s and, 101–102
  rise of gangs in, 93
  significant court cases in, 94–95
  survival of racial minorities in, 92–93
  War on Poverty and, 102
  see also civil rights movement
poverty, 100, 101, 102, 180–181, 196
  culture of, 182–183

Presidential Advisory Commission on Educational Excellence for Hispanic Americans, 196
profiling and testing of students, 76–81
progressivism, 73–75, 76–77, 161
Public Education in the United States, 71
public schooling
   achievement gap in, 4–5, 12, 222–223
   bilingual education in, 36, 192–193, 198–199, 220–221
   dropouts from, 193–195, 201–202, 221
   funding for, 37, 99, 189–191
   increasing racial diversity in, 2, 4, 6, 11–12, 118–119
   language, pedagogy and rights in, 191–193
   Latinization of, 2, 4, 11–12, 118–119, 221
   Lyndon Johnson and increased funding for, 99
   new century struggles in, 206–212
   predominantly White teachers in, 5
   as stagnant and stale, 7–8
   standardization of, 23
   system structure of, 6–7, 86–87
   see also American education
Puerto Ricans, 2–3, 4, 69–70, 91, 117, 122, 123, 216
   American takeover of Puerto Rico and, 148–149
   high school boycott by, 101
   see also Latinos
Pygmalion effect, 81

Q

Quakers, 41, 42

R

Race Matters, 82
racism, 73–76
   scientific, 27, 77, 181–182

Ravitch, Diane, 103, 109
Reagan, Ronald, 106
Reconstruction Era, 51–52, 144
reform, educational, 207, 226–227
   Charles W. Eliot and, 70–71
   early, 69–76
   fallacy of, 81–83
   Latinos and, 179–184, 196–197
   national goals in, 107–109
   A Nation at Risk report and, 104, 105–107
   No Child Left Behind (NCLB) and, 109–111
   stratified education and, 71–72
Regional Conference for the Education of the Spanish-speaking People in the Southwest, 160
Reign of Error, 109
re. Rodríguez case, 176–178
Revolutionary War, 17, 19, 45
   minority populations after, 144
Reynolds study, 172
Richman, Julia, 86–87
Riley, Richard J., 195
riots, 1960s, 101–102
Roberts, Benjamin, 59
Roberts v. The City of Boston, 59–60
Rodríguez, L. F., 201
Roosevelt, Franklin D., 165, 178
Rush, Benjamin, 18–19, 33
Ryan, William, 81, 184

S

SAMS, 92–93
San Antonio ISD v. Rodríguez, 190
Sánchez, George I., 30, 173, 217
San Miguel, G., Jr., 139, 141
Santayana, George, 16
Schurz, Carl, 36
Schurz, Margaretha Meyer, 36
scientific racism, 27, 77, 181–182
Secada, Walter, 194, 196
second-class schooling for Latinos, 168–174

Second Great Awakening, 32, 33, 41–42
Second Reconstruction, 98
segregation, 28, 30, 60–61
   as disenfranchisement, 83–87
   Jones Report on, 82–83
   of Latinos, 60–61, 118–119, 161
   reformers and, 73
   scholarship on effects of, 74–75
   unabated, 164–168
   see also dual systems
Seguín, Juan, 2
self-determination, 163
self-hatred, 74, 142
self-reliance, 163
Shaw, George Bernard, 91
Shook-Up Generation, The, 93
Sizemore, Barbara, 211
Society of Jesus, 130–131
socio-emotional learning (SEL), 224
Souls of Black Folks, The, 74, 82
South Africa, 226
Spanish-American War, 29, 121–122, 147
Spanish colonialism, 120–122, 126–129
   education in, 129–132
Spring, Joel, 142–143
Stand and Deliver, 184
Stanford University, 71
Stanley, Grace, 170–171
Stowe, Harriett Beecher, 39
stratified education, 71–72
Subtractive Schooling, 140
Sumner, Charles, 59

T

Takaki, R., 29
Tape v. Hurley, 28
Tashima, A. Wallace, 200
teachers
   early American, 24–25
   predominance of white, 5, 167
Terkel, Studs, 3
Terman, Lewis M., 78, 182
testing and profiling of students, 76–81
Thirteenth Amendment, 53
Thomas, Hugh, 129
Thorndike, E. L., 182
Time, 1
Toraño, María Elena, 196
Trail of Tears, 20
Treaty of Guadalupe Hidalgo, 65–66, 121, 132, 141, 176, 177, 220
Tribal Colleges and Universities (TCUs), 42–43
tripartite system
   educational contradictions in, 162–164
   polarization during *Plessy* and, 157–162
   unabated segregation in, 164–168
   see also dual systems
Truman, Harry, 203
Tudico, Christopher, 202
Tuley High School boycott, 101
Twain, Mark, 53
Two Nations: Black and White, Separate, Hostile and Unequal, 82
Tyack, David, 8, 10, 78, 86
Tydings-McDuffie Act of 1935, 29

U

Uncle Tom's Cabin, 39
United States v. Reynolds, 52
University of Alabama, 96–97
Untouchables, The, 3
Uprooted, The, 46
U.S. News & World Report, 196
utilitarian education, 164

V

Valencia, R. R., 139, 141, 171
Valenzuela, Angela, 64, 140
Vargas, Z., 166
Vietnam War, 102
Violent Gang, The, 93

W

Walkout, 101
Wallace, George, 97
Ward, Lester Frank, 69–70
War on Poverty, 102, 180–181, 183, 196
Warren, Earl, 94, 95, 96, 211
Washington, Booker T., 71
　impact of, 162–164
Washington, George, 19
Weber, David, 130
Webster, Daniel, 122
Webster, Noah, 33, 35, 43
West, Cornel, 82, 222
West Side Story, 93, 216
White, Christian, and Protestant educational focus in America, 45–46
White flight, 4
White Man's Burden, The, 149
White nationalism, 26–27
Wilde, Oscar, 189
Wilkerson, Doxey A., 87, 90
Wilson, Woodrow, 73
Woodson, Carter, 72, 74, 119, 142, 144, 149–150, 164
Works Progress Administration (WPA), 165
World War I, 36, 52, 54, 78, 117, 122, 159, 169
World War II, 32, 72, 73, 75, 92–94, 97, 104, 112, 117, 161, 166, 169, 206, 225

Y

Yerkes, Robert, 182

Yolanda Medina and Margarita Machado-Casas
GENERAL EDITORS

Critical Studies of Latinos/as in the Americas is a provocative interdisciplinary series that offers a critical space for reflection and questioning what it means to be Latino/a living in the Americas in twenty-first century social, cultural, economic, and political arenas. The series looks forward to extending the dialogue to include the North and South Western hemispheric relations that are prevalent in the field of global studies.

Topics that explore and advance research and scholarship on contemporary topics and issues related with processes of racialization, economic exploitation, health, education, transnationalism, immigration, gendered and sexual identities, and disabilities that are not commonly highlighted in the current Latino/a Studies literature as well as the multitude of socio, cultural, economic, and political progress among the Latinos/as in the Americas are welcome.

To receive more information about CSLA, please contact:

Yolanda Medina (ymedina@bmcc.cuny.edu) &
Margarita Machado-Casas (Margarita.MachadoCasas@utsa.edu)

To order other books in this series, please contact our Customer Service Department at:

(800) 770-LANG (within the U.S.)
(212) 647-7706 (outside the U.S.)
(212) 647-7707 FAX

Or browse online by series at:

WWW.PETERLANG.COM